HARRY POTTER
A History of Magic

BLOOMSBURY

Contents

Introduction

Julian Harrison LEAD CURATOR, *Harry Potter: A History of Magic*

J.K. Rowling's Harry Potter novels are a global phenomenon. The stories have sold millions of copies worldwide, have been translated into dozens of languages and inspired countless readers, young and old. But how many of those readers have paused to reflect on the magical traditions that lie at the heart of Harry Potter's world?

Opening at the British Library in October 2017, *Harry Potter: A History of Magic* is the first major exhibition to explore this rich and diverse aspect of J.K. Rowling's stories. From ancient amulets to medieval mandrakes, from unicorns (they really did exist) to bubbling cauldrons, there are often historical and mythological antecedents for the characters and scenes in the Harry Potter series. The exhibition strives to tell some of these stories and to celebrate the inspiration behind J.K. Rowling's own spellbinding creations.

The exhibition features many precious artefacts relating to the Harry Potter books and magic through the ages. First and foremost are items associated with J.K. Rowling. These include fascinating early drafts of *Harry Potter and the Philosopher's Stone* and *Harry Potter and the Deathly Hallows*; original drawings by the author; and intricately worked-out plot plans for *Harry Potter and the Order of the Phoenix*. Each and every one of these treasures bears testament to the author's creativity and craftsmanship, and to the enduring appeal of Harry Potter himself.

We are also delighted to showcase some of the original artwork of the artist Jim Kay. Kay has illustrated the first three Harry Potter novels for Bloomsbury (*The Philosopher's Stone*, *The Chamber of Secrets* and *The Prisoner of Azkaban*) to widespread international acclaim. We are extremely grateful to him and to Olivia Lomenech Gill, artist of the new illustrated edition of *Fantastic Beasts and Where to Find Them*, for their generous involvement and support.

It is an equal pleasure to present items from the British Library's own unrivalled collections, many of which have never previously been considered in this wider, magical context. On display are Greek papyri, Ethiopian talismans and Anglo-Saxon centaurs, Chinese oracle bones, French phoenixes and Thai horoscopes. Harry Potter fans can pore over Leonardo da Vinci's notebook, marvel at the Dunhuang Star Atlas, and gaze in amazement at the snowy owl in Audubon's *Birds of America*. To complement these British Library objects, we are also thrilled to have secured some amazing loans from a number of institutions and private individuals.

Harry Potter: A History of Magic is framed around some of the subjects studied at Hogwarts School of Witchcraft and Wizardry. There is Potions (and its more

advanced cousin, Alchemy), Herbology, Charms, Astronomy, Divination, Defence Against the Dark Arts and Care of Magical Creatures. Focusing on each of these subjects has enabled the exhibition curators to delve deeper into the theme of enchantment through the ages. Potion-making, fortune-telling, harvesting herbs and spells to make you invisible all make an appearance. In the process, we have uncovered intriguing facts about many of the exhibits. Did you know, for example, that Leonardo da Vinci believed that the Sun rotated round the Earth? Were you aware that the 'Abracadabra' charm first originated as a cure for malaria? How many people knew that a 'real' mermaid was presented to the British Museum in 1942? Some of these facts, quite frankly, border on the absurd – according to *The Old Egyptian Fortune-Teller's Last Legacy*, which we examine in Divination, 'a mole on the buttock denotes honour to a man and riches to a woman'.

The Harry Potter stories are rooted in centuries of popular tradition. Predicting the future, for instance, has a long history. The oldest items in the British Library's collections are Chinese oracle bones, which date as far back as 1600 BC. These ancient bones were used for a divination ritual at the court of the Shang Dynasty. In order to foretell upcoming events, the bone would have been engraved and then heated with metal sticks, causing it to crack – the diviners then examined the patterns of the fractures to interpret the future. One of these humble-looking bones is actually the oldest exactly datable object in the exhibition. On the front, the diviners observed that nothing of great significance would happen in the immediate future. On its reverse, however, the bone recorded a lunar eclipse, viewable at Anyang in China between 21:48 and 23:30 (give or take seventeen minutes) on the night of 27th December, 1192 BC. In order to have been inscribed in this way, the bone must have been in existence at that very same time. These artefacts have been known historically as 'dragon bones', emphasising their magical qualities.

The ancient art of alchemy is at the heart of the first story, *Harry Potter and the Philosopher's Stone*. In that book, the mysterious Stone in question had been taken in secret to Hogwarts School, where it was being guarded by a monstrous three-headed dog, named Fluffy, and a series of protective spells placed upon it by the teachers. It was Hermione Granger who was the first to realise the significance of a certain Nicolas Flamel. Having spent several frustrating weeks with Harry and Ron Weasley in the library, she suddenly pulled out an old book that she had put aside for a bit of light reading.

'Nicolas Flamel,' she whispered dramatically, 'is the ***only known maker of the Philosopher's Stone!'***

According to this ancient tome, Flamel was a noted alchemist and opera-lover, aged 665, who was living quietly in Devon with his wife, Perenelle. What readers of the Harry Potter stories may not have realised is that Flamel was a real person, a wealthy landlord who lived in medieval Paris, where he died in 1418. One of the star items in the exhibition is the actual headstone that marked the real Flamel's tomb, on loan from the Musée national du Moyen Âge in Paris.

Firenze the centaur was another to play a significant part in *Harry Potter and the Philosopher's Stone*, saving Harry from danger in the Forbidden Forest before going on to teach Divination at Hogwarts in the later books. In Greek mythology, Chiron was the greatest of all centaurs, renowned as a physician and astrologer. According to a medieval herbal in our exhibition, the plants known as *Centauria major* and

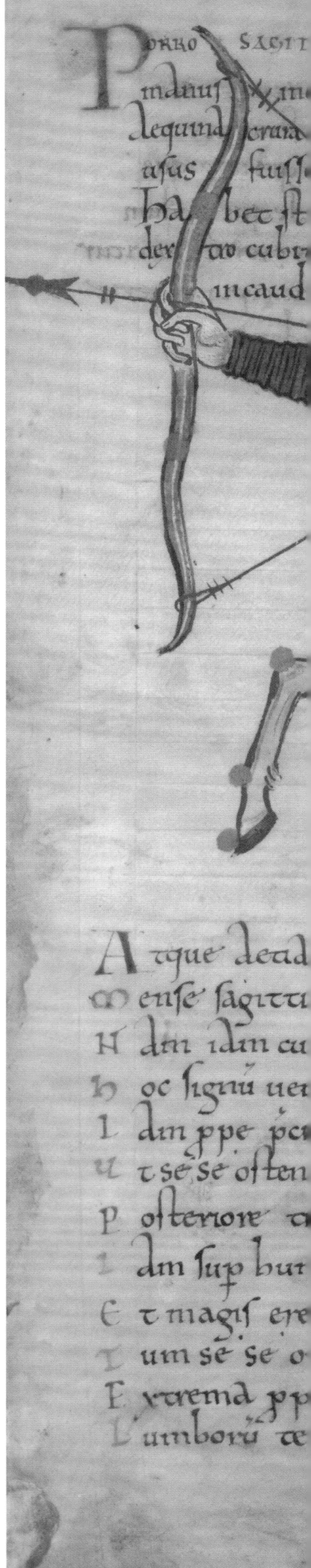

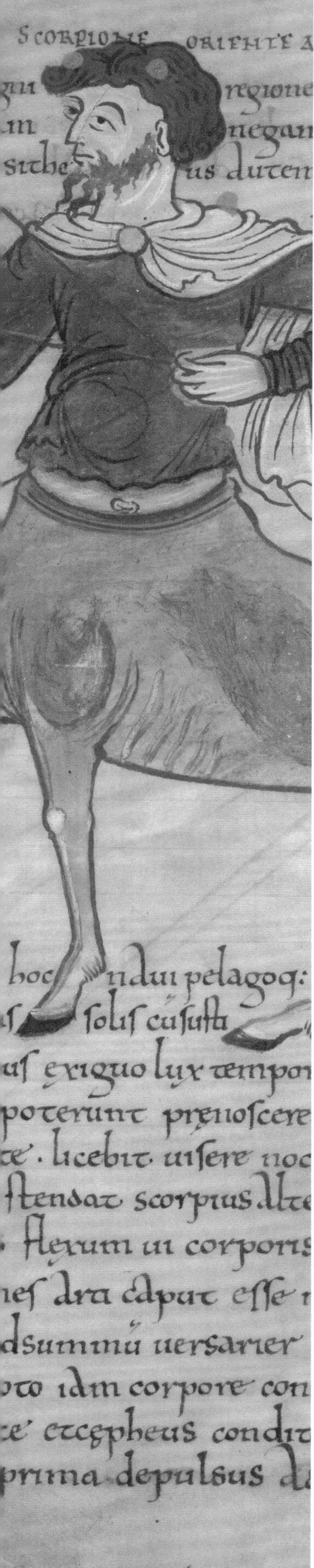

Centauria minor (greater and lesser centaury) were named after Chiron. He is shown in that manuscript handing over these plants to Asclepius, the god of medicine and healing. Centaury was renowned as a remedy for snakebite. I am particularly pleased to reveal that we are also displaying one of my favourite medieval books, an 11th-century Anglo-Saxon manuscript containing an illustration of the constellation Sagittarius. This constellation takes its name from the Latin word for 'archer', and is depicted in these pages as a bearded centaur, with a white cloak draped round its shoulders, and drawing back its bow. This Anglo-Saxon manuscript is a precious survivor from another age, when our ancestors set great store in tracking the movements of celestial bodies.

Witches and wizards have long been associated with cauldrons and broomsticks. There are two historical cauldrons on show in *Harry Potter: A History of Magic*, on generous loan from the British Museum and the Museum of Witchcraft and Magic in Boscastle. One of those cauldrons, made almost 3,000 years ago, was found in the River Thames at Battersea, London, in the 1860s. Despite having rested in the silt for countless centuries, the Battersea Cauldron is extraordinarily well preserved. The other cauldron, in contrast, is no longer in pristine condition. It exploded when a group of modern-day Cornish witches were using it to brew a potion on the beach. These two items give real meaning to the first printed image of witches with a cauldron, found in a book published in Cologne in 1489. This illustration shows two elderly women placing a snake and a cockerel into a large cauldron, in a bid to summon up a hailstorm. Popular perceptions of witches as ugly, haggard and demonic can ultimately be traced to this highly influential publication.

Every witch or wizard, so we have always been led to believe, should be able to fly on a broomstick. As Kennilworthy Whisp noted in *Quidditch Through the Ages*, 'No Muggle illustration of a witch is complete without a broom'. We are very happy to be showing in our exhibition a traditional witch's broomstick with an elaborately coloured handle. Its former owner, Olga Hunt of Manaton in Devon, used this broomstick for magical purposes – on a Full Moon she is said to have leaped around Haytor Rocks on Dartmoor, much to the alarm of courting couples and campers. There is also a little book entitled *The History of the Lancashire Witches*, describing that English county as 'famous for witches and the very strange pranks they have played'. Alongside a picture of a jolly witch mounting a broomstick, the anonymous author declares, 'Lancashire witches chiefly divert themselves in merriment and sport' and are 'more sociable than any others'. Any Yorkshire witches out there are probably already cursing in dismay.

Harry Potter fans will be familiar with the hazardous properties of mandrakes. According to medieval herbals, mandrakes could cure headaches, earache and insanity, but their roots grew in human form and would shriek when torn. A 15th-century British Library manuscript shows the approved way to harvest that plant, by attaching one end of a cord to the plant and the other to a dog. The dog would be encouraged to move forward by sounding a horn or enticing it with meat, dragging the mandrake with it. There were a number of comparable drawings that we could have shown alongside this manuscript, but we plumped eventually for a 14th-century illustrated herbal, containing an Arabic translation of the writings of Pedanius Dioscorides, a physician in the Roman army. Dioscorides was one of the first to distinguish between the male and female mandrake (or maybe we should rename them the 'mandrake' and the 'womandrake'). Sadly for the romanticists among us, modern science now dictates that this identification is incorrect –

1
3
4
2

there is more than one mandrake species native to the Mediterranean, rather than two separate sexes of the same plant.

This exhibition is alive with tales of human enterprise and endeavour. The discovery of phosphorus by the German alchemist Hennig Brand is shown in a magnificent painting by Joseph Wright of Derby, kindly loaned by Derby Museum and Art Gallery. Brand's discovery came about after he boiled down vast quantities of urine in a failed attempt to manufacture gold. The by-product was phosphorus, not quite every alchemist's dream. Elizabeth Blackwell illustrated, engraved and hand-coloured her *Curious Herbal* to raise funds to have her husband, Alexander, released from a debtors' prison. Alexander Blackwell assisted by identifying the plants she had drawn at Chelsea Physic Garden in London, until such time as she had absolved the debt. Once released he repaid his wife's kindness by leaving for Sweden, entering the service of King Frederick I, and getting himself executed for his involvement in a political conspiracy. The poignant copy of *A Curious Herbal* on display in *Harry Potter: A History of Magic* has been annotated in Elizabeth Blackwell's own hand.

Some magical advice dispensed over the centuries now seems rather quaint in a modern context. Quintus Serenus Sammonicus, physician to the Emperor Caracalla, recommended that the 'Abracadabra' charm should be worn as an amulet around the neck, fixed with either flax, coral stones or the fat of a lion. An Ethiopian charm for changing oneself into various animals, and for which there is no counter-charm, reads as follows:

With red ink, write these secret names on a piece of white silk. To transform yourself into a lion, tie the silk to your head; to become a python, tie it on your arm; to turn into an eagle, tie it on your shoulder.

Magical creatures abound in the Harry Potter novels. Many of these fantastic beasts are J.K. Rowling's own creations, but others have illustrious precedents. Did you know that the French author Guy de la Garde devoted an entire study to the phoenix, entitled *L'Histoire et description du Phoenix*? The British Library's copy of this book is printed on vellum and contains a hand-coloured picture of a phoenix emerging from a burning tree. A 13th-century bestiary also describes the 'Fenix' in great detail. According to that manuscript, this mythical bird is so called because its colour is 'Phoenician purple', it is native to Arabia, and it can live for 500 years. In old age, the phoenix is said to create its own funeral pyre from branches and leaves, before fanning the flames with its own wings, in order to be consumed by the fire. After the ninth day, it rises again from the ashes.

In the second task of the Triwizard Tournament, relayed in *Harry Potter and the Goblet of Fire*, Harry encountered a choir of merpeople in the black lake at Hogwarts. Merpeople were also once intended to feature at the beginning of *Harry Potter and the Chamber of Secrets*, before the author had a change of mind. In a draft chapter subsequently rewritten by J.K. Rowling, the Ford Anglia flown by Ron and Harry originally crashed into the lake rather than into the Whomping Willow, leading them to see their first mermaid:

Her lower body was a great, scaly fishtail the colour of gun-metal; ropes of shells and pebbles hung about her neck; her skin was a pale, silvery grey and her eyes, flashing in the headlights, looked dark and threatening.

This description, although never published, echoes historical accounts of mermaids and mermen, creatures that were renowned, somewhat sinisterly, for luring people into the sea. One of my favourite exhibits is the specimen of a mermaid that had allegedly been caught in Japan in the 18th century. The creature has large staring eyes and a wide open mouth, reminiscent of Edvard Munch's painting *The Scream*. In actual fact it is a fake, a bizarre curiosity brought about by fusing together the upper body of a monkey and the tail of a fish.

No exhibition about the world of Harry Potter would be complete without mentioning the most magical of mythical creatures, the unicorn. Unicorns – and unicorn blood – played a key part in Voldemort's continued survival in *Harry Potter and the Philosopher's Stone*. The blood, hair and horn of the unicorn have long been supposed to have medicinal properties, according to medieval folklore. In mythology, the creature came in all shapes and sizes. A poem by the Byzantine writer Manuel Philes described the unicorn as a wild beast with the tail of a boar and a lion's mouth, while Pierre Pomet's *Histoire générale des Drogues* illustrated five species, including one, somewhat ironically, with two horns, known as the pirassoipi.

When I discover a beautifully imagined unicorn that has been hidden for centuries inside the pages of a bestiary, carefully unfurl an illuminated scroll that promises to reveal the secrets of the Philosopher's Stone, or breathe in the earthy pages of a centuries-old herbal, my connection to our magical past becomes tangible and real. Now I invite you to share in this rare enchantment. Many treasures await – whether you are curled up on the sofa with this book upon your lap or exploring the exhibition at the British Library. As you gaze at the astonishing collection of artefacts in *Harry Potter: A History of Magic*, we hope you will be spellbound, too.

Julian Harrison

You were wondering, of course, how to make yourself invisible. According to one 17th-century manuscript entitled *The Book of King Solomon called The Key of Knowledge*, you simply have to recite the following words. Go ahead and try, but please don't blame us if the charm doesn't work!

Stabbon, Asen, Gabellum, Saneney, Noty, Enobal, Labonerem, Balametem, Balnon, Tygumel, Millegaly, Juneneis, Hearma, Hamorache, Yesa, Seya, Senoy, Henen, Barucatha, Acararas, Taracub, Bucarat, Caramy, by the mercy whitch you beare towardes mann kynde, make me to be invysible.

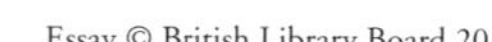

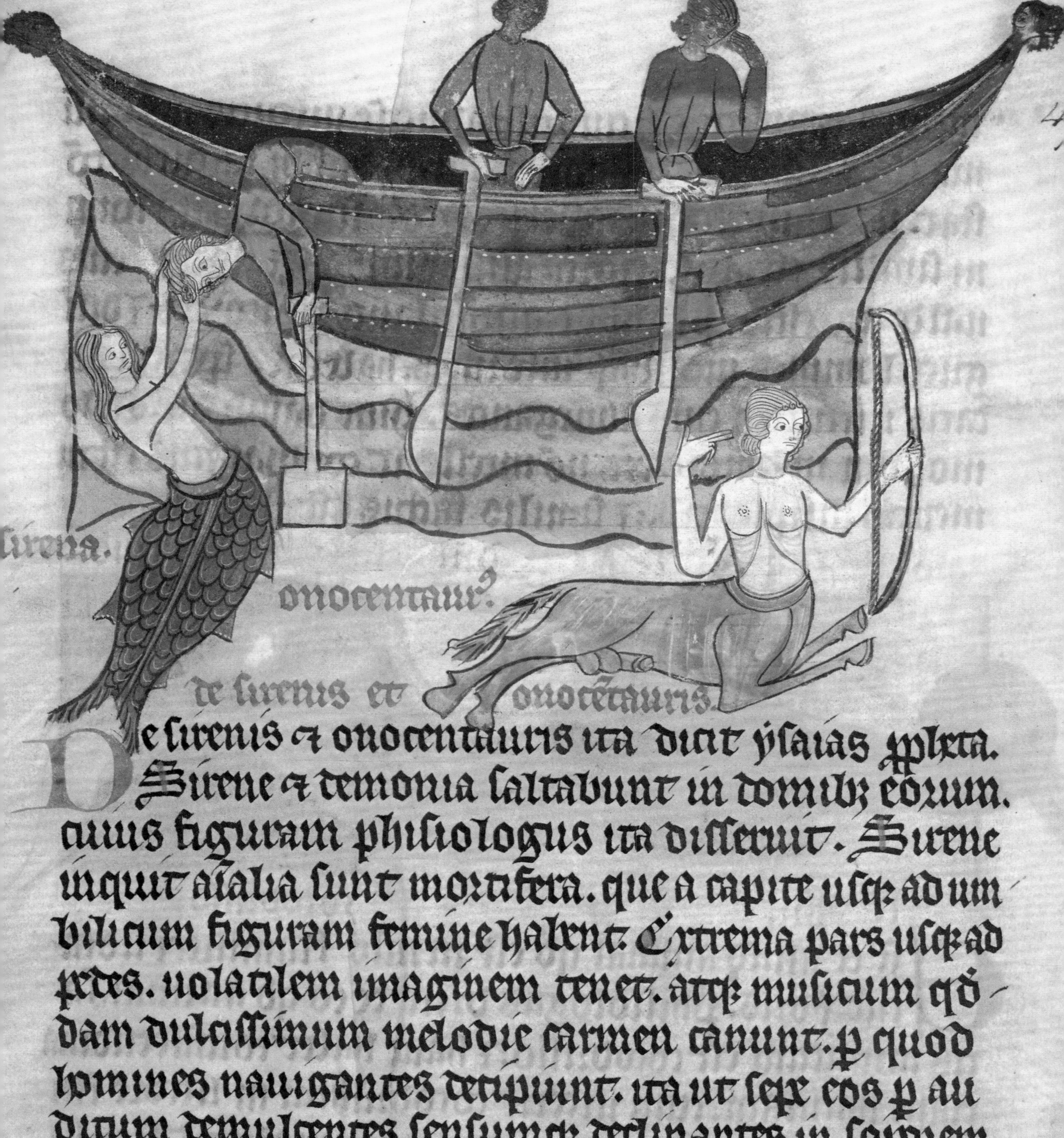

De sirenis et onocentauris ita dicit ysaias propheta.
Sirene et demonia saltabunt in domibus eorum.
cuius figuram phisiologus ita disseruit. Sirene
inquit animalia sunt mortifera. que a capite usque ad um
bilicum figuram femine habent. Extrema pars usque ad
pedes. uolatilem imaginem tenet. atque musicum quo
dam dulcissimum melodie carmen canunt. per quod
homines nauigantes decipiunt. ita ut sepe eos per au
ditum demulcentes sensumque declinantes in soporem
uertant. Et tunc ille uidentes eos sopitos. inuadunt

PROF. ALBUS DUMBLEDORE

The Journey

The Journey

Julia Eccleshare

Julia Eccleshare is Director of Hay Children's Festival, contributing children's books editor of the Guardian, and a regular radio commentator. In addition to chairing the judges of the Guardian Children's Book Prize she is the founder and chair of the Branford Boase Award. Her books include A Guide to the Harry Potter Novels, The Rough Guide to Teenage Books and 1001 Children's Books to Read Before You Grow Up. She was appointed MBE for services to children's literature in 2014 and is currently Head of Public Lending Rights Policy and Engagement at the Britsh Library.

The story of Harry Potter, a boy on the brink of his eleventh birthday at the beginning of a journey of self-discovery and adventure in a magical world, came to Joanne Rowling as she was stuck on a train from Manchester to London in 1990. 'All of a sudden the idea for Harry just appeared in my mind's eye,' she later said. 'I can't tell you why or what triggered it. But I saw the idea of Harry and the wizard school very plainly.' And so, Harry Potter, the most famous fictional character of the 21st century, was born.

A great reader as a child and a student of Classical and European literature, Rowling knew the traditions of fictional heroes and richly invested them in Harry. As a result, the structure of the story is familiar – orphaned Harry, brought up by his cruel relatives, is rescued and transported to an extraordinary boarding school awash with magic where he gradually discovers that he has a great destiny. In essence, there was nothing so very out of the ordinary about Rowling's idea; any experienced reader might have felt they had read such a story before. But those readers should have known better. Rowling's ambition for her hero was immense and she laid it out at the beginning of the very first book. As she leaves the baby on his relatives' doorstep, Professor McGonagall says, 'These people will never understand him! He'll be famous – a legend [...] there will be books written about Harry – every child in our world will know his name!'

But when *Harry Potter and the Philosopher's Stone* was first published, no one knew his name and that grand destiny. The incredible magic of Hogwarts School was confined to the book; it showed no particular signs of becoming anything else. As publishers are when they have an exciting new author and a book with a 'high

JK

concept', Barry Cunningham was passionate about its qualities before publication. Having recently set up the children's list at Bloomsbury he was looking for stories with strong child-appeal. Despite its length, in *Harry Potter and the Philosopher's Stone* he was sure that he had found such a title. The whole of Bloomsbury was galvanised by excitement about the book, and began a campaign to spread the word. Pre-publication proofs were dispatched to all parts of the book trade in the search for endorsement and a prominent place in the bookshops. I received a proof and read it several times, first as a submission for inclusion in a book club where the selection committee – adults all – were enchanted by the magical events of the story and liked Harry as a character. However, they were as much struck by its traditional themes as by its originality and certainly missed spotting its huge potential. It was a fun book to read, we thought its target audience would enjoy it and, much to its credit and an important part of Rowling's vision for it, we wanted to know what happened next.

I read the story again when it was submitted for the Nestlé Smarties Book Prize. Still unpublished, by this point there was a lot of talk about the book. It was beginning to be seen as 'special' particularly because a six-figure sum had been paid for the US rights, a handsome figure for a first novel. Chairing a panel of judges, again all adults, the response to the book was very enthusiastic. Rowling's originality was highly praised, and the universal view was that children would love it. And so it proved. When, several months later, children in schools across the country cast their votes for the 1997 Nestlé Smarties Book Prize Gold Medal, this unknown and still very new author was the runaway winner. Her readers had spoken. They had found a book they adored and the reader-to-reader, word-of-mouth story sharing that has been such a significant feature of the whole sequence had begun.

On publication, *Harry Potter and the Philosopher's Stone* was quietly but well received. A review in the *Scotsman* published two days later described Harry as 'a hugely likeable child, kind but not wet, competitive but always compassionate'. Yet Rowling's name was misspelt in the review and she was so unknown that it was barely noticed. At that moment it would have been hard to identify the book as the blue touchpaper for a publishing phenomenon that would go on to change perceptions of writing for children. More praise followed, including a rave review in the *Sunday Times*, and Bloomsbury secured a book-of-the-month slot for July 1997 across Ottakar's bookstores (now part of Waterstones). Sales began to build as word of mouth spread. But certainly no one predicted the subsequent 'must read' status of Rowling's titles and how that would benefit so many other books for children. Nor did anyone imagine how the series would subtly change how future publishing would engage young people by making reading an experience of belonging and sharing.

Although in 1997 all Rowling's readers had to love was one book, they were already so captivated by the diverse and inventive cast of characters, the originality of everything about Hogwarts and especially Quidditch, that they eagerly awaited the second title. Long held views about the need for a central character to remain one age were instantly upturned by Rowling's bold and unusual decision to allow Harry and his friends to grow up during the stories. For the purpose of Harry's personal destiny it made perfect sense. For readers, it played a big part in tying them into the whole extended narrative. Here was a story to grow up with, a story that kept pace with their own emotional development, a story they could own and inhabit.

And so Professor McGonagall's prophecy came true.

Harry Potter became a legend not just within the stories, but across the real world, too. Rowling gave readers a whole new place to play in – one rich in imagination, vivid in adventure and deep in emotion. She offered big ideas about identity, parental love, bravery, insecurity and much more, deftly wrapping everything up with magic. Her readers were spellbound.

Julia Eccleshare

THE BOY WHO LIVED

In this preparatory sketch by Jim Kay, Harry Potter is shown with his glasses taped up at the bridge and dark hair that just never *would* lie flat. He looks askance to the side, with a cheeky glint in his eyes, reminiscent of his father's mischievous nature. At this stage no colour has been added to the image, because Kay often digitally layers colour over the original drawing – we cannot see the green colour of Harry's eyes, a reminder of his mother, Lily. Harry Potter's youth and unworldliness at the beginning of the story is captured perfectly in this image, but it also looks like he may be the possessor of a wonderful secret. Kay's sketch invites us to reflect on the development of Harry's character throughout the books, from the wide-eyed child to the brave young man who stands up against Lord Voldemort.

➢ PORTRAIT OF HARRY POTTER
BY JIM KAY
Bloomsbury

"Jim Kay's portrait brings to life a young boy who seems both innocent and fragile. His large, expressive eyes, however, suggest a depth of character hidden beneath the surface. We get the feeling that there is a lot more about Harry Potter for us to discover ..."

JOANNA NORLEDGE
Curator

Harry looked up into the fierce, wild, shadowy face and saw that the beetle eyes were crinkled in a smile. 'Las' time I saw you, you was only a baby,' said the giant. 'Yeh look a lot like yer dad, but yeh've got yer mum's eyes.'

Harry Potter and the Philosopher's Stone

Synopsis

Harry Potter lives with his aunt, uncle and cousin because his parents died in a car-crash - or so he has always been told. The Dursleys don't like Harry asking questions; in fact, they don't seem to like anything about him, especially the very odd things that keep happening around him (which Harry himself can't explain).

The Dursleys' greatest fear is that Harry will discover the truth about himself, so when letters start arriving for him near his eleventh birthday, he isn't allowed to read them. However, the Dursleys aren't dealing with an ordinary postman, and at midnight on Harry's birthday the gigantic Rubeus Hagrid breaks down the door to make sure Harry gets to read his post at last. Ignoring the horrified Dursleys, Hagrid informs Harry that he is a wizard, and the letter he gives Harry explains that he is expected at Hogwarts School of Witchcraft and Wizardry in a month's time.

To the Dursleys' fury, Hagrid also reveals the truth about Harry's past. Harry did not receive the scar on his forehead in a car-crash; it is really the mark of the great dark sorcerer Voldemort, who killed Harry's mother and father but mysteriously couldn't kill him, even though he was a baby at the time. Harry is famous among the witches and wizards who live in secret all over the country because Harry's miraculous survival marked Voldemort's downfall.

So Harry, who has never had friends or family worth the name, sets off for a new life in the wizarding world. He takes a trip to London with Hagrid to buy his Hogwarts equipment (robes, wand, cauldron, beginners' draft and potion kit) and shortly afterwards, sets off for Hogwarts from Kings Cross Station (platform nine and three quarters) to follow in his parents' footsteps.

Harry makes friends with Ronald Weasley (sixth in his family to go to Hogwarts and tired of having to use second-hand spellbooks) and Hermione Granger (cleverest girl in the year and the only person in the class to know all the uses of dragon's blood). Together, they have their first lessons in magic - astonomy up on the tallest tower at two in the morning, herbology out in the greenhouses where the mandrakes and wolfsbane are kept, potions down in the dungeons with the loathsome Severus Snape. Harry, Ron and Hermione discover the school's secret passageways, learn how to deal with Peeves the poltergeist and how to tackle an angry mountain troll: best of all, Harry becomes a star player at Quidditch (wizard football played on broomsticks).

What interests Harry and his friends most, though, is why the corridor on the third floor is so heavily guarded. Following up a clue dropped by Hagrid (who, when he is not delivering letters, is Hogwarts' gamekeeper), they discover that the only Philosopher's Stone in existance is being kept at Hogwarts, a stone with powers to give limitless wealth and eternal life. Harry, Ron and Hermione seem to be the only people who have realised that Snape the potions master is planning to steal the stone - and what terrible things it could do in the wrong hands.
For the Philospher's Stone is all that is needed to bring Voldemort back to full strength and power... it seems Harry has come to Hogwarts to meet his parents' killer face to face - with no idea how he survived last time...

SYNOPSIS OF *HARRY POTTER AND THE PHILOSOPHER'S STONE*
BY J.K. ROWLING (1995)
J.K. Rowling

THE AUTHOR'S SYNOPSIS

This is the original synopsis of the first Harry Potter book, typed to accompany the opening chapters of *The Philosopher's Stone* and circulated among prospective agents and publishers. It was this synopsis that was submitted to Bloomsbury, persuading them to offer J.K. Rowling her first contract. With folded corners, tea stains and crumpled grip marks at the bottom, it is a document that has clearly been read and handled a great deal. From the very beginning, the lessons at Hogwarts were part of what makes Harry Potter's world so captivating. In just a few short lines, J.K. Rowling makes learning magic sound like amazing fun. Who wouldn't want to study Astronomy 'in the tallest tower at two in the morning' and Herbology in the greenhouses 'where the mandrake and wolfsbane are kept'?

A CRITICAL MOMENT FOR THE PHILOSOPHER'S STONE

Prior to being accepted for publication by Bloomsbury, the manuscript of *Harry Potter and the Philosopher's Stone* was famously offered to some eight publishers, all of whom rejected it. The Bloomsbury editorial staff presented J.K. Rowling's manuscript to their colleagues in the form of a scroll, and filled it with Smarties, a nod to the leading children's book award at that time (the Smarties Prize). Nigel Newton, founder and Chief Executive of Bloomsbury, took the scroll home and gave it to his eight-year-old daughter, Alice. Alice read the chapters, which went as far as Diagon Alley, and then gave her verdict, as preserved in this charming note. For long after she pestered her father to bring home the remainder of the manuscript. Alice's intervention was crucial: at the following day's acquisitions meeting, of which he was chairman, Nigel Newton approved editor Barry Cunningham's proposal that *The Philosopher's Stone* be published by Bloomsbury, leading to what is widely regarded as the most successful venture in children's publishing history.

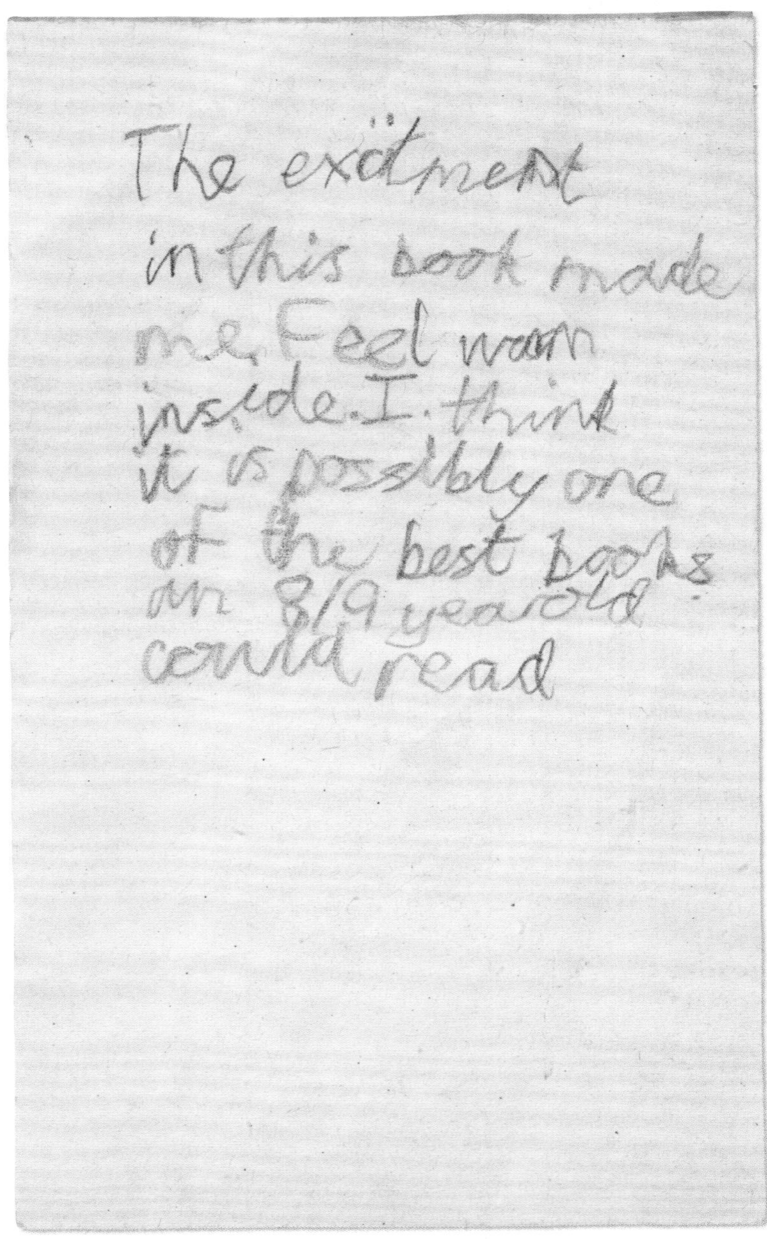

The exitment in this book made me Feel warm inside. I think it is possibly one of the best books an 8/9 year old could read

➢ READER'S REPORT OF ALICE NEWTON, AGED EIGHT, ON *HARRY POTTER AND THE PHILOSOPHER'S STONE*

Nigel Newton (Chief Executive, Bloomsbury Publishing Plc)

The excitement in this book made me feel warm inside. I think it is possibly one of the best books an 8/9 year old could read.

Alice Newton

HARRY POTTER AND THE DURSLEYS

Harry Potter's journey began at four, Privet Drive, the house of Vernon and Petunia Dursley. One morning, the Dursleys woke up to find baby Harry placed on their doorstep. This drawing is a family portrait of Mr and Mrs Dursley, their son Dudley, and Harry. The Dursleys' sour expressions are in contrast to that of their nephew. Despite the misery he experienced living at Privet Drive, Harry is the only person who seems able to raise a smile. The boy's baggy T-shirt emphasises his frailty in comparison to his sturdier relatives. Dudley Dursley has been drawn with his arms folded in a permanent sulk, and a large piggy nose that makes him appear particularly beastly. Uncle Vernon stands glaring behind, while Aunt Petunia protectively clasps her son's shoulder.

> *"This early drawing by J.K. Rowling was made several years before* The Philosopher's Stone *was published. It is an expressive picture that makes it instantly clear that Harry does not belong in the Dursley family."*
>
> JOANNA NORLEDGE
> *Curator*

A DRAWING OF HARRY POTTER AND THE DURSLEYS BY J.K. ROWLING (1991)
J.K. Rowling

6 HOURS SLEEP IN THREE DAYS.

THE HOGWARTS EXPRESS

This painting by Jim Kay is a preliminary version of the artwork featured on the front cover of the illustrated edition of *The Philosopher's Stone*. It shows the busy platform nine and three-quarters at King's Cross as students board the Hogwarts Express at the beginning of term. Harry Potter is singled out, standing with his loaded trolley and Hedwig amidst the hustle and bustle of families seeing off their children. The Hogwarts Express has a fierce, fire-breathing animal head decorating the top of its chimney and a shining bright light – a small winged hog sits at the very front, a nod to the name of Hogwarts. This journey marked Harry's transition to the world of magic, away from the Muggle-realm of the Dursleys.

STUDY OF PLATFORM NINE AND THREE-QUARTERS BY JIM KAY
Bloomsbury

A scarlet steam engine was waiting next to a platform packed with people.

Harry Potter and the Philosopher's Stone

WELCOME TO HOGWARTS

This annotated sketch by J.K. Rowling shows the layout of Hogwarts School of Witchcraft and Wizardry, complete with the giant squid that lives in the lake. In an accompanying note addressed to her editor, J.K. Rowling stated, 'This is the layout as I've always imagined it.' Another map of Hogwarts, the Marauder's Map, also plays an important role in the stories. The sketch provides a vital stepping stone between the author's imagination and the world she has brought to life for so many readers. The majority of the novels take place primarily at Hogwarts – this is the playground in which Harry learns about the wizarding world and, ultimately, realises his destiny.

➢ SKETCH OF HOGWARTS
BY J.K. ROWLING
Bloomsbury

"The positioning of the buildings and trees on the map are integral to the storylines of the Harry Potter books. Note how the author insists that the 'Whomping Willow must stand out', recognising its significance in The Chamber of Secrets *and* The Prisoner of Azkaban.*"*

JOANNA NORLEDGE
Curator

Slipping and stumbling, they followed Hagrid down what seemed to be a steep, narrow path [...] There was a loud 'Oooooh!'. The narrow path had opened suddenly on to the edge of a great black lake. Perched atop a high mountain on the other side, its windows sparkling in the starry sky, was a vast castle with many turrets and towers.

Harry Potter and the Philosopher's Stone

N

W E

S

Forbidden forest is massive, stretches out of sight.

Southern approach over lake (castle stands on high cliff above lake/loch) – station's on other side)

To reach the school by stagecoach, go right round lake to front entrance at North.

Giant squid in lake.

Seats all around Quidditch pitch – 3 long poles with hoops on at either end.

There can be other trees/bushes dotted around lawns but Whomping Willow must stand out.

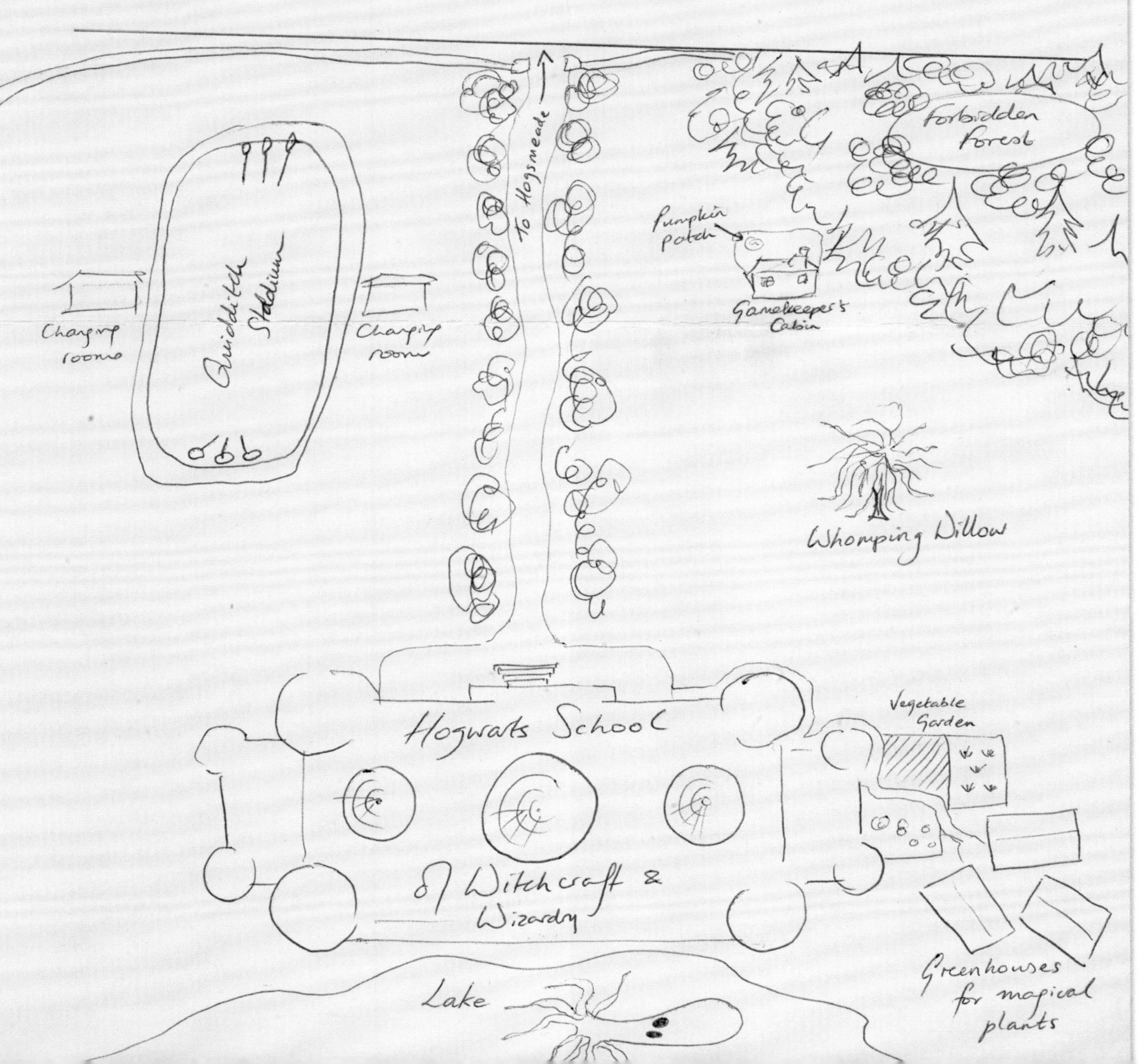

PROFESSOR DUMBLEDORE

This portrait of Professor Albus Percival Wulfric Brian Dumbledore shows him gazing intently towards the right with bright blue eyes. A gargoyle vase sits on the table containing the dried branch of the plant of *Lunaria annua* or 'honesty', known for its translucent seedpods. There is also a small flask, containing what might well be dragon's blood, referring to the wizard's achievement of discovering all twelve uses of the magical substance. Dumbledore's favourite sweets, lemon sherbets, feature as one of the passwords to his office. His knitting lies to one side, the orange wool curling across the table. Jim Kay's portrait captures the complexity of Dumbledore's personality – the powerful and serious wizard with a penchant for sweets and knitting.

PORTRAIT OF PROFESSOR ALBUS DUMBLEDORE BY JIM KAY
Bloomsbury

"Albus means 'white' in Latin. Hagrid's first name Rubeus means 'red'. Harry's two father figures symbolically represent different stages of the alchemical process needed to create the Philosopher's Stone."

JOANNA NORLEDGE
Curator

PROFESSOR McGONAGALL

Professor Minerva McGonagall is Deputy Headmistress, Head of Gryffindor House and Transfiguration teacher at Hogwarts. Dressed in dark green with her hair drawn back in a severe bun, this portrait captures her intelligence and no-nonsense attitude. Her glasses sit low on her nose, ideal for peering piercingly at students. As a registered Animagus, she can transform into a cat. Becoming an Animagus is a complex process that involves holding a mandrake leaf in your mouth for a month. She is named 'Minerva' after the Roman goddess of wisdom – her surname echoes the notoriously bad Scottish poet, William McGonagall. The juxtaposition of giving such a highly capable and intelligent character the surname of a hopelessly awful poet is an example of the humour and wit employed throughout the world of Harry Potter.

PORTRAIT OF PROFESSOR MINERVA McGONAGALL BY JIM KAY
Bloomsbury

A tall, black-haired witch in emerald-green robes stood there. She had a very stern face and Harry's first thought was that this was not someone to cross.

Harry Potter and the Philosopher's Stone

THE TALES OF BEEDLE THE BARD

In the final Harry Potter novel, Dumbledore bequeaths his own copy of *The Tales of Beedle the Bard,* written in runes, to Hermione Granger. It contains several bedtime fairy stories told widely in the magical world, equivalent to Muggle stories. One particular tale, 'The Tale of the Three Brothers', plays a vital role in helping Harry, Hermione and Ron to uncover three legendary magical objects known as the Deathly Hallows – the Elder Wand, the Resurrection Stone and the Invisibility Cloak. This copy of *Beedle the Bard* was handwritten by J.K. Rowling and embellished with rhodochrosite stones, associated with love and balance. It was originally gifted to Barry Cunningham, who accepted the first Harry Potter book for publication by Bloomsbury. This copy also features small illustrations, such as the stump featured in 'Babbitty Rabbitty and her Cackling Stump'.

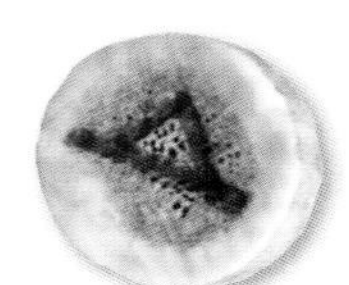

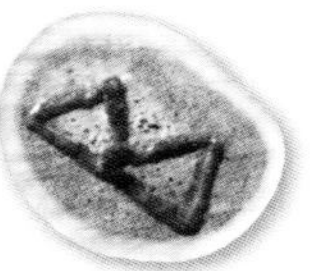

DIVINATION RUNES

Runes are the characters of an early Germanic writing system, used in parts of northern Europe from roughly the 2nd century AD to the early 16th century. They have long been understood to possess magical qualities. The common Germanic root of the word 'rune' is *run*, which meant 'mystery' or 'secrecy' in the languages – Old Norse, Old High German, Old English – that employed these characters. Although runes are no longer written today, their symbols are still commonly used in magic. Made from antler, these divination discs are inscribed with red runes, with the intention that they be scattered and then interpreted.

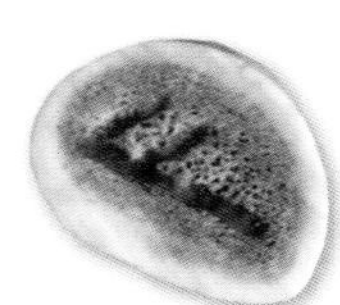

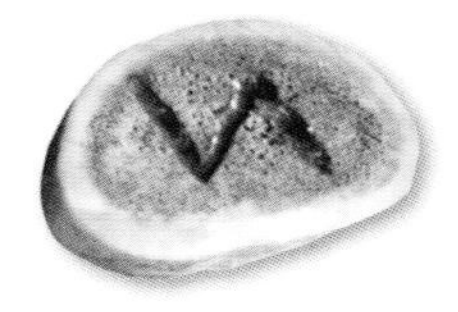

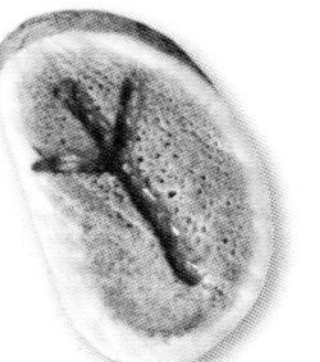

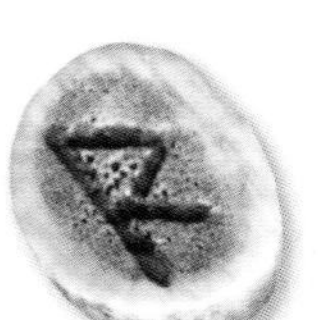

RUNE ANTLER DISCS
The Museum of Witchcraft and Magic, Boscastle

◁ *THE TALES OF BEEDLE THE BARD*
BY J.K. ROWLING ▽
Private Owner

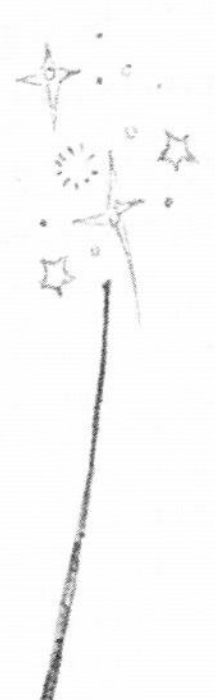

Babbitty Rabbitty
and her Cackling Stump

A long time ago, in a far off land, there lived a foolish King, who decided that he alone should have the power of magic.

heed for this thy fire
The fire with water brent shall be
And water with fire wash shall he
Then earth on fire shall be put
And water with aire shall be knitt
The which whiteness is forever abiding
Lo here is a very full finishing
Of the white Stone & the red
Here is the very true deed.
The Red Lyon
The green Lyon
The mouth of Collerick beware
Here is the last of the Red. And the begining to put away the Dead, The Elixir Vitæ
father that Phœbus hight
th so high in Majesty
s beames that shines so bright
ces were they be
father of all things
ner of life to crop & roote
seth nature for to spring
he wiffe being sothe
salve to every sore
about this precious work
d heed unto this lore
unto lewd & clerk
Divide thou Phœbus in many parts
With his beams that be so bright
And thus with nature him conjoin
The which is mirrour of all light
This Phœbus know hath many a name
Which that is full hard to know
And but thou take the very same
The Philosophers Stone thou shalt not know
Therefore I councell thee ere thou begin

POTIONS AND ALCHEMY

Potions and Alchemy

Roger Highfield

Roger Highfield is the Director of External Affairs at the Science Museum Group, and author of The Science of Harry Potter: How Magic Really Works. Former Editor of New Scientist and Science Editor of the Daily Telegraph, Roger was the first person to bounce a neutron off a soap bubble. He has written two bestsellers and won various prizes for journalism, notably a British Press Award.

'You are here to learn the subtle science and exact art of potion-making.'

Surrounded by wooden desks, steaming cauldrons, potions bottles, apothecary jars and brass scales in the dungeons of Hogwarts, Harry Potter learned much during Severus Snape's classes about wormwood, puffer-fish eyes, wolfsbane and other peculiar ingredients.

The cauldrons used to concoct potions are one of the most potent symbols of witchcraft. Snape himself was entranced by the 'beauty of the softly simmering cauldron with its shimmering fumes, the delicate power of liquids that creep through human veins, bewitching the mind, ensnaring the senses'. They have been used for a long time – one magical example, dredged out of the Thames in 1861, was forged from riveted bronze sheets dating from the late Bronze Age/early Iron Age, between 600 and 800 BC. It would take the publication of *On Witches and Female Fortune Tellers* in 1489 however, the earliest illustrated treatise on witchcraft, to demonstrate one in use by witches. Two elderly women are shown using a cauldron to conjure up a hailstorm with the help of a snake and a cockerel. The treatise influenced attitudes to nature and women, even more so when it was reproduced widely as a result of a relatively newfangled technology known as printing.

Even in the Muggle world, there are many old books packed with the kind of recipes favoured by witches and wizards, reflecting how, though polar opposites, the worlds of science and magic shared the same inspiration long ago, in this case through the quest for cures. Strange treatments dating back a millennium can be found in Bald's Leechbook (nothing to do with hair restoration but the name of the original owner, a 10th-century Anglo-Saxon physician). Written in Old English, you can browse all sorts of 'Potions and leechdoms against poison'. There is a handy antidote to snakebite, for example – simply smear earwax around the puncture wounds left by the reptile's fangs and recite the prayer of St John. One can get an intuitive grasp of how treatments which sound bizarre today could take hold long

ago – of all the people bitten by snakes every year only a tiny fraction end up as fatalities, so if every one of them had smeared earwax and chanted prayers, the vast majority would have survived to tell their friends that this prescription really had worked.

In the wizarding world, Snape mentioned another way to counter poisons that would have been familiar to Muggles long ago, and a few still use them today. A 'stone' consisting of a hairball or mass of indigestible material found in the stomach of an animal such as a goat or antelope was thought to be an antidote. Called a bezoar after the Persian word for 'counter poison', its potency depends on the animal that produced it, according to *A Compleat History of Druggs* (1694). The best stones of all were hoarded by popes, kings and noblemen. From the 18th century onwards, the bezoar's magical healing properties were increasingly questioned, but a recent study conducted at the Scripps Institution of Oceanography, San Diego, suggested that the stones might have the capacity to bind arsenic poison to the minerals and degraded hair they contain. Harry Potter's graffitied copy of *Advanced Potion-Making* gave the following succinct advice on how to deal with poisoning:

Just shove a bezoar down their throats.

If you wanted to become immortal, you required something more powerful. Only the Philosopher's Stone had transformative properties also capable of turning base metals into gold. Voldemort craved this Elixir of Life, but thanks to Harry's intervention, the Dark Lord would end up joining a legion of disappointed people who tried and failed in the age-old quest for the Stone, ranging from Chinese rulers to Holy Roman emperors, with armies of alchemists in between.

Just as astrologers focused on humanity's relationship with the stars, alchemists focused on our relationship with terrestrial nature, blending chemistry with magic. Lacking a common language for their concepts and processes, they borrowed signs and symbols from mythology and astrology, so that even a basic recipe read like a magic spell. The one used to create the Philosopher's Stone was a closely guarded secret that early alchemists kept deliberately obscure.

The endeavour to find the Elixir of Life was not entirely in vain, however. Through careful study of alchemical formulae, pictures and codes, and by attempting to recreate those early experiments, historians and scientists have discovered that some leading alchemists helped lay the foundations of scientific chemistry.

One of the most beautiful and symbolic representations of the alchemical process can be seen in the intricate Ripley Scroll. The scroll was named after the English alchemist George Ripley, a canon at Bridlington Priory in Yorkshire. Only 23 are known to exist – one was only identified as recently as 2012 by the Science Museum – and all are thought to be copies and variations upon a lost 15th-century original. When the entire scroll is unfurled one can see dragons, toads and a robed, bearded figure (perhaps Ripley himself?), clutching an alchemical vessel.

J.K. Rowling deftly draws on historical fact with the character of Nicolas Flamel. Flamel was a real person who lived in the 14th century. His work was known to influential 17th-century alchemists such as Robert Boyle and Sir Isaac Newton. He supposedly prepared the Philosopher's Stone (it did eventually become clear that the idea of one element being turned into another was not so potty after all in 1932,

when atom splitting apparatus was used to carry out the first true transmutation by John Cockcroft and Ernest Walton at the Cavendish Laboratory in Cambridge). The real-world Flamel was also believed to have made the Elixir of Life. Alas the elixir did not seem to do him much good, however – history tells us that Nicolas actually died in around 1418. His gravestone now belongs to the Musée national du Moyen Âge.

The German alchemist Hennig Brand also spent years in search of the Philosopher's Stone. That quest was a stretch too far, but in around 1669 he did manage to isolate phosphorus from urine. He decided to name the element after the Greek word for 'light-bearer'. The find made a deep impression at the time. Such was the impact of Brand's feat that, more than a century later, English artist, Joseph Wright of Derby, captured the breakthrough in his painting *The Alchymist, In Search of the Philosopher's Stone, Discovers Phosphorus, and prays for the successful Conclusion of his operation, as was the custom of the Ancient Chymical Astrologers.*

Alchemy began to give way to chemistry with the publication of *The Sceptical Chymist* by Boyle in 1661, suggesting that matter consists of atoms. After this came pioneering work by French nobleman Antoine-Laurent Lavoisier and the Russian Dmitri Mendeleev, who created a periodic table in 1869. As if to underline how chemistry had by then eclipsed alchemy, Mendeleev's table could be used to predict the properties of elements that had yet to be discovered.

In the centuries since, Muggles have thrived on the scientific culture of evidence-gathering, scepticism, testing and provisional consensus-forming. Just take a moment to think about what we take for granted today in terms of life expectancy, for example. We can predict important chemical reactions, such as how a drug will work in the body. We can anticipate eclipses, plot the course of a spacecraft across the Solar System, and forecast the weather. We can apply science in many diverse and incredible innovations, from iPads and DNA tests to reusable rockets and the Web. This is true wizardry for, as Arthur C. Clarke once remarked, any sufficiently advanced technology is indistinguishable from magic.

THE POTIONS MASTER

Harry Potter's first glimpse of Professor Snape is of a man 'with greasy black hair, a hooked nose and sallow skin'. In this portrait by Jim Kay, Snape looks listlessly down at something out of sight, with half a sneer contorting one side of his face. The bottled mole signifies his role as a spy for the Order of the Phoenix, while the lilies by his hands represent his enduring love for Harry's mother, Lily. The scissors refer to *Sectumsempra*, the Dark Magic spell Snape had invented. A snake pattern decorates his shirt, while a snake clasp pins his cloak at the neck. His green cravat and the table top echo the colour of his house, Slytherin. J.K. Rowling has explained elsewhere that, in the novels, Dark Magic is often represented by the colour green.

PORTRAIT OF PROFESSOR SEVERUS SNAPE BY JIM KAY
Bloomsbury

"This formal portrait captures the sneering Professor Snape that Harry so mistrusts in the first book, but the objects scattered in front of him hint at his complex character and his role in the stories."

JOANNA NORLEDGE
Curator

At the start-of-term banquet, Harry had got the idea that Professor Snape disliked him. By the end of the first Potions lesson, he knew he'd been wrong. Snape didn't dislike Harry – he ***hated*** *him.*

Harry Potter and the Philosopher's Stone

A POTIONS CLASS

This medieval book, *Ortus Sanitatis*, is the first printed encyclopedia of natural history, featuring sections devoted to plants, animals, birds, fish and stones. The title is Latin for 'The Garden of Health'. In this woodcut engraving we are shown a Potions master instructing a group of students. The page appears at the beginning of the section called '*De Lapidibus*' (On Stones), and it has been coloured by hand. The Potions master is shown wearing an ermine-lined grey cloak, clutching a stick in his left hand, with his assistant before him holding open a book of recipes.

"The Ortus Sanitatis *is an important scientific book, but this illustration is also packed with wonderful human detail. Work is in progress in this scene, but it is questionable how much attention the students are paying to their teacher."*

JULIAN HARRISON
Lead Curator

JACOB MEYDENBACH, *ORTUS SANITATIS* (MAINZ, 1491)
British Library

De Lapidibus.

Prohemiū.

Ca. primū.

Operationes.

¶ Ulricus. Dico q̄ nō possunt. nisi quādo ⁊ q̄bus ac inq̄ntum
a deo ex causa maiestatē suā mouente eisdem ꝯceditur ¶ Sigis
mundus. Super quo fundas hanc ꝯclusionē ¶ Ulricus. Su
per prius deductis. Insup Johānes damascenus libro scd̄o ait
Non habent demones virtutes aduersus aliquē nisi a deo dis
pensante ꝯcedatur. sicut in Job patuit. ⁊ etiā in porcis quos di
uina ꝑmissione submerserunt in mari. vt ptz in euangelio Etiā
habent potestatem transformādi seu transfigurādi se in quācūq
volunt figurā ſm ymaginē. i. ſm fantasiam. Item Gregorius
in dyalogo libro tercio ait. Absq omnipotentis dei concessio
E i

FIRE BURN AND CAULDRON BUBBLE

Although the association of cauldrons with witches dates back to at least the 6th century, this motif did not gain widespread acceptance until *On Witches and Female Fortune Tellers* was published in 1489. Ulrich Molitor's book is the earliest illustrated treatise on witchcraft. It contains the first printed depiction of witches with a cauldron. This page shows two elderly women placing a snake and a cockerel into a large flaming pot, in a bid to summon a hailstorm. The book was so widely reproduced, it helped to consolidate modern impressions of how witches were supposed to behave. Molitor addressed *On Witches* to Sigismund III, Archduke of Austria and Tyrol, who wished to refute witchcraft and demonic practices.

ULRICH MOLITOR, *DE LANIIS ET PHITONICIS MULIERIBUS … TRACTATUS PULCHERRIMUS* (REUTLINGEN, 1489)
British Library

'I don't expect you will really understand the beauty of the softly simmering cauldron with its shimmering fumes, the delicate power of liquids that creep through human veins, bewitching the mind, ensnaring the senses'

Professor Snape, Harry Potter and the Philosopher's Stone

"The woodcut illustration in this book was massively influential. The image of women gathered around a cauldron established a powerful visual iconography for witchcraft that has lasted for centuries. Not everybody can read words, but anyone can read a picture."

ALEXANDER LOCK
Curator

THE BATTERSEA CAULDRON

Cauldrons are one of the most potent symbols of witchcraft. They probably came in all shapes and sizes, and were used historically for different purposes, including creating potions. This magnificent example was not necessarily associated with witches, but still has a fascinating history. It is almost three thousand years old and was created by riveting together seven plates of sheet bronze. The craftsmanship is so fine that it can only have been made for a wealthy owner. Sometime around 1861, more than two millennia after it had been manufactured, this cauldron was fished out of the River Thames at Battersea in South London.

"The Battersea Cauldron is a true survivor. Even today, its condition remains superb. It seems unlikely that the cauldron was dropped into the Thames by accident. It may have been deposited as a votive offering."

JULIAN HARRISON
Lead Curator

Hermione threw the new ingredients into the cauldron and began to stir feverishly. 'It'll be ready in a fortnight,' she said happily. *Harry Potter and the Chamber of Secrets*

THE BATTERSEA CAULDRON
(C. 800–600 BC)
British Museum

MEDIEVAL MEDICINE

Few manuscripts have as exotic a name as Bald's Leechbook, so called after its first owner – 'Bald owns this book, which he ordered Cild to compile'. Bald's work is an attempt to incorporate everything that is known about medicine from the Anglo-Saxon and Mediterranean world. This chapter begins, 'Potions and leechdoms against poison', dealing in particular with antidotes to snakebite. One remedy prescribes putting 'so much betony as weighs three pennies' into three bowls full of wine, then giving it to the bitten man to drink. Snakebite could also be treated by smearing earwax around the wound and reciting the prayer of St John. Don't try this at home!

> *"Scientists have subsequently tested some of Bald's recipes. Far from being naive, many of the medical practices revealed useful applications for the modern world. One was even shown to counteract the MRSA virus."*
>
> JULIAN HARRISON
> *Lead Curator*

Snape put them all into pairs and set them to mixing up a simple potion to cure boils. He swept around in his long black cloak, watching them weigh dried nettles and crush snake fangs, criticising almost everyone except Malfoy, whom he seemed to like.

Harry Potter and the Philosopher's Stone

➢ BALD'S LEECHBOOK (ENGLAND, 10TH CENTURY)
British Library

- sealfe clænsian þ dolh
sealf wiþ cancre. genim
þe læt weorþan to flete
wætre on wætre. nim sigel
un wyrtne doclane cnua
þære butan þam don on wan
l swiþe awring wel þurh clað
cancer adle. ac wind on
wþan. 7 meng wyrt mid þe
- weard. cum gliffe mid þo
ela gecnua to duste. do hunig
nig do begea ... fela gemeng
clam ondone cancer ne do

XLV.

cas 7 læcedomas. betonican
finul. pedic. cnua on ealað
ætwre betonican 7 þa sina
doon halig wæter drince þ
a. wid ælcum ætwre. pedic
neg þe nanman ætwre
elcum ætwre biscop wyrt

ni þe wearð 7 geleh tre. 7 springwyrt mid þe
eoforþrotan 7 elatan. awyl on ealað sele d
gelome. Gif nædre slea man þone blac
snægl awesc on halig wætre sele drincan
hwæt hwega þæs þe swa scottum come.
wegbrædan gecnid swiþe drinc on wine
nædran bite betonican þ te þry wingæras
wyrte don þry bollan fulle wines sele dri
Wiþ nædran bite læt wif leafe awringe cnu
win gemenged god biþ to drincanne.
nædran bite læt æcele þonne gecnu fulade
ce on niht nestig. iii. bollan fulle. W
nædran slege springwyrt. ætorlaþan
eoforþrotan. biscopwyrt wyrte to drin
Wiþ þon þe mon hæbbe ætor. genim þa hara
hunan gewyrc micelne dæl 7 nædder wyr
cnua togædere 7 wring þ seaw do wines
mel on 7 sele drincan. Wiþ nædran s
nim wegbrædan 7 agrimonian 7 nædder
wyrt sele gecnidene on wine drincan.
wyrc sealfe of þam ilcum wyrtum. 7 nim þ

'It's Veritaserum, a colourless, odourless potion that forces the drinker to tell the truth,' said Hermione.

'Very good, very good!' said Slughorn, beaming at her. 'Now, this one here is pretty well-known… featured in a few Ministry leaflets lately, too… who can -?'

he continued pointing at the cauldron nearest the Ravenclaw table

Hermione's hand was fastest once more.

'It's Polyjuice Potion, sir,' she said.

Harry, too, had recognised the slow-bubbling, mud-like substance in the second cauldron, but did not resent Hermione getting the credit for answering the question; she, after all, was the one who had succeeded in making it, back in their second year.

'Excellent, excellent! Now, this one here… yes, my dear?' said Slughorn, now looking slightly bemused, as Hermione's hand punched the air again.

'It's Amortentia!'

'It is indeed. It seems almost foolish to ask,' said Slughorn, who was looking mightily impressed, 'but I assume you know what it does?'

'It's the most powerful love potion in the world!' said Hermione.

'Quite right! You recognised it, I suppose, by its distinctive mother-of-pearl sheen?'

'And the steam rising in characteristic spirals,' said Hermione. *

'May I ask your name, my dear?' said Slughorn, ignoring these signs of embarrassment.

'Hermione Granger, sir.'

'Granger? Granger? Can you possibly be related to Hector Dagworth-Granger, who founded the Most Extraordinary Society of Potioneers?'

'No, I don't think so, sir. I'm Muggle-born, you see.'

* 'and it's supposed to smell differently to each of us, according to what attracts us, and I can smell freshly-mown grass and new parchment and –'
But she turned slightly pink and did not complete the sentence

175

HARRY POTTER AND THE HALF-BLOOD PRINCE

These two pages show annotations by J.K. Rowling and her editor on a typed draft of *Harry Potter and the Half-Blood Prince.* The action on the first page takes place in Professor Slughorn's class. The wizard presents a series of potions, which Hermione, naturally, is able to identify as Veritaserum, Polyjuice Potion, Amortentia and Felix Felicis. The detail marked by an asterisk reveals the smells that Hermione finds attractive, including the scent of 'new parchment'. The second page is the draft of a scene in which Harry consults the Half-Blood Prince's copy of *Advanced Potion-Making* to find out how to brew more Felix Felicis. He notices another spell, *Sectumsempra,* that he has been itching to try out, only later realising the danger of using an unknown spell.

DRAFT OF *HARRY POTTER AND THE HALF-BLOOD PRINCE,* ANNOTATED BY J.K. ROWLING AND HER EDITOR (C. 2004–2005?)
Bloomsbury

"These marked-up pages offer a real insight into the editing process. I particularly love the additional detail that has been worked in at this late stage. The insertion of Hermione's favourite scents adds depth to the character."

JOANNA NORLEDGE
Curator

'How many times have we been through this?' she said wearily. 'There's a big difference between needing to use the room and wanting to see what Malfoy needs it for –'

'Harry might need the same thing as Malfoy and not know he needs it!' said Ron. 'Harry, if you took a bit of Felix, you might suddenly feel the same need as Malfoy –'

'Harry, don't go wasting the rest of that Potion! You'll need all the luck you can get if Dumbledore takes you along with him to destroy a,' she dropped her voice to a whisper, 'horcrux – so you just stop encouraging him to take a slug of Felix every time he wants something!' she added sternly to Ron.

'Couldn't we make some more?' Ron asked Harry, ignoring Hermione. 'It'd be great to have a stock of it… have a look in the book…'

Harry pulled his copy of *Advanced Potion-Making* out of his bag and looked up *Felix Felicis.*

'Blimey, it's seriously complicated,' he said, running an eye down the list of ingredients. 'And it takes six months… you've got to let it stew…'

'Dammit,' said Ron.

Harry was about to put his book away again when he noticed that the corner of a page turned down; turning to it, he saw the 'Sectumsempra' spell, captioned 'for Enemies,' that he had marked a few weeks previously. He had still not found out what it did, mainly because he did not want to test it around Hermione, but he was considering trying it out on McLaggen next time he came up behind him unawares.

The only person who was not particularly pleased to see Katie Bell back at school was Dean Thomas, because he would no longer be required to fill her place as Chaser. He took the blow stoically enough when Harry told him, merely grunting and

A TRIP TO THE APOTHECARY

This illustration of an apothecary's shop appears in a 14th-century French manuscript that was created for a surgeon. The apothecary is perhaps the figure in the centre wearing a grey cowl who has handed a striped jar to his seated customer. There is a flat dish hanging from a hook fixed to the ceiling that would be used for mixing his ingredients. This manuscript has passed through numerous hands, from Amiens in northern France all the way to the library of King Henry VIII of England. It was eventually acquired by the physician and collector, Sir Hans Sloane – the man after whom Sloane Square in London is named.

AN APOTHECARY'S SHOP, IN A SURGEON'S MANUSCRIPT (FRANCE, 14TH CENTURY)
British Library

"An apothecary was a medical professional, the equivalent to a modern pharmacist, who dispensed supplies to physicians and their patients. The blue pigment used in the illustration still looks bright and vibrant, hundreds of years after it was first applied."

JULIAN HARRISON
Lead Curator

AN APOTHECARY'S SIGN

Throughout history, the blood, hair and horns of unicorns were believed to possess powerful medicinal properties. Because of their rarity, they commanded very high prices. In *The Philosopher's Stone*, Voldemort survives on unicorn blood, and potions are made from 'silver unicorn horns' that in Diagon Alley cost 'twenty-one Galleons'. This 18th-century sign from an apothecary's shop features a very handsome unicorn. The expertly carved sign shows the prosperity of the apothecary and his ability to acquire precious and exotic cures. Although the ivory horn looks like it belongs to a genuine unicorn, this example is actually made from a narwhal's tusk. Known as the 'unicorn of the sea', narwhal tusks were often sold and marketed in this way.

A PHARMACY SIGN IN THE SHAPE OF A UNICORN'S HEAD (18TH CENTURY)
Science Museum

'It's not easy ter catch a unicorn, they're powerful magic creatures. I never knew one ter be hurt before.'

Harry Potter and the Philosopher's Stone

THE BEZOAR GOAT

In his very first Potions lesson, Professor Snape asked Harry Potter, 'where would you look if I told you to find me a bezoar?' Bezoars are a mass of undigested fibre formed in the stomach of animals, which are believed to be an antidote to poison. They have been found in the guts of cows and even elephants, but mostly they come from the 'bezoar goat'. According to *A Compleat History of Druggs*, first published in French in 1694, the medicinal strength of the bezoar depended on the animal that produced it. '*Bezoar* Stones taken from Cows,' for instance, 'have nothing near the good Qualities' of the true bezoar goat. On the other hand, a mere two grains of 'the *Bezoar* that is found in Apes' will have a far greater effect than that of a mere goat.

◁ PIERRE POMET, *A COMPLEAT HISTORY OF DRUGGS*, 2ND EDN (LONDON, 1725)
British Library

"There are lots of interesting stories and anecdotes about bezoars. Scrapings of the stone were swallowed in a bid to cure a range of illnesses. Repelling poison may not have been such a stretch, as ingesting the stone would be likely to cause sickness."

ALEXANDER LOCK
Curator

A REAL BEZOAR STONE

Bezoars were first introduced into medieval Europe by Arabic physicians. Although doubts were sometimes cast over their properties, the demand continued well into the 18th century. Wealthy collectors spent considerable sums to acquire the best 'stones', which were kept in elaborate cases. Later, in *The Half-Blood Prince*, Harry put his learning to good effect. In his copy of *Advanced Potion-Making*, Harry had noticed the instruction, 'Just shove a bezoar down their throats.' He did exactly that when Ron Weasley drank some poisoned mead, thereby saving his friend's life.

A BEZOAR STONE IN A GOLD FILIGREE CASE
Science Museum

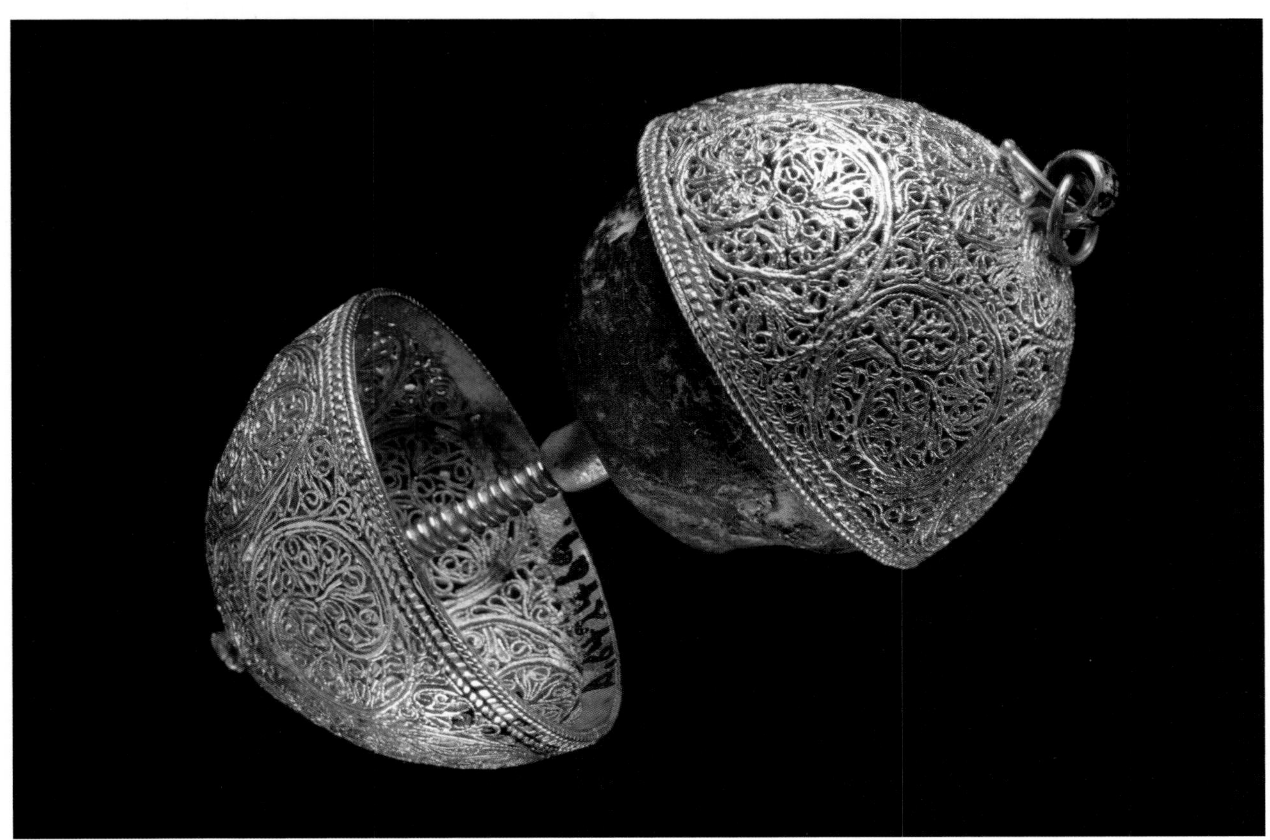

'Blimey, it was lucky you thought of a bezoar,' said George in a low voice.

'Lucky there was one in the room,' said Harry, who kept turning cold at the thought of what would have happened if he had not been able to lay hands on the little stone.

Harry Potter and the Half-Blood Prince

A SET OF APOTHECARY JARS (SPAIN?, 17TH OR 18TH CENTURY)
Science Museum

APOTHECARY JARS

As early as 1500 BC, the ancient Egyptians recognised that glass was an excellent vessel for storing chemical substances – it is non-absorbent and will not adulterate the contents. These glass apothecary jars used this ancient technology to store a selection of medicinal ingredients. The jar labelled 'Vitriol. Coerul.' contained copper sulphate, while that marked 'Ocul. Cancr.' stored 'crab's eyes' – stony concretions taken from the stomachs of putrefied crayfish, prescribed to aid digestion! The jar named 'Sang. Draco.V.' once stored 'Dragon's Blood'. It contained a potent red resin that is still widely used in medicine, magic, art and alchemy.

A PENCIL SKETCH OF POTIONS BOTTLES BY JIM KAY
Bloomsbury

POTIONS BOTTLES

This preliminary sketch by Jim Kay, in preparation for the illustrated edition of *Harry Potter and the Philosopher's Stone*, shows the intricate detail of a selection of potions bottles. Each bottle seems full of life even before the vibrant colours have been applied, and the highly ornate design illustrates the imaginative scope of what they could contain.

BOOK OF THE SEVEN CLIMES

Abū al-Qāsim Muhammad ibn Ahmad al-ʻIrāqī was an author of books on alchemy and magic. Al-ʻIrāqī's *Book of the Seven Climes* is the earliest known study focused wholly on alchemical illustrations. This picture was supposedly taken from a 'Hidden Book' attributed to Hermes Trismegistus, a legendary sage-king of ancient Egypt, who was believed to have mastered the secrets of alchemy and recorded them in hieroglyphs on the walls of tombs. Al-ʻIrāqī gave each element an alchemical interpretation, but in actual fact this illustration has no meaning. Unknown to al-ʻIrāqī, the picture reproduces an ancient monument erected in memory of King Amenemhat II, who ruled Egypt around 1922–1878 BC.

◅ ILLUSTRATION OF THE ALCHEMICAL PROCESS, IN ABŪ AL-QĀSIM AL-ʻIRĀQĪ, *KITĀB AL-AQĀLĪM AL-SABʻAH (BOOK OF THE SEVEN CLIMES)* (18TH CENTURY)
British Library

> *"Al-ʻIrāqī was known as al-Sīmāwī, which means 'the practitioner of natural or white magic'. He lived in Egypt in the 13th century, during the reign of the Mamluk sultan, Baybars I al-Bunduqdārī."*
>
> BINK HALLUM
> *Curator*

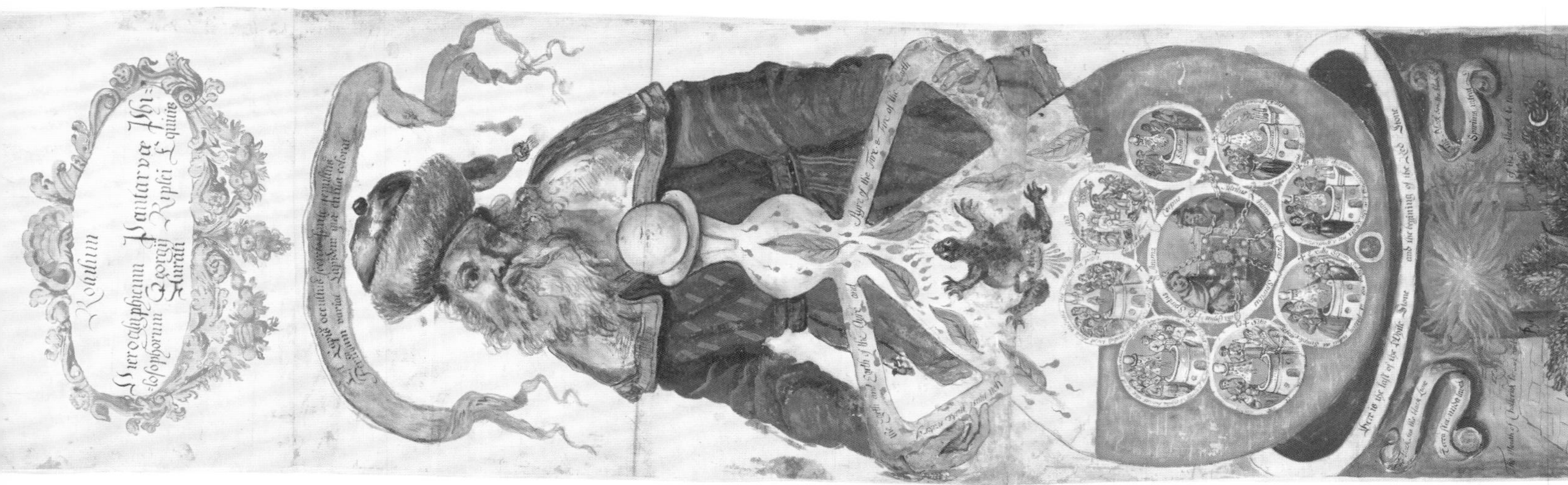

'The ancient study of alchemy is concerned with making the Philosopher's Stone, a legendary substance with astonishing powers. The Stone will transform any metal into pure gold. It also produces the Elixir of Life, which will make the drinker immortal.'

Harry Potter and the Philosopher's Stone

▲ THE RIPLEY SCROLL (ENGLAND, 16TH CENTURY)
British Library ▼

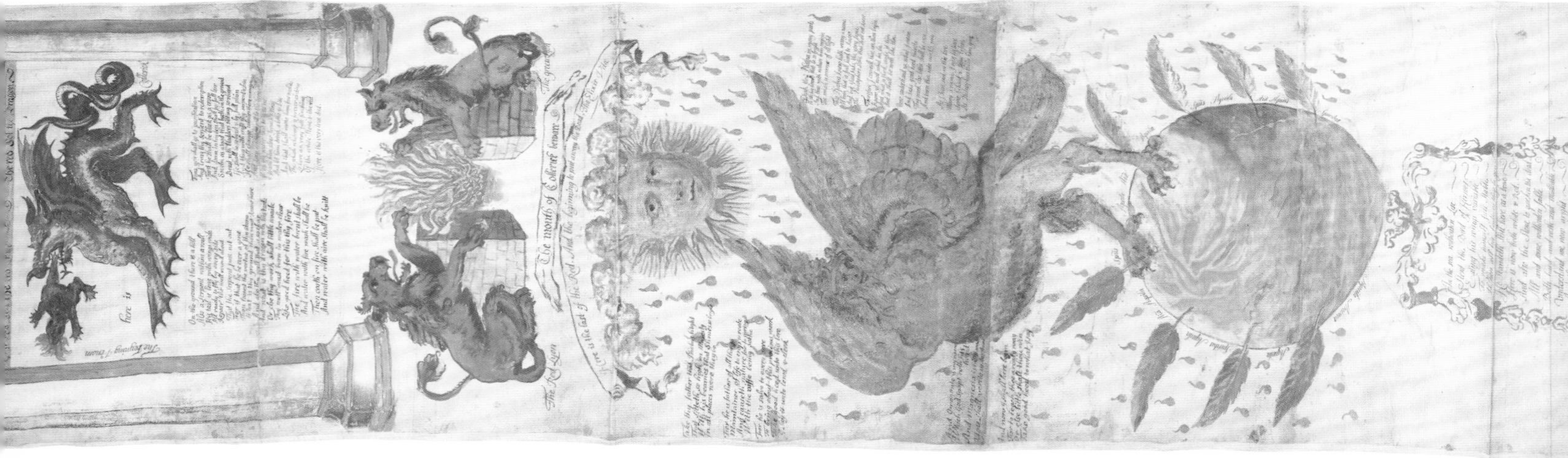

THE RIPLEY SCROLL

The Ripley Scroll is the name given to a mystical alchemical treatise that features a series of verses about the Elixir of Life. The scroll takes its name from George Ripley, a canon at Bridlington Priory in Yorkshire and a skilled alchemist. Ripley had reportedly studied alchemy in Italy and at the University of Louvain, in modern-day Belgium. He subsequently wrote a book on how to make the Philosopher's Stone, known as *The Compound of Alchymy*. This manuscript is based on Ripley's teachings, and stretches almost six metres in length. It features beautiful illustrations of dragons, toads and a winged bird captioned, 'The Bird of Hermes is my name, Eating my Wings to make me lame'. At the head of the scroll is a robed, bearded figure holding an alchemical vessel. Inside two figures can be seen lifting up the so-called 'Book of Philosophy'.

"Very few people have seen the Ripley Scroll in its fullest extent, simply because it is such an enormous document. The manuscript in its entirety is full of symbolism – richly decorated with creatures and motifs that represent the alchemical process."

JULIAN HARRISON
Lead Curator

SPLENDOR SOLIS

Perhaps the most beautiful of all illuminated manuscripts about alchemy was made in Germany in 1582. The book contains the work known as *Splendor Solis* or 'Splendour of the Sun'. The authorship of *Splendor Solis* is unknown, but it has often been attributed in error to Salomon Trismosin, a man who claimed to have used the Philosopher's Stone to conquer old age. This page shows an alchemist holding a flask filled with a golden liquid. A black scroll emerges out of the flask, inscribed with the words '*Eamus quesitum quatuor elementorum naturas*'. This is Latin for 'Let us ask the four elements of nature'.

➢ *SPLENDOR SOLIS* (GERMANY, 1582)
British Library

> *"The splendid gold border on this page is equally as impressive as the portrait in the centre. The frame has been painstakingly decorated with pictures of flowers, birds and animals – among them a peacock, a stag and an owl."*
>
> JULIAN HARRISON
> *Lead Curator*

'A stone that makes gold and stops you ever dying!' said Harry. 'No wonder Snape's after it! Anyone would want it.'

Harry Potter and the Philosopher's Stone

NICOLAS FLAMEL, ALCHEMIST

In *The Philosopher's Stone*, Harry, Hermione and Ron spent some considerable time in the library at Hogwarts, trying to identify a certain Nicolas Flamel. Eventually Hermione pulled out an old book she had put aside for a bit of light reading. '"Nicolas Flamel," she whispered dramatically, "is the *only known maker of the Philosopher's Stone*!"' According to this ancient tome, Flamel was a noted alchemist and opera-lover, aged 665, who lived quietly in Devon with his wife, Perenelle. In reality, Flamel spent his life in medieval Paris, and according to some sources died in 1418. Flamel was a landlord, sometimes said (incorrectly) to have been involved in the book trade. This illustration shows a memorial to the Holy Innocents commissioned by Nicolas and Perenelle, with the Flamels praying at the top beside the saints.

WATERCOLOUR ILLUSTRATIONS TO A MEMOIR OF NICOLAS FLAMEL AND HIS WIFE (FRANCE, 18TH CENTURY)

British Library

"Nicolas Flamel is a fascinating character – an intersection in history between myth, legend and the magic of Harry Potter. Almost everything we knew about him was incorrect. The real Flamel wasn't an alchemist, yet after his death this fantastical story somehow rose up around his name."

JULIAN HARRISON

Lead Curator

FLAMEL'S TOMBSTONE

At his reputed death in 1418, the real-life Nicolas Flamel was buried in the church of Saint-Jacques-de-la-Boucherie in Paris. His grave was marked by this small medieval tombstone. The upper scene shows Christ flanked by Saints Peter and Paul, along with the Sun and the Moon. The deceased lies below the main transcription, which has been carved in French. In J.K. Rowling's story, Nicolas Flamel eventually agreed with his friend Albus Dumbledore that the Philosopher's Stone should be destroyed. Flamel and his wife had 'enough Elixir stored to set their affairs in order' before finally being laid to rest.

TOMBSTONE OF NICOLAS FLAMEL (PARIS, 15TH CENTURY)
Musée national du Moyen Âge, Paris

*'To one as young as you, I'm sure it seems incredible, but to Nicolas and Perenelle, it really is like going to bed after a very, **very** long day. After all, to the well-organised mind, death is but the next great adventure.'*

Professor Dumbledore, Harry Potter and the Philosopher's Stone

THE AGE-OLD CHEMICAL WORK

Nicolas Flamel's reputation as an alchemist derives ultimately from posthumous accounts of his life. According to these 16th- and 17th-century legends, Flamel had a prophetic dream that led him to discover a rare manuscript revealing the true composition of the Philosopher's Stone. First published in Germany in 1735, the *Uraltes Chymisches Werck* ('Age-Old Chemical Work'), reputedly by the rabbi Abraham Eleazar, claimed to be a translation of this lost text. In this picture, a serpent and a crowned dragon form a circle, head-to-tail. This is a common alchemical illustration, which symbolises the unification of *materia* (primary matter) with *spiritus universalis* (the universal spirit). This unification was considered essential in the creation of the Stone.

R. ABRAHAMI ELEAZARIS URALTES CHYMISCHES WERCK (ERFURT, 1735)
British Library

"Although scholars continue to debate whether the work is genuine and question whether Eleazar even existed, the 'Age-Old Chemical Work' nevertheless attempts to show how to make the Philosopher's Stone."

ALEXANDER LOCK
Curator

'See?' said Hermione, when Harry and Ron had finished. 'The dog must be guarding Flamel's Philosopher's Stone! I bet he asked Dumbledore to keep it safe for him, because they're friends and he knew someone was after it. That's why he wanted the Stone moved out of Gringotts!'

Harry Potter and the Philosopher's Stone

SEEING FLUFFY

In this original drawing by J.K. Rowling, Neville, Ron, Harry, Hermione and 'Gary' (later renamed Dean and cut from this scene) are faced with a terrifying, huge three-headed dog. Each student has a detail appropriate to their character – note Neville's bunny pyjamas, Ron's freckles and Hermione's large front teeth. This early drawing shows us how the characters might have appeared in the author's mind. Originally designed to be part of Chapter Seven, 'Draco's Duel', this scene eventually became Chapter Nine and was renamed 'The Midnight Duel'. Only Hermione has the composure to spot that 'Fluffy' is guarding a trapdoor, leading Harry to realise that they have found the hiding place of Hagrid's mysterious package from Gringotts vault 713.

➢ PEN AND INK DRAWING OF HARRY AND HIS FRIENDS BY J.K. ROWLING (1991)

J.K. Rowling

▲ EDWARD BURNE-JONES, *PSYCHE THROWING THE HONEY CAKES TO CERBERUS* (C. 1880)

Birmingham Museum and Art Gallery

CERBERUS

In Greek mythology, Cerberus was the monstrous, three-headed dog that guarded the gates to the Underworld, preventing the dead from leaving. Cerberus features in many ancient legends, including the tale of the lovers, Cupid and Psyche. In the story, Psyche was sent on a quest to the Underworld, where she had to use cakes baked with honey to distract the dreaded hound. This wood engraving by Edward Burne-Jones was designed to illustrate a lavish publication of William Morris's *The Earthly Paradise*. The proofs were made at the Chiswick Press in the 1880s, but the project was abandoned. Burne-Jones shows Psyche throwing cakes at the drooling figure of Cerberus.

They were looking straight into the eyes of a monstrous dog, a dog which filled the whole space between ceiling and floor. It had three heads. Three pairs of rolling, mad eyes; three noses, twitching and quivering in their direction; three drooling mouths, saliva hanging in slippery ropes from yellowish fangs.

Harry Potter and the Philosopher's Stone

THE ALCHYMIST

The study of alchemy has fascinated people worldwide for centuries. In 1771, the English artist Joseph Wright of Derby completed his painting entitled *The Alchymist Discovers Phosphorus*, which was later reworked in 1795. In this picture, Wright shows an alchemist accompanied by two young apprentices, observing a flask in which a quantity of urine has been boiled down. The flask bursts into light as the phosphorus ignites spontaneously in air. It has often been suggested that this scene refers to the discovery of phosphorus by the German alchemist, Hennig Brand, in Hamburg in 1669. The setting of Wright's painting has Gothic-style arches, vaults and windows. Some have compared the setting to a medieval church, as if bestowing the alchemist's discovery with religious significance.

"In this picture, Wright recreated a historical event that had taken place a century before his own lifetime. It is important to note that the discovery of phosphorus was, however, accidental. Brand's chief aim, like all alchemists, was to find gold."

JULIAN HARRISON
Lead Curator

THE ALCHYMIST, IN SEARCH OF THE PHILOSOPHER'S STONE, DISCOVERS PHOSPHORUS, AND PRAYS FOR THE SUCCESSFUL CONCLUSION OF HIS OPERATION, AS WAS THE CUSTOM OF THE ANCIENT CHYMICAL ASTROLOGERS BY JOSEPH WRIGHT OF DERBY (1771–95)
Derby Museum and Art Gallery

'You know, the Stone was really not such a wonderful thing. As much money and life as you could want! The two things most human beings would choose above all – the trouble is, humans do have a knack of choosing precisely those things which are worst for them.'

Professor Dumbledore, Harry Potter and the Philosopher's Stone

QUIRRELL AND THE PHILOSOPHER'S STONE

This handwritten draft of 'The Man with Two Faces', Chapter Seventeen of *The Philosopher's Stone*, shows J.K. Rowling's writing in biro, on unlined paper. While you can see some small deletions in the text, much of the dialogue in this early draft remains the same as the published text. On discovering that Professor Quirrell was behind the attempts to steal the Philosopher's Stone, not Snape as he had suspected, Harry is given this defiant line: 'You haven't got the stone yet [...] Dumbledore will be here soon. He'll stop you.' This and Quirrell's next line was cut during the editorial process, in which the confrontation was reorganised. In the published version, Quirrell discloses that he had let the troll into the school immediately after he had bound Harry in ropes.

Chapter Seventeen

The Man with Two Faces.

It was Quirrell.

"You!" said Harry.

Quirrell smiled, and his face wasn't twitching at all.

"Me," he said calmly.

"But I thought – Snape –"

"Severus?" Quirrell laughed and it wasn't his usual quivering treble either, but cold and sharp. "Yes, Severus does seem the type, doesn't he? So useful to have him swooping around like an overgrown bat. Next to him, who would suspect me? P-p-poor st-st-stuttering P-P-Professor Quirrell."

"But he tried to kill me –"

"No, no, no," said Quirrell. "I was trying to kill you. Your friend Miss Granger accidentally knocked me over as she rushed to set fire to Snape. It broke my eye contact with you. Another few seconds and I'd have got you off that broom. I'd have managed it before then if Snape hadn't been muttering a counter-curse, trying to save you."

"He was trying to save me?"

"Of course," said Quirrell coolly. "Why do you think he wanted to referee your next match? He was trying to make sure I didn't do it again. Funny, really... he needn't have bothered. I couldn't do anything with Dumbledore watching. All the other teachers thought Snape was trying to stop Gryffindor winning, he did make a fool of himself... ~~and he needn't have bothered~~ and what a waste of time, when after all that ~~in the end~~, I'm going to kill you tonight."

Quirrell snapped his fingers. Ropes sprang out of thin air and wrapped themselves tightly around Harry.

"Now, you wait there, Potter, while I examine this interesting mirror –"

It was only then that Harry realised what was standing behind Quirrell. It was the Mirror of Erised.

"You haven't got the stone yet –" said Harry desperately. "Dumbledore will be here soon. He'll stop you –"

"For someone who's about to die, you're very talkative, Potter," said Quirrell, feeling his way around the Mirror's frame. "This mirror is the key to finding the stone, it won't take me long – and Dumbledore's in London, I'll be gone far away by the time he gets here –"

All Harry could think of was to keep Quirrell talking.

"That troll at Hallowe'en –"

"Yes, I let it in. I was hoping some foolhardy student would get themselves killed by it, to give me time to ~~get to~~ the Stone. Unfortunately, Snape found out. I think see what was guarding

"J.K. Rowling has expressed how much she loves writing dialogue, and this draft shows how small changes in dialogue can have a powerful effect on characterisation."

JOANNA NORLEDGE
Curator

A DRAFT OF *HARRY POTTER AND THE PHILOSOPHER'S STONE*, CHAPTER SEVENTEEN, HANDWRITTEN BY J.K. ROWLING
J.K. Rowling

that ghost with ~~his head hanging off~~ the loose head tipped
him off. Snape came straight to the third floor corridor to
head me off ... and you didn't get killed by the troll!
That was why I tried to finish you at the Quidditch
match — but blow me if I didn't fail again."

Quirrell rapped the Mirror of Erised impatiently.
"Dratted thing ... trust Dumbledore to come up with
something like this ..." He stared, [wrigging] into the mirror. "I see the
stone," he said. "I'm presenting it to my Master ... but where
is it?"

He went back to feeling his way around the mirror.
~~A sudden thought struck~~ Harry's B mind was racing.
B
"What I want more than anything else in the world, at this moment,"
he thought, "is to find the Stone before Quirrell does. So if I
look in the mirror, I should see myself finding it — which
means I'll see where it's hidden. But how can I look
without him realising what I'm up to? & I've got to play for
time ..."

"I saw you and Snape in the forest," he blurted out.
"Yes," said Quirrell idly, walking around the mirror to
look at the back. "He was onto me. Trying to find out
how far I'd got. He suspected me all along. Tried to
frighten me — as though he could scare me, when I had
Lord Voldemort on my side."
"But Snape always seemed to hate me so much—"
"Oh, he does," Quirrell said casually. "Heavens, yes.
He was at ~~school~~ Hogwarts with your father, didn't you
know? They loathed each other. But he didn't
want you *dead*."
"And that warning burned into my bed—"
"Yes, that was me," said Quirrell, now feeling the
Mirror's clawed feet. "I heard you and Weasley in my class,
talking about Philosopher's Stones. I thought you
might try and interfere. Pity you didn't heed my
warning, isn't it? Curiosity has led you to your doom, Potter."
"But I heard you a few days ago, sobbing—
I thought Snape was threatening you—"
For the first time, a spasm of fear flitted across
Quirrell's face.
"Sometimes—" he said, "I find it hard to follow my
Master's instructions — he is a great man and I am weak—"
"You mean he was there in the classroom with you?"
Harry gasped.
"He is with me wherever I go," said Quirrell softly.
"I met with him when I travelled round the world, a
foolish young man, full of ridiculous ideas about good and evil.
Lord Voldemort showed me how wrong I was. There is no
good and evil. There is only power, and those too
weak to seek it ... Since then, I have served him faithfully,
though I have let him down many times. He has had to be very
hard on me." Quirrell shuddered suddenly. "He does not
forgive mistakes easily. When I failed to steal the stone from

HERBOLOGY

Herbology

Anna Pavord

Anna Pavord's books include her bestseller, The Tulip, and most recently Landskipping. In The Naming of Names, also published by Bloomsbury, she considered the search for order in the world of plants, a quest begun by the ancient Greeks and still continuing today. For more than 40 years Anna has lived in Dorset where she gardens on a steep sunny slope among arisaemas and magnolias.

There's a screech as a child trips over a stinging nettle. We search for a dock leaf to wrap around the hot, itchy rash. This is perhaps the last, widely disseminated piece of plant lore that still exists in Britain. Generally, if we need a remedy, we reach for a pill or an expensively packaged potion. Mostly forgotten are the uses, for good or for ill, of all the wild worts that used to be gathered from pastures, riverbanks and woods – barrenwort, birthwort and butterwort (rubbed on cows' udders both as protection and cure); masterwort, milkwort and mugwort (*Artemisia vulgaris*), revered throughout Europe as a herb both medical and magical. Everyone knew that 'yf it be within a house there shall no wicked sprite abyde'. It is one of the plants carved into the roof bosses of Exeter cathedral. 'Wort' quite often crops up as part of the common name of a British native plant, indicating that it was once used as a kind of medicine.

At Hogwarts, Herbology, the study of plants and their uses, quite rightly sits at the centre of the curriculum, one of the seven core subjects that all students must study. Classes are taken by Professor Pomona Sprout. *One Thousand Magical Herbs and Fungi* by Phyllida Spore is one of the set texts for First Years, duly purchased by new boy Harry Potter at the Flourish and Blotts bookshop in Diagon Alley.

But even Muggles, unable to get hold of this compendious herbal, could learn about plants such as the asphodel, dittany and wormwood, that Hogwarts pupils study. If they were interested in such things, they would be able to field Professor Snape's question about the difference between monkshood and wolfsbane. The answer is that there is none. They are the same plant, known by many different names throughout Europe. To the ancient Greeks, this was *akoniton*, which grew plentifully in Crete and Zakynthos. The root, pounded when dry, was a deadly and effective poison with few antidotes. The time it took to kill was equal to the time

I.
Helleborus niger legi timus.
II.
Leucoium bulbosum triphyll
Maius Byzantinum:
III.
Leucoium bulbosum triphyll
Minus.
IIII.
Leucoium bulbosum hexaphyll
V.
Leucoium bulbosum hexaphyllon
Minus:
Georg Mack 1614

that elapsed since it had been gathered. Writing about it in around AD 77, the Greek doctor Dioscorides reckoned the best remedy for akoniton poisoning was to swallow a mouse whole.

Dioscorides had joined the Roman army as a physician and travelled widely in the Near East. His book *De materia medica* was a kind of field guide that would help him identify medicinal plants, and give a summary of the complaints and problems that each plant might cure. For the next 1,500 years it was revered as the ultimate authority on plants. But like a game of Chinese whispers, the manuscripts produced in Britain during the Middle Ages drifted further and further from Dioscorides' brisk, practical original. *The Lay of the Nine Healing Herbs* was typical of the work produced by these medieval copyists, imbued with magic and Anglo-Saxon superstition about elf-shot (the sudden pain in the side which we call a stitch, they ascribed to malevolent supernaturals) and flying venom: 'smite four strokes towards the four quarters with an oaken brand, make the brand bloody, throw away and sing this three times'.

Travellers, for instance, were warned it would be foolish to set out on a journey without their mugwort or St John's wort (*Hypericum perforatum*). Bringing it was not enough – they had to know that this particular wort was effective only when worn under the left armpit. If used in this way, it could be a powerful antidote against second sight, enchantment, witchcraft and the evil eye. Users also had to know when, where and how the herbs had been gathered. Their efficacy depended on the correct rites being observed. Never was this more imperative than when dealing with a mandrake.

There was potent sympathetic medicine in the fanged roots of the mandrake, perceived to have been created in human form. It is a native of northern Italy and Greece, but its dried roots could be found in apothecary shops throughout Europe. Mandrake is a powerful plant – hallucinogenic and widely recommended in early herbals as a painkiller. And an aphrodisiac. It was said to scream as it was pulled from the earth. Medieval manuscripts described the complex rituals involving ivory tools, phases of the Moon and hungry dogs that had to be observed during harvesting. We might see this as a clever protection racket worked by the herb gatherers, but at Hogwarts the young wizards wore earmuffs when handling the mandrakes in the greenhouse.

Inevitably, because it commanded such a high price, fake mandrake began to flood the market. The German botanist Leonhart Fuchs said the roots were often carved from roots of canna. The English herbalist, John Gerard, talked of so-called mandrake that was actually the root of wild bryony fashioned by 'idle drones that have little or nothing to do but eate and drinke'.

Gerard's *Herball*, published in 1597, contained details of even more plants than Phyllida Spore's compendium. Though a plagiarist and a crook, he and his book succeeded because the academic carapace that fostered the study of plants on the Continent – botanic gardens attached to universities, scholarly books issued by well-established printers, inspirational teachers, superb illustrations of plants, such as those made by artists working in northern Italy in the 15th century – did not exist in Britain.

Gerard, who grew mandrake in his Holborn garden (unsurprisingly, it was killed by a winter frost), dismissed as 'ridiculous tales' the superstitions surrounding it. And yet in his book he included details of the barnacle tree, a miraculous thing that grew on Orkney and bore geese rather than leaves. He even gave it a 'proper' Latin name, *Britannica concha anatifera.* Like other observers at the time, he was trying to explain natural phenomena that were not yet understood. Nobody knew that birds migrated each year. Where then did these magical flocks of geese suddenly come from? In the context of the time, the barnacle tree seemed to provide as good an explanation as any other.

We poor Muggles may never have the chance to be properly initiated into the magical properties of the Bouncing Bulb and the Whomping Willow. Yet some of the old lore lives on. Students at Hogwarts are taught which plants and fungi have the power to protect them from Dark forces. Near where I live, you'll still occasionally find a branch of our native rowan wedged over the porch of a farmhouse, to protect against witches. Just in case.

Anna Pavord

HERBOLOGY AT HOGWARTS

Herbology classes at Hogwarts took place in the greenhouses in the castle grounds. This is a meticulous drawing by Jim Kay of one of the Herbology greenhouses, showing the structural sections and glass panels. Anyone who has seen the Palm House, the Temperate House and the Alpine House at Kew Gardens, where the artist once worked, will recognise these drawings as specialised greenhouses designed to provide varying environments for the plants.

"The greenhouses in Kay's vision are clearly designed around the plants' needs – some hang, some will creep up walls, some will grow in water, others spread out in the shade."

JOANNA NORLEDGE
Curator

DRAWING OF A HOGWARTS GREENHOUSE BY JIM KAY
Bloomsbury

Harry, Ron and Hermione left the castle together, crossed the vegetable patch and made for the greenhouses, where the magical plants were kept.

Harry Potter and the Chamber of Secrets

Professor Sprout was a squat little witch who wore a patched hat over her flyaway hair; there was usually a large amount of earth on her clothes, and her fingernails would have made Aunt Petunia faint.

Harry Potter and the Chamber of Secrets

A SQUAT LITTLE WITCH

J.K. Rowling's early drawing of Professor Sprout, made seven years before the publication of *Harry Potter and the Philosopher's Stone*, shows the character surrounded by the plants studied in her Herbology class. At Hogwarts, Herbology included the study of normal plants as well as magical ones. Are the tendrils spreading from one of the pots actually sneaky Venomous Tentacula, looking for something to chew on? Professor Sprout herself is pictured in her witch's hat, with a spider hanging from its tip, handy for keeping her greenhouses free from plant-eating insects.

A PEN AND INK DRAWING OF PROFESSOR POMONA SPROUT BY J.K. ROWLING (30TH DECEMBER, 1990)

J.K. Rowling

CULPEPER'S HERBAL

When seeking inspiration for naming her herbs and potions, J.K. Rowling used the herbal of the apothecary Nicholas Culpeper. The book was first published in 1652 as *The English Physician*. It has subsequently appeared in over 100 editions, and was the first medical book to be published in North America. Culpeper's herbal provides a comprehensive list of native medicinal herbs, indexed against specific illnesses, and prescribes the most effective forms of treatment and when to take them. Culpeper was an unlicensed apothecary, disliked by the medical profession who jealously guarded their monopoly to practise medicine in London. He came into conflict with the College of Physicians, and in 1642 was apparently tried, but acquitted, for practising witchcraft.

CULPEPER'S ENGLISH PHYSICIAN; AND COMPLETE HERBAL (LONDON, 1789)
British Library

> *"Culpeper was concerned to inform the less educated members of society, and so he wrote in English rather than the traditional Latin."*
>
> ALEXANDER LOCK
> *Curator*

CULPEPER's
ENGLISH PHYSICIAN;
AND COMPLETE
HERBAL.
TO WHICH ARE NOW FIRST ADDED,
Upwards of One Hundred additional HERBS,
WITH A DISPLAY OF THEIR
MEDICINAL AND OCCULT PROPERTIES,
PHYSICALLY APPLIED TO
The CURE of all DISORDERS incident to MANKIND.
TO WHICH ARE ANNEXED,
RULES for Compounding MEDICINE according to the True SYSTEM of NATURE:
FORMING A COMPLETE
FAMILY DISPENSATORY,
And Natural SYSTEM of PHYSIC.
BEAUTIFIED AND ENRICHED WITH
ENGRAVINGS of upwards of Four Hundred and Fifty different PLANTS,
And a SET of ANATOMICAL FIGURES.
ILLUSTRATED WITH NOTES AND OBSERVATIONS,
CRITICAL AND EXPLANATORY.

By E. SIBLY, Fellow of the Harmonic Philosophical Society at PARIS; and Author of the Complete ILLUSTRATION of ASTROLOGY.

HAPPY THE MAN, WHO STUDYING NATURE'S LAWS,
THROUGH KNOWN EFFECTS CAN TRACE THE SECRET CAUSE. DRYDEN.

LONDON:
PRINTED FOR THE PROPRIETORS, AND SOLD BY GREEN AND CO. 176, STRAND.
MDCCLXXXIX.

Three times a week they went out to the greenhouses behind the castle to study Herbology, with a dumpy little witch called Professor Sprout, where they learnt how to take care of all the strange plants and fungi and found out what they were used for.

Harry Potter and the Philosopher's Stone

Mr NICHOLAS CULPEPER Born 18th Oct. 11 m P.M. 1616 DEPARTED this Life 10th of January 1654

MAGICAL GARDENING IMPLEMENTS

Herbology is a mandatory subject taken by all students at Hogwarts, reflecting the importance of plants to magic, medicine and herbal lore. These gardening implements, made from bone and antler, were used specifically for sowing and harvesting. It was essential that these tools were formed entirely from natural resources so that they did not corrupt the plants being harvested. The materials also had symbolic importance. Tools shaped from antlers, which rise upwards above the head, were considered to connect the Earth with the higher spirit world. As antlers are shed and regrown annually, they symbolise the magic of regeneration and renewal.

GARDENING IMPLEMENTS MADE FROM ANTLER AND BONE
The Museum of Witchcraft and Magic, Boscastle

"Tools like these have been used for thousands of years. Many plants are harvested not only for their medicinal qualities, but for their alleged supernatural powers – in such cases, the rituals involved in gathering them are extremely important."

ALEXANDER LOCK
Curator

THE PLANT COLLECTOR

Gherardo Cibo was an Italian naturalist and illustrator, who made this visual diary to record his plant-collecting excursions. In his early years he travelled widely between Rome, Germany, Spain and the Low Countries, but from around 1540 he spent most of his life at home in Rocca Contrada, Italy. Cibo was widely praised for his observations and detailed coloured drawings of plants. Unlike other botanists, who employed their own artists, he did his own illustrations, frequently showing the naturalist at work. This illustration shows two men collecting specimens on an Italian hillside, equipped with a mattock, a sickle and a sack.

◄ HERBAL ILLUSTRATED BY GHERARDO CIBO (ITALY, 16TH CENTURY)
British Library

'Oh, hello there!' Lockhart called, beaming around at the assembled students. 'Just been showing Professor Sprout the right way to doctor a Whomping Willow! But I don't want you running away with the idea that I'm better at Herbology than she is! I just happen to have met several of these exotic plants on my travels ...'

Harry Potter and the Chamber of Secrets

REMEDY FOR SNAKEBITE

What was one of the most effective remedies for snakebite? This 12th-century manuscript advises the afflicted to seek out two plants known as *Centauria major* and *Centauria minor*. The 'greater' and 'lesser' centaury were named after the ancient Greek centaur Chiron. In Greek mythology, Chiron was renowned as a physician, astrologer and oracle. Among his pupils was Asclepius, the god of medicine and healing, who had been rescued as a baby and was taken to Chiron to be reared. In this pen and ink drawing, Chiron is shown handing over the two plants to the toga-wearing Asclepius. A snake can be seen slithering away from under their feet.

➢ CENTAURY IN A HERBAL (ENGLAND, 12TH CENTURY)
British Library

They had their Herbology exam on Wednesday (other than a small bite from a Fanged Geranium, Harry felt he had done reasonably well)

Harry Potter and the Order of the Phoenix

turitu. Itali

...nul contrita facies
mirabiliter sanat.
...uicula que in ingui-
nascitur. Herba
...natiuum contusa
...no in ligno sic ut
...axungia facies
...onis panicula
recludit. legis
...uria maior.
...unci dicit Abus-
...as dicit. Alii
...nas. Itali fel terre
...us in uino
...s dolorem.
...ca splenem psa-

nat nos ipsi experti sumus. Ad uulnera et canceromata. Herba centaurie maior contrita & apposita. tumorem fieri non patitur. Ad suggillaciones & liuores. Herbe centaurie suci puncti summe facit. Ad uulnera recentia. Herbe centaurie puluis missus plagas conglutinat. ut eciam carnes coerescant. ł. centauria maior in aqua decocta. inde uulnera foueantur. Nomen herbe centauria minor. Omoeos. Illebontes. Prophete. Coa heracleos. Egiptii. Amarach. Daci. Str sozila. Itali. Febrifugia. Alii. Fel terre. Romani. Amaritudo. Has herbas duas dicunt ciro centaurum inuenisse & eas asclepio dedisse. unde nomen centauria acceperunt. Nascitur locis solidis & fortibus.

Ad uipere morsum. Herbe centaurie minore contrita puluis eius aut

DRAGON AND SERPENT

During the Middle Ages, many scholars compiled manuscripts for their own practical use, recording and illustrating the properties of individual plants. This magnificently decorated herbal was made in Lombardy, northern Italy, around the year 1440. It was most probably compiled for a wealthy landowner. Each page has been filled with life-like drawings of plants and short notes explaining their names. On the right-hand side we can see snakeroot. The author has recorded some of the species' Latin names beside it – '*Dragontea*', '*serpentaria*' and '*viperina*' reveal the plant's ability to cure snakebite. A hissing green serpent can also be seen curling around the plant's root. A snarling dragon called in Latin '*Draco magnus*' is perched to its left, painted with a forked tongue and an elaborately knotted tail.

➢ SNAKEROOT IN A HERBAL
(ITALY, 15TH CENTURY)
British Library

> *"The term 'snakeroot' is applied today to various plants with medicinal qualities, such as plantain. A poultice of plantain applied to a wound is widely believed to accelerate the healing process."*
>
> JULIAN HARRISON
> *Lead Curator*

Dragontea. a'. serpentaria. a'. asclepias.
.a'. colubraria ul' uiperina a'. auricula asi
nina. a'. iacas. a'. lus uocant.
.Draco magnus.

GERARD'S HERBAL

John Gerard was an English herbalist, whose most famous work was entitled *The Herball or Generall Historie of Plantes*. Gerard maintained his own garden in Holborn, London. He cultivated all manner of plants there, including exotic specimens such as the potato. *The Herball* contains more than 1,800 woodcut illustrations. Only sixteen of these were actually original to Gerard's work, the remainder having been taken (without acknowledgement) from a book printed in Germany six years previously. Gerard documented where scarce varieties of plant grew in England. In this copy of *The Herball*, a former owner has annotated the pages referring to speedwell: 'This harb cureth the yealowe jaundies and causeth on[e] to pisse well … Yt comforteth the stomake … and is singular ag[a]inst the migrane and disines in the heade.'

➢ SPEEDWELL, IN *THE HERBALL OR GENERALL HISTORIE OF PLANTES. GATHERED BY JOHN GERARDE OF LONDON, MASTER IN CHIRURGERIE* (LONDON, 1597)
British Library

Professor Sprout took a large key from her belt and unlocked the door. Harry caught a whiff of damp earth and fertiliser, mingling with the heavy perfume of some giant, umbrella-sized flowers dangling from the ceiling.

Harry Potter and the Chamber of Secrets

500 THE SECOND

* *The de*

3 This Whitelowe graſſe hath ſmall iagged lea
where it groweth : among which riſeth vp a ſlend
next the ground, but leſſer. The flowers growe at
and roótes are alſo like.

4 The fourth kinde of *Paronychia*, hath ſmall, th
reſembling the ſmall leaues of Rue, but a great de
the leaues alſo; but the caſes wherin the ſeed is
Scorpioides, or Chickweede Scorpion graſſe.

There is another ſort of Whitlow graſſe or Nai
a ſmall tough roote, with ſome threddie ſtrings an
tough ſtalkes, ſet with little narrowe leaues confu
of doubtleſſe theſe be kindes; alongſt the ſtalkes
come the ſeedes in ſmall buttons, of the bigneſſe c

* *The*

Theſe ſmall, baſe, and lowe herbes growe vpo
which are growen to haue much moſſe vpon then
It groweth plentifully vpon the bricke wall in C
thampton, in the ſuburbes of London, and ſundri

* *The*

Theſe flower many times in Ianuarie and Febr
no more to be ſeene all the yeere after.

* *The*

The Grecians haue called theſe plants παρωνυχ
kindes of plants, called by the ſaid name of *Parony*
the true kinde: but you may very boldly take th
or raiſed vp ſome new plant, approching neerer vr
we may call them in Engliſh Naile woort, and W

* *The temperat*

A As touching the qualitie hereof, we haue noth
the diſeaſe of the nailes called a Whitlowe, where

Of Fluellen the female, or

* *The*

There be two ſortes of female Fluellens.

* *The de*

1 THe firſt kinde of *Elatine*, being of *Fuch*
male Fluellen, ſhooteth from a ſmall an
diſperſed flat vpon the ground, ramping
the leaues of *Elatine* are of an hoarie, hairie, an
foorth many ſmall flowers, of a yellow colour n
dragon, hauing a certaine taile or ſpur faſtened v
ſpur. The lower iawe or chap of the flower is of
low; which being paſt, there ſucceedeth ſmall bla

2 The ſecond kinde of *Elatine* hath ſtalkes, bra
leaues are faſhioned like *Eryſimum*, and ſomewha
at the point: but the ſpurre or taile of the flower i
in the flower.

cut, lying flat vpon the wall or earth
reupon do growe such leaues as those
hose of the last described. The seede

leaues, cut into three diuisions, much
The stalks are little like the former, &
e like vnto the seed vessels of *Myositis*

t is likewise a low or base herb, hauing
o: from which rise vp diuers slender
se of the smallest Chickweede, wher-
ery little white flowers, after which
ead.

stone wals, vpon olde tiled houses,
ome shadowie and drie muddie wals.
ne, belonging to the Earle of Sou-
s.

hen hot weather approcheth, they are

cero calleth *Reduuia*. There be many
hath caused many writers to doubt of
the same, vntill time hath reuealed
: which I thinke will neuer be, so that
sse.

ues.

vne: onely it hath been taken to heale
is name.

ll. Chap. 187.

olus called *Veronica fœmina*, or the fe-
ot many flexible and tender branches,
with leaues like *Nummularia*, but that
greene colour; among which come
little purple, like vnto the small Snap-
ch flower, like the herbe called Larkes
lour, and the vpper iawe of a faire yel-
ontained in round huskes.
vers, and rootes, like the first, but the
g a broad arrow head, which is sharpe
d more purple mixed with the yellowe

1 Veronica

1 *Veronica fœmina Fuchsij, siue Elatine.*
The female Fluellen.

2 *Elatine altera.*
Sharpe pointed Fluellen.

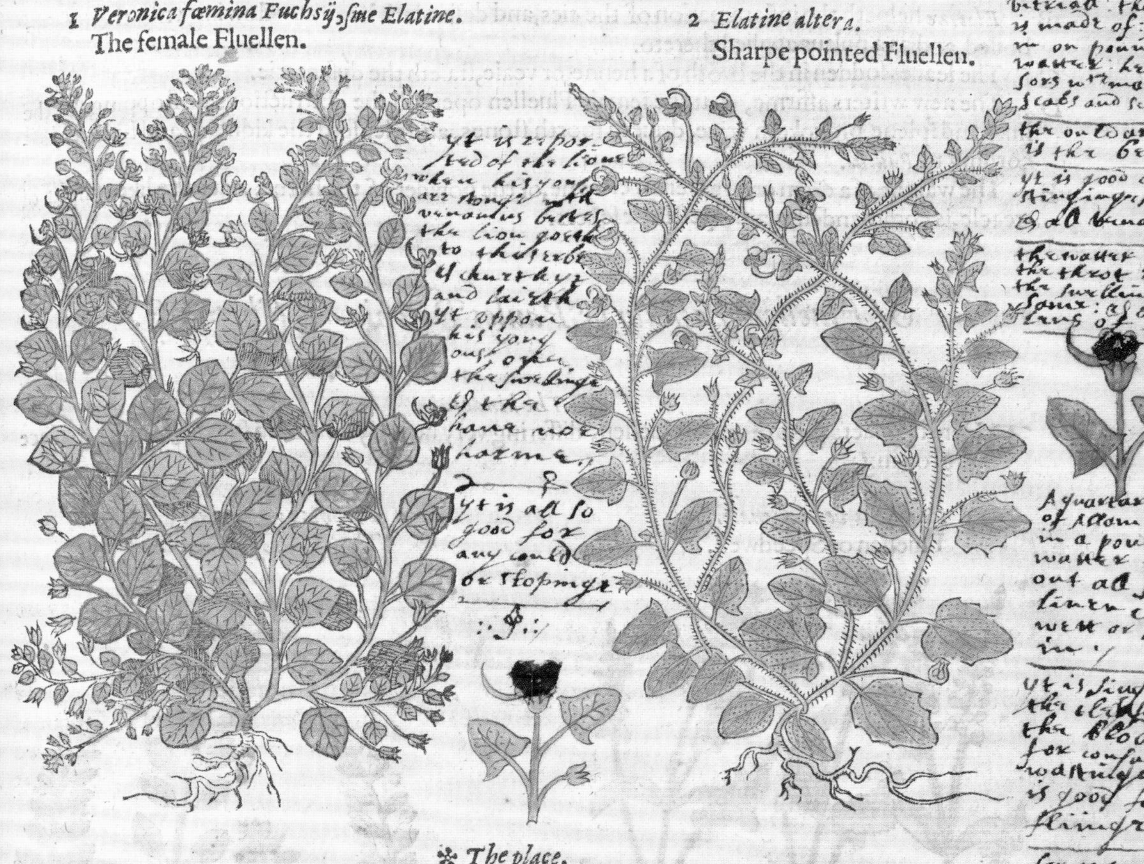

✲ *The place.*

Both these plants I haue founde in sundrie places where corne hath growen, especially Barley, as in the fieldes about Southfleete in Kent, where within sixe miles compasse there is not a fielde wherein it doth not grow.

Also it groweth in a fielde next vnto the house sometime belonging to that Honorable gentleman Sir *Fraunces Walsingham*, at Barne-elmes, and in sundrie places of Essex; and in the next fielde vnto the churchyarde at Cheswicke neere London, towards the midst of the fielde.

✲ *The time.*

They flower in August and September.

✲ *The names.*

Their seuerall titles set foorth their names as well in Latine as English.

✲ *The nature and vertues.*

A These plants are not onely of a singular astringent facultie, and thereby helpe them that be greeued with the dysenterie and hoat swelling; but of such singular efficacie to heale spreading & eating cankers, & corosiue vlcers, that their vertue in a maner passeth all credit in these fretting sores vpon sure proofe done vnto sundrie persons, & especially vpon a man whom *Pena* reporteth to haue his nose eaten most greeuously with a canker or eating sore, who sent for the Phisitions and Chirurgions that were famously knowen to be the best, & they with one consent concluded to cut the saide nose off, to preserue the rest of his face: among these Surgeons and Phisicions came a poore sorie Barbar, who had no more skill than he had learned by tradition, and yet vndertooke to cure the patient. This foresaide Barbar standing in the companie and hearing their determination, desired that he might make triall of an herbe which he had seene his master vse for the same purpose, which herbe *Elatine*, though he were ignorant of the name whereby it was called, yet he knewe where to fetch. To be short, this herbe he stamped, & gaue the iuice of it vnto the patient to drinke, and outwardly applied the same plaisterwise, and in very short space perfectly cured the man, and staied the rest of his bodie from further corruption, which was readie to fall into a leprosie.

Elatine

JOHN EVELYN'S PLANT SPECIMENS

Although he was only an amateur scientist, John Evelyn made many important contributions to the study of botany and horticulture. He first introduced the term 'avenue' into the vocabulary of the English landscape, and for much of his life was engaged in writing an encyclopedic history of gardening, which ultimately was never published. He developed an interest in botany in Padua in 1645, where he made this album of dried plant samples taken from the city's public botanic garden. Once vibrant with colour, the album contains real plant specimens such as dorian woundwort, mandrake and hellebore, the key ingredient that Harry forgot to put in his 'Draught of Peace'.

> *"Evelyn's friend, the diarist Samuel Pepys, certainly found this album useful. He judged it to be 'better than any Herball'."*
>
> ALEXANDER LOCK
> *Curator*

Explanation of Letters.

1 The Number, Latine & Greeke name of the plant
2 Pl: place where it growes.
3 T. Tyme of Flowring.
4 V. Vertue.
P. Mr Parkinsons Herbal, whither you are limited by the page: for the full description.

(1)
Small codded Loose strife.

Place; Alpes: Eng: in shady places. &c.
Tyme. June & July.
Virtue, Astringent, bloud, Fluxes, Wounds &c.
Parkinson: pag: 540.

▲ JOHN EVELYN, *HORTUS HYEMALIS* (PADUA, 1645) ➤
British Library

THE GARDEN OF EICHSTÄTT

Commissioned in 1611 by Johann Konrad von Gemmingen, Prince Bishop of Eichstätt in Bavaria, the *Hortus Eystettensis* is a magnificent catalogue of the plants grown in the bishop's palace garden. The book was produced by Basilius Besler, a botanist from Nuremberg, who supervised both the garden and the artists who drew the plants. This book was a major undertaking, with the flowers having to be illustrated as they bloomed throughout the seasons. It contains 367 hand-coloured engravings, and was printed on the largest paper then available. Harry Potter may have forgotten the hellebore in his 'Draught of Peace', but it was well known to Besler, who cultivated several varieties of the plant in the garden. One, *Helleborus niger* (black hellebore), had been used as a medicine since antiquity, although today it is considered a poison.

BASILIUS BESLER, *HORTUS EYSTETTENSIS* (ALTDORF, 1613)
British Library

His heart sank. He had not added syrup of hellebore, but had proceeded straight to the fourth line of the instructions after allowing his potion to simmer for seven minutes.

Harry Potter and the Order of the Phoenix

A CURIOUS HERBAL

A Curious Herbal is a book with a remarkable history. This work was illustrated, engraved and hand-coloured by Elizabeth Blackwell in order to raise sufficient funds to have her husband, Alexander, released from a debtors' prison. The book was issued in weekly parts between 1737 and 1739, containing images of 500 of 'the most useful plants, which are now used in the practice of physick'. Elizabeth made her drawings at Chelsea Physic Garden in London. She then took her drawings to Alexander in prison, where he identified the plants in question. Although the venture raised enough income to secure the release of her husband, he eventually left for Sweden, where he was executed for treason, having become involved in a political conspiracy. Elizabeth died alone in England in 1758.

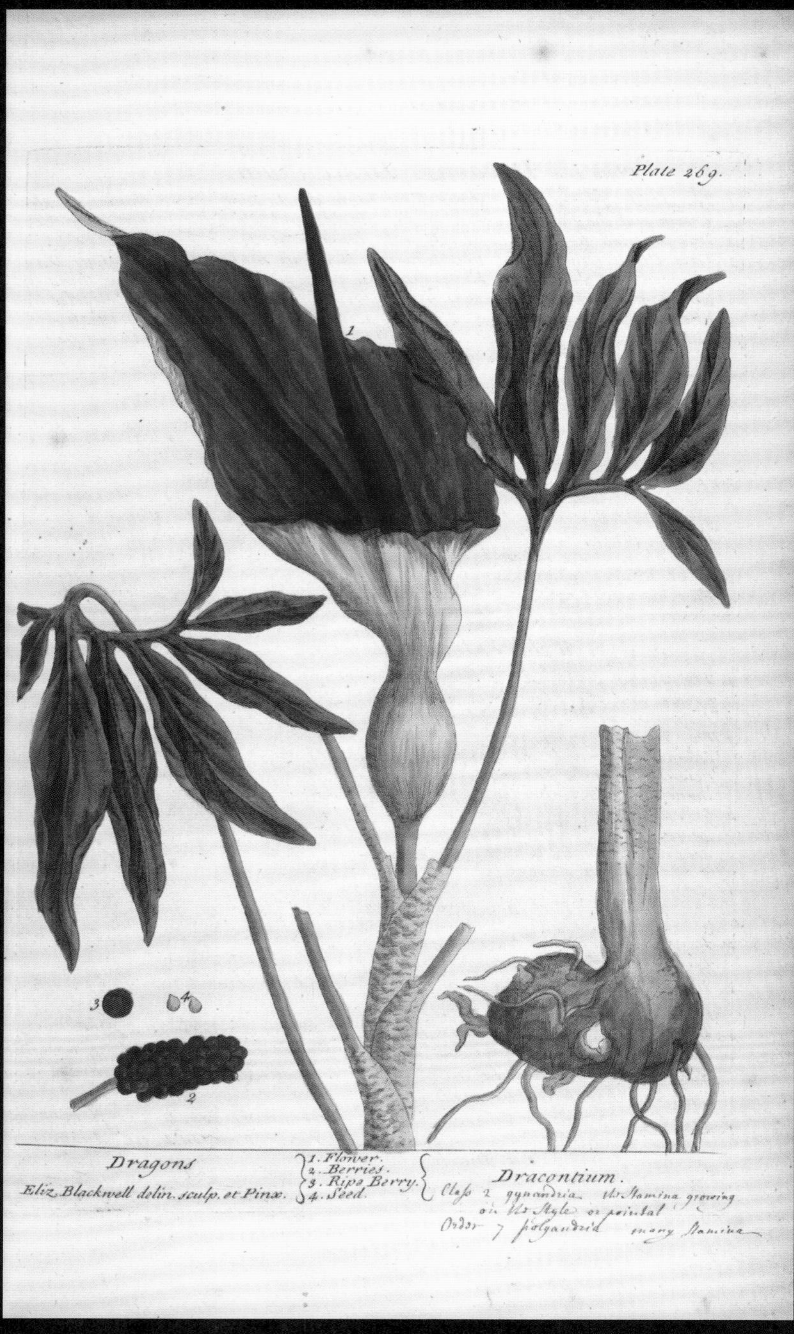

➢ DRACONTIUM, IN ELIZABETH BLACKWELL, *A CURIOUS HERBAL, CONTAINING FIVE HUNDRED CUTS OF THE MOST USEFUL PLANTS WHICH ARE NOW USED IN THE PRACTICE OF PHYSIC*, 2 VOLS (LONDON, 1737–9)

British Library

And so the three witches and the forlorn knight ventured forth into the enchanted garden, where rare herbs, fruit and flowers grew in abundance on either side of the sunlit paths.

The Tales of Beedle the Bard

THE TEMPLE OF FLORA

Described as a 'visually magnificent failure', this elaborate book on botany nearly bankrupted its author, the physician and botanist, Robert John Thornton. *The Temple of Flora* represents an attempt to produce the most impressive botanical book ever published. Using a range of modern printing techniques, Thornton employed teams of master engravers and colourists to reproduce 28 highly dramatised paintings of flora from across the world. Such an undertaking seriously undermined his finances – despite being granted a licence from Parliament to hold a fundraising lottery, Thornton never recovered his investment.

➢ DRACONTIUM, IN ROBERT JOHN THORNTON, *THE TEMPLE OF FLORA* (LONDON, 1799–1807)
British Library

> *"This exquisite black flower is called 'dragon arum'* (Dracunculus vulgaris)*, also known by the somewhat less appealing name 'stink lily'. It produces the smell of putrefying meat to attract flies for pollination."*
>
> ALEXANDER LOCK
> *Curator*

Instead of roots, a small, muddy and extremely ugly baby popped out of the earth. The leaves were growing right out of his head. He had pale green, mottled skin, and was clearly bawling at the top of his lungs.

Harry Potter and the Chamber of Secrets

STUDY OF MANDRAKES BY JIM KAY
Bloomsbury

A STUDY OF MANDRAKES

This preparatory sketch by Jim Kay shows a baby mandrake alongside a fully grown adult. The roots of the plant seamlessly form the adult mandrake's body, with leaves growing from its head. The mature mandrake also has berries sprouting amongst the leaves. In Kay's vision, the root forms the spine of the baby mandrake. This drawing appears to be drawn from life – Jim Kay was previously a curator at the Royal Botanic Gardens, Kew – and it references the natural studies of plants that are typically found in any botanical library.

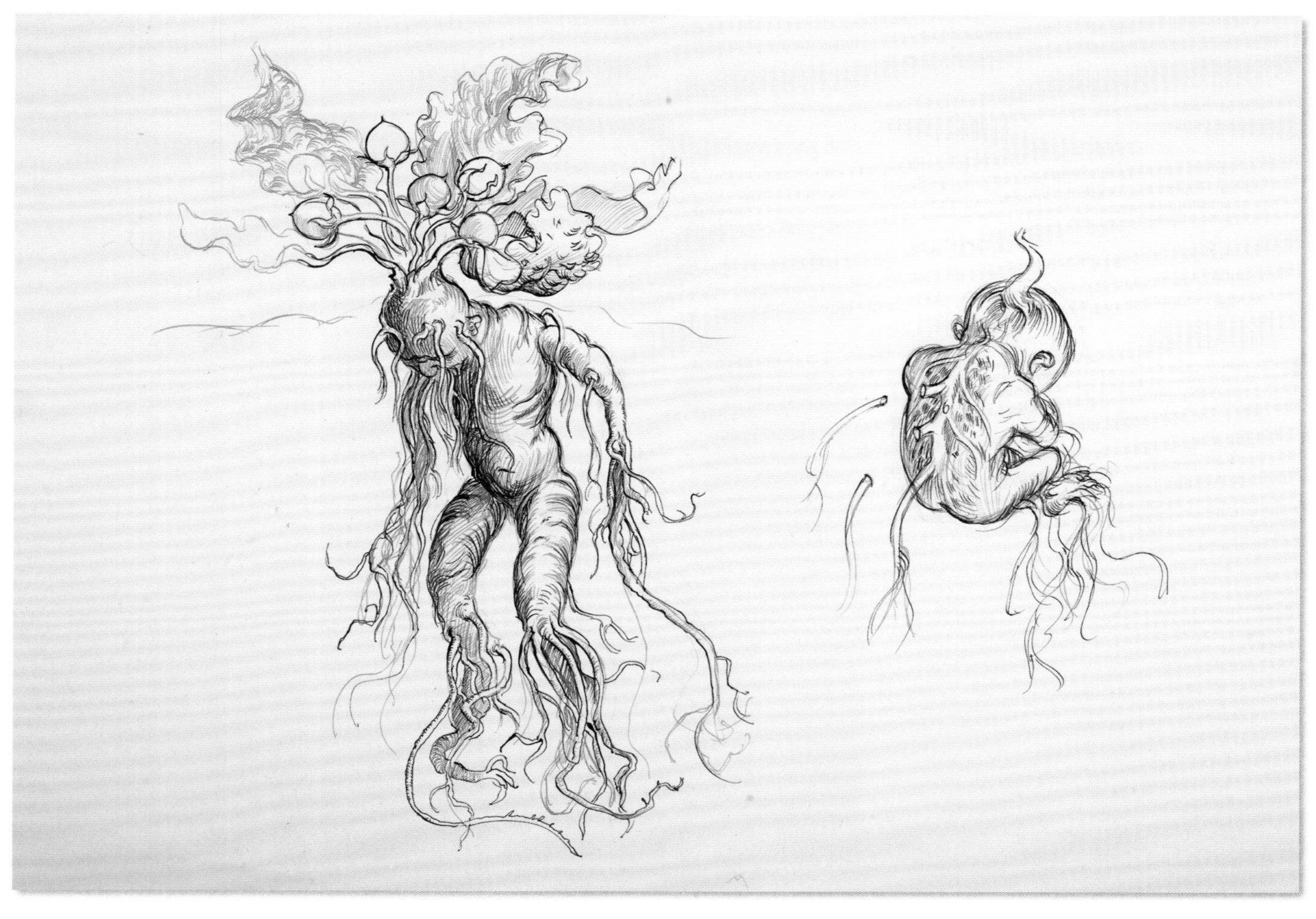

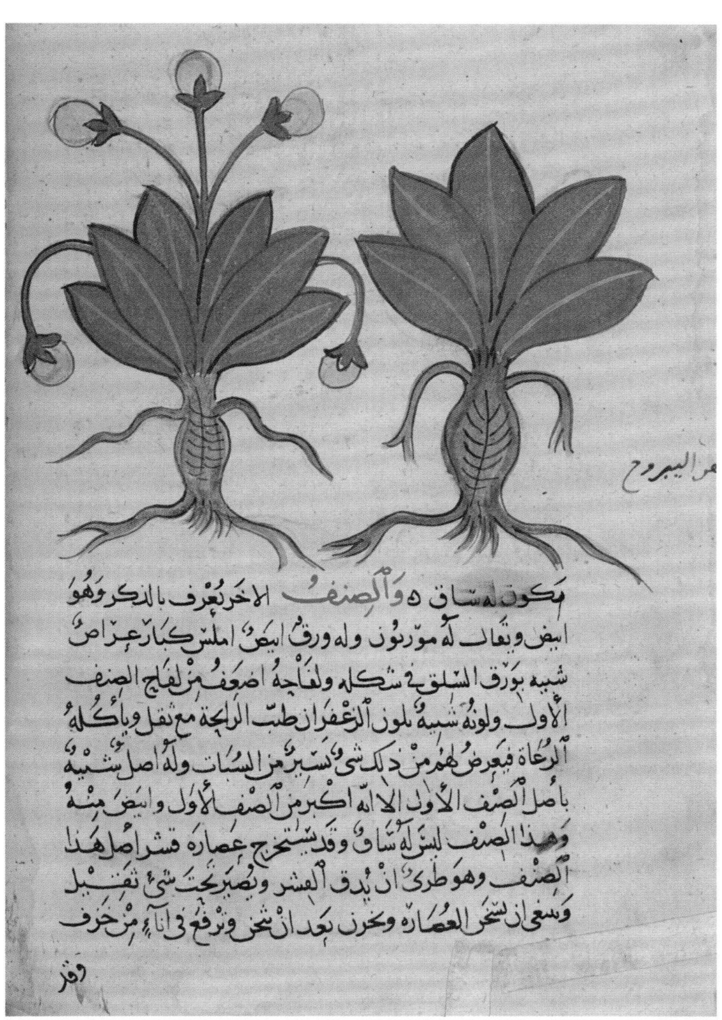

THE MALE AND FEMALE MANDRAKE

This illuminated manuscript contains an Arabic version of Books Three and Four of *De materia medica* ('On medical material'), originally written in Greek by Pedanius Dioscorides. Dioscorides was a botanist and pharmacologist, working as a physician in the Roman army. The manuscript contains no fewer than 287 colour illustrations of plants, together with spaces left blank for a further 52 drawings. Dioscorides was one of the first authors to distinguish between the male and female mandrake, as shown here. One should almost refer to them as the 'mandrake' and 'womandrake'. In fact, this identification is based on there being more than one species of mandrake native to the Mediterranean.

THE MALE AND FEMALE MANDRAKE, IN *KITĀB MAWĀDD AL-'ILĀJ* (BAGHDAD, 14TH CENTURY)
British Library

A MANDRAKE ROOT

Harry and his friends first came face-to-face with a mandrake in Greenhouse Three, which contained the most 'interesting and dangerous plants' at Hogwarts. As Hermione Granger immediately knew, 'Mandrake, or Mandragora, is a powerful restorative [...] used to return people who have been transfigured or cursed, to their original state [...] The cry of the Mandrake is fatal to anyone who hears it'. While the mandrakes encountered by Harry, Hermione and Ron are still young, this specimen has the appearance of a bearded old man. The resemblance of mandrakes to the human form has influenced many cultures over the centuries. In reality, the mandrake's root and leaves are poisonous and it can induce hallucinations.

A MANDRAKE ROOT (ENGLAND, 16TH OR 17TH CENTURY)
Science Museum

HARVESTING A MANDRAKE

According to medieval herbals, mandrakes were said to cure headaches, earache, gout and insanity, among other ailments. Harvesting them, however, has long been deemed an extremely hazardous business. The best way to obtain the plant safely was to unearth its roots with an ivory stake, attaching one end of a cord to the mandrake and the other to a dog. The dog could be encouraged to move forward by blowing a horn, dragging the mandrake with it. The sound of the horn would also serve to drown out the plant's terrible shriek.

➢ GIOVANNI CADAMOSTO'S ILLUSTRATED HERBAL (ITALY OR GERMANY, 15TH CENTURY)
British Library

> *"A macabre feature of the mandrake in the foreground of this image is the two severed hands growing out of its stems. These symbolise the plant's use as an anaesthetic during amputations."*
>
> JULIAN HARRISON
> *Lead Curator*

'As our Mandrakes are only seedlings, their cries won't kill yet,' she said calmly, as though she'd just done nothing more exciting than water a begonia.

Professor Sprout, Harry Potter and the Chamber of Secrets

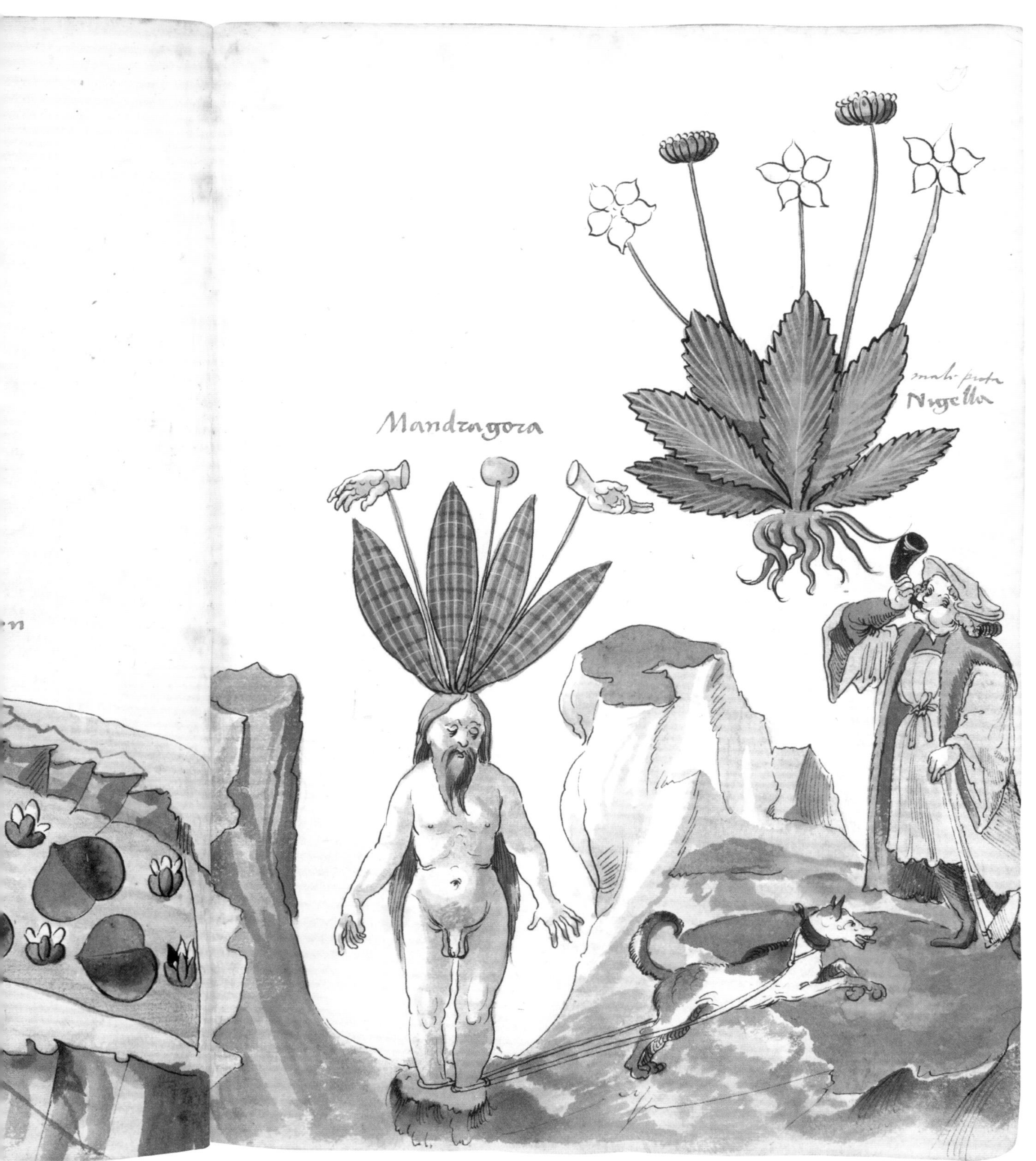
Mandragora
Nigella

A STUDY OF GNOMES

The garden gnome *Gernumbli gardensi*, in the world of Harry Potter, was a pest that could swiftly get out of hand if left unchecked. Gnomes grow to be roughly one foot tall, burrowing their gnomeholes in gardens and creating unsightly mounds of earth on the lawn. They do not appear to have much intellect – when de-gnoming began at the Weasley household, some of the gnomes came out of their holes to see what was happening, only to be flung from the garden themselves. Jim Kay's study captures the ugliness of these creatures, with their potato-like heads and dim expressions of confusion.

A STUDY OF GNOMES BY JIM KAY
Bloomsbury

It was small and leathery-looking, with a large, knobbly, bald head exactly like a potato. Ron held it at arm's length as it kicked out at him with its horny little feet

Harry Potter and the Chamber of Secrets

GNOME ALONE

August Heissner is often credited with being the inventor of the garden gnome. He began to make them in his workshop at Gräfenroda, Germany, in 1872, where production continues to the present day. This example was made around the year 1900, and is the very essence of a traditional garden gnome – he wears a pointy red hat and sports a long, white beard. In *Harry Potter and the Chamber of Secrets*, Ron remarked on the Muggle craze for garden gnomes, describing them as 'fat little Father Christmases with fishing rods' – not unlike this jolly chap.

A FISHING GNOME (GERMANY, C. 1900)
The Garden Museum, London

DEVIL'S TONGUE

This beautifully illustrated Chinese manuscript deals with the topic of poisonous and medicinal plants. The picture shows a lily with an elegant, single bloom called devil's tongue, also known as 'konjac', 'voodoo lily' or 'snake palm'. Today, devil's tongue is used in making weight loss supplements and facial massage products. The exotic-looking flower is a member of the same genus as Titan Arum, the worst-smelling plant on Earth.

➢ DEVIL'S TONGUE, IN *DU CAO* (CHINA, 19TH CENTURY)
British Library

Lily waited until Petunia was near enough to have a clear view, then held out her palm. The flower sat there, opening and closing its petals, like some bizarre, many-lipped oyster.

Harry Potter and the Deathly Hallows

7

毒草

蒟蒻開寳本草始著録湖南山中有之雲南園圃尤多根大者
重十餘斤形如芋而扁發葶宛似笋籜漸長色黒黄斑駁如染
梢開三杈杈上分枝舒葉如芹菜葉春初忽有抽葶上作一長
苞小者如錐大者如巨燭而抒上色黒紫深皺内空楞似鋪粉
絮蓋其花也花下有跗如斜旗形外駮内赤詭状可駭旬餘即
萎湘中曰鬼芋一曰磨芋滇曰鬼廟又曰軟菜秋冬間採根拭
去粗皮磨研成漿煮之用大匕攪和不令成餅俟熟用石灰水
點之待凝畫成塊味甘滑其芽又名鬼鼻五六月間以竹竿拍

'Careful, Weasley, careful!' cried Professor Sprout, as the beans burst into bloom before their very eyes.

Harry Potter and the Prisoner of Azkaban

"Herbal medicine has a long history in China. According to tradition, it originated with the mythical emperor, Shen Nong (the 'Divine Farmer'), who is believed to have been the inventor of agriculture and medicine, as well as the author of the first book on the subject, the Bencaojing."

EMMA GOODLIFFE
Curator

ted in that chapter, sprinkle yt also wth water; and yf yt be nece-
sary to make a cyrcle, let such an one be made as ys appoynted, a
towching the same. If any other Ceremonyes be required in this e
peryment doe them. When all theis bee fynisshed, say the coniu
cyon, wch thy Art doth teache the, and in the ende therof saye
Pater noster, Rerax, Terson, Syletim, I adiure you by t
holy name Ioth, He, Vau, wch is wrytten wth 12. letters
by this present experyment we may see the truthe; Ia, Ia, I
ya, yah, cause theis spirittes to shewe vs our desyer. I coniure
aforenamed spirittes, by all that is aforesayde, and by hym to w
all creatures doe obay, that ymmediatly you shewe vs the thi
that we requyre; or else hym that toke yt awaye. If yf to doe
experyment, yt be requisite, to write letters and figures, they
to bee wrytten, as ys prescribed in the seconde booke; note that by
whatsoeuer meanes, experyments for thefte are made or done, req
yt ys, that there bee other experyments besides this, as ys aboue sa

Howe experyments to be invysible must bee preparedd, Cap. 7.

Yf thou wylt haue an experiment to bee invysible, yf yt yt be n
ded to write thy experiment, then write yt all in virgyn parc
mente, and wyth penn and ynke, as shalbe appoynted in the ch
ter of penn and ynke, yf furdermore a coniuration be requyred,
then before yor coniuration say privyly as followethe.
Stabbon, Asen, Gabellum, Saneney, Noty, Enobal, Labo
rem, Balametem, Balnon, Tygumel, Millegaly, Iu
neis, Hearma, Hamorache, Yesa, Seya, Senoy, Hen
Barucatha, Acararas, Taracub, Bucarat, Caram
by the mercy whiche you beare towardes man kynde, make me to
invysible; Afterward make yor inuocations, and yf you must ma
a cyrcle, make such an one as is appoynted in the chapter o
makyng a cyrcle: yf you must wryte any figures, and letter
wryte such as are prescribed in the chapiter, as towching carac
notes, or fygures, yf you must wryte wyth any bloode, vse
such, as is also hereafter appoynted, when this is prepared
yf you must vse any coniuratio in ye ende of yt, saye as followethe

Charms

Charms

Lucy Mangan

Lucy Mangan is a journalist and columnist. She was educated in Catford and Cambridge. She studied English at the latter and then spent two years training as a solicitor, but left as soon as she qualified and went to work much more happily in a bookshop instead. She is now a columnist for Stylist magazine, features journalist and author of four books with a fifth – Bookworm, a memoir of childhood reading – soon to be published. She also does various bits of radio and television presenting, but does not have the chutzpah to call herself a broadcaster just yet.

Charms are, by and large, quite … charming. J.K. Rowling has said that they are potentially 'the most imaginative form of magic because you are adding properties to an object', rather than changing it completely. To sum it up in her words, 'turning a teacup into a rat would be a spell, whereas making a teacup dance would be a charm'. Thus most of the charms mentioned in the Harry Potter books provide delightful shortcuts through the boring bits of life. Summoning Charms (*Accio*) mean wizards never suffer the frustration that is so familiar to Muggles of mislaying things. A Scouring Charm will save you from the tedium of housework. Any glasses wearer yearns to be able to perform an Impervius Charm that will keep the rain off his or her lenses. An Undetectable Extension Charm will give you an endlessly capacious handbag, and if you're too young yet to realise the value of this – well, my friends, YOU WILL.

And so they are generally benevolent in intention (Cheering Charms, Hover Charms, Tickling Charms, the Bubble-Head Charm, the Shield Charm to deflect minor curses – although all these of course can be put to negative use if the wizard is so inclined). The same could be said for Charms in the Muggle world, including the most famous of them all, 'Abracadabra'. This ancient incantation has been in use since perhaps the third century AD, originally attached to a charm with healing powers.

In the general run of things, however, charms are small, manageable spells executed suitably gently. A wave and flick with a wand is usually all that is

12
11

required (hence swishy willow wands like Lily Potter's being so good for charm work), along with the correct words correctly pronounced, of course. Remember all the trouble Hermione had teaching Ron how to say *Wingardium Leviosa* ('make the "gar" nice and long') when they were trying to get their feathers to fly in one of Professor Flitwick's classes in the first book? Historically, here in the real world, you might sometimes need an amulet, or a special stone or some kind of talisman to help magical powers along, but in Harry's world these additions are rarely necessary.

In the Harry Potter books, charms add a great deal of fun to the narrative. They are the building blocks of the advanced magic Harry, Ron and Hermione come to learn about and master, and the care and detail with which J.K. Rowling adds and delineates each one is a microcosm of the meticulous planning that was done for the books as a whole. There is such pleasure, always, in the consistency of Harry's world and the charms are no different. It is fitting perhaps that this (generally) light, bright form of magic is taught by the tiny, squeaky Professor Filius Flitwick (an appropriately light, bright name).

It makes sense that the powers of these entry-level pieces of magic are usually temporary (thus hippogriff owners, we discover in *Fantastic Beasts and Where to Find Them*, are bound by law to conceal their animals with a Disillusionment Charm that must be performed daily so that it doesn't wear off at an inopportune moment). And the limits of those powers are reliably circumscribed by their creator – the charm wears off the Spell-Checking Quills bought in the Weasley twins' joke shop just like the batteries/ink/fart noises run out of most things bought in our real-world ones. Tough manticore skin can repel most charms. Invisibility fields cannot, without great cleverness and effort, extend beyond the article itself – and then, as Hermione notes of the Headless Hats in *Harry Potter and the Order of the Phoenix*, the little spell's lifespan will be even shorter. This is all part of J.K. Rowling's commitment to the internal logic that makes Harry's world, though magical, so entirely credible.

And it is this blend of wild adventure and invention with realism that has helped make J.K. Rowling's books such a success. A world with its own, consistent rules, even if they are different from our own, is a world you can imaginatively inhabit – and roam safely. This is a world and an author that is never going to break its contract with the reader. Things will be worked out properly – not necessarily easily or without sadness – but thoroughly, fairly and legitimately. All readers want this, but it's generally only writers for children who can be trusted to honour the pact. Thus does Harry charm every age, and surely through the ages to come.

L. Mangan

INTO THE ALLEY

This drawing reveals, in six stages, how the entrance arch to Diagon Alley appears when tapped three times by Hagrid's umbrella at the beginning of *The Philosopher's Stone*. This fully worked-out visualisation shows how J.K. Rowling rooted the magic in the book as closely as possible to real-world logic. The concept of bricks reorganising themselves into an archway is far more plausible than an opening simply appearing out of the blue. These imaginative touches, and the serious considerations that have gone in to explaining magical processes, underline what makes J.K. Rowling's world so vivid and real to so many readers.

DRAWING OF THE OPENING TO DIAGON ALLEY BY J.K. ROWLING (1990)
J.K. Rowling

The brick he had touched quivered – it wriggled – in the middle, a small hole appeared – it grew wider and wider – a second later they were facing an archway large enough even for Hagrid, an archway on to a cobbled street which twisted and turned out of sight.

Harry Potter and the Philosopher's Stone

A TRIP TO THE SHOPS

Jim Kay created fantastically meticulous drawings showing the panorama of the shops along Diagon Alley. The atmosphere of this renowned street is captured in the uneven cobbles and the fountainhead beneath the street sign. The shop in the foreground of the drawing above has hung a vast array of wares all over the building. Why limit yourself to a window display when magic can adorn the whole shop front?

DRAWING OF DIAGON ALLEY
BY JIM KAY
Bloomsbury

"Kay chose clever, fun and personal names for the shops. 'Twinkles Telescopes', for example, was inspired by a theatrical store from his childhood called Sally Twinkles. The nut store, 'Tut's Nuts', was named after the seeds taken from Tutankhamun's tomb and stored in Kew Gardens where the artist once worked."

JOANNA NORLEDGE
Curator

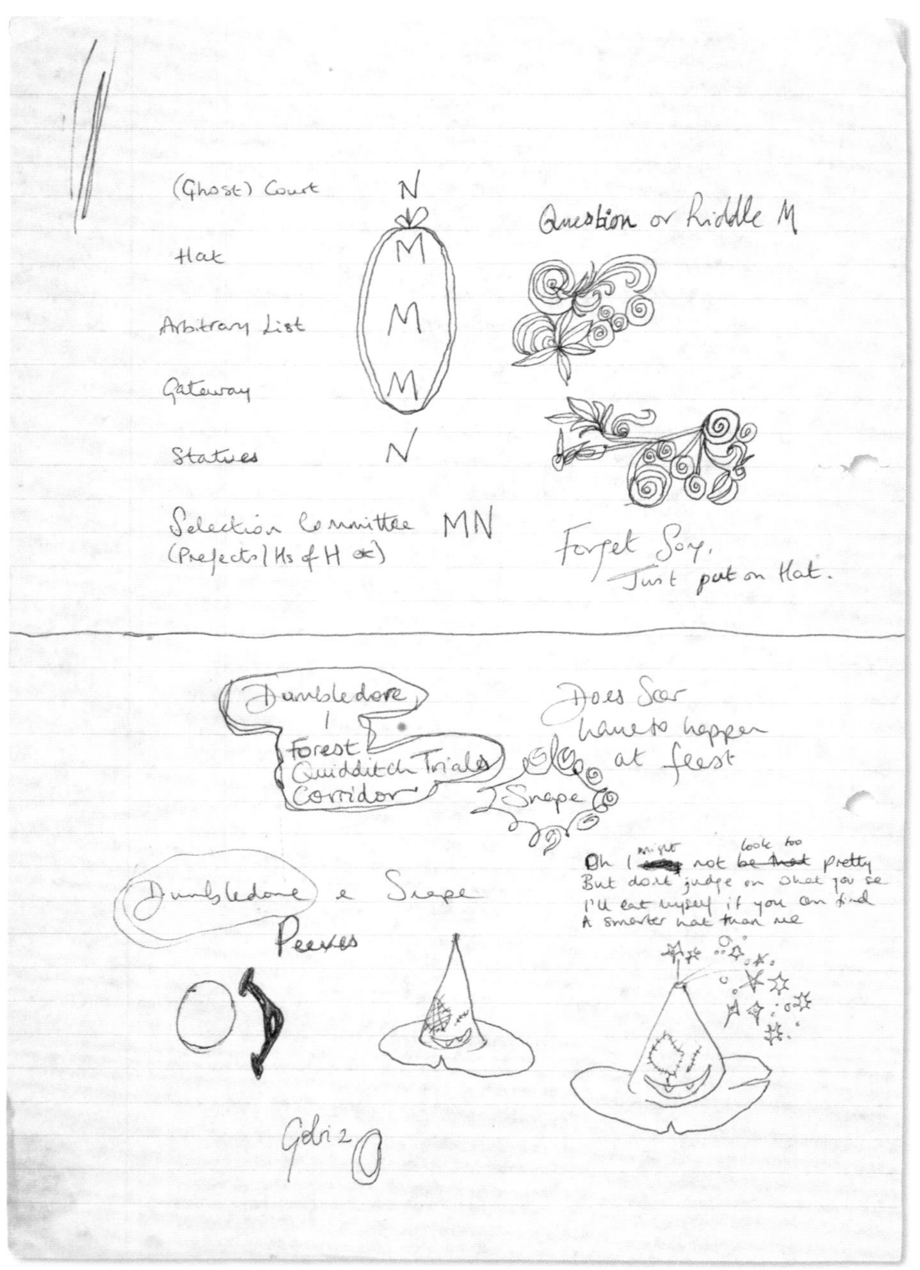

DECIDING ON A SORTING HAT

J.K. Rowling spent five years planning out Harry Potter's world and his story. She decided that Hogwarts would have four school houses – Gryffindor, Ravenclaw, Hufflepuff and Slytherin – with distinct qualities attributed to each. After that she had to work out how the students would be sorted in to the houses. These notes show the author listing some possible ways. The note 'statues' represents her idea that four statues of the founders in the Entrance Hall might come alive and select students from the group in front of them. Other ideas included a ghost court, a riddle, or prefects choosing students. The Sorting Hat is also shown here, complete with rips, patches and a grinning mouth.

◄ NOTES ON SORTING THE STUDENTS BY J.K. ROWLING

J.K. Rowling

> *"Finally, I wrote a list of the ways in which people can be chosen: eeny meeny miny mo, short straws, chosen by team captains, names out of a hat – names out of a talking hat – putting on a hat – the Sorting Hat."*

J.K. Rowling on Pottermore

Oh, you may not think I'm pretty
But don't judge on what you see
I'll eat myself if you can find
A smarter hat than me
You can keep your bowlers black
Your top hats sleek and tall
For I'm the Hogwarts Sorting Hat
And I can cap them all
~~None can tell you the~~
There's nothing hidden in your ~~head~~
The Sorting Hat can't see
So try me on and I will tell you
Where you ought to be.
You might belong in Gryffindor
Where dwell the brave at heart
~~It's daring, nerve and chivalry~~
~~Or Huffl~~ ~~If you have not~~
Their daring, nerve and chivalry
Set Gryffindors apart
You might belong in Hufflepuff
Where they are just and loyal
The patient Hufflepuffs are true
And unafraid of toil
~~You may Or Ravenclaw could be your house~~
~~The house for~~
might belong in Ravenclaw
ere all quick wits are found
e wisest and most learned minds

THE SORTING HAT SONG

At the start of every academic year at Hogwarts, new students are sorted in to their houses by the Sorting Hat. This is J.K. Rowling's original, handwritten draft of the song that the hat sings at Harry's Sorting Ceremony in his first year. The draft contains some crossings-out and additional edits, but most of these lines survived in the final published text of *The Philosopher's Stone.*

THE SORTING HAT SONG
BY J.K. ROWLING
J.K. Rowling

"The Sorting Ceremony begins when the hat sings a song explaining the qualities favoured by each of the houses. A new song is composed every year. It's not until his fourth year at Hogwarts that Harry finally attends another Sorting Ceremony."

JOANNA NORLEDGE
Curator

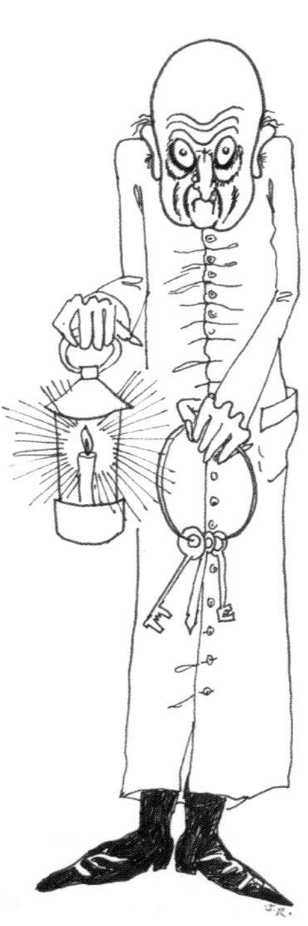

ARGUS FILCH

Argus Filch, the caretaker at Hogwarts, often came close to discovering Harry Potter on his night-time adventures around the school. Harry only escaped detection thanks to his Invisibility Cloak, which once belonged to his father, James Potter. The lamp held by Filch while he was patrolling the school corridors, shown here in a sketch by J.K. Rowling, enabled him to spot any students wandering the castle when they should have been tucked up in bed. This drawing shows Filch with several worry lines on his forehead, perhaps caused by years of chasing after misbehaving pupils. 'Argus' or 'Argos' is a name from Greek mythology for a many-eyed or one-hundred-eyed giant whose epithet, 'Panoptes', means 'all-seeing'.

◄ SKETCH OF ARGUS FILCH
BY J.K. ROWLING (1990)
J.K. Rowling

MAKE ME TO BE INVYSIBLE

For those who won't inherit an Invisibility Cloak, other methods of disappearing must be found instead. *The Key of Knowledge* was an instructional text on magic that was spuriously attributed to King Solomon. Here it cites a charm to achieve invisibility. The method proposed exists in several guises, because the book was widely shared, copied and recopied by students of magic. This manuscript once belonged to the English poet Gabriel Harvey. Care should be taken when reciting this spell, however – *The Key of Knowledge* does not include a charm to make yourself reappear again!

Howe experyments to be invysible must bee prepared, Cap. 7

► 'HOW EXPERIMENTS TO BE INVISIBLE MUST BE PREPARED', IN *THE BOOK OF KING SOLOMON CALLED THE KEY OF KNOWLEDGE* (ENGLAND, 17TH CENTURY)
British Library

A CLOUD OF KEYS

These two draft sketches show how Jim Kay created some of his illustrations, using a detailed pencil sketch which was then digitally coloured in or overlaid with a watercolour painting. Here you can see him experimenting with the design and colours of the winged keys, capturing the 'whirl of rainbow feathers' described in *The Philosopher's Stone*. Each key is beautifully detailed. They have been charmed by Professor Filius Flitwick. The winged keys were one of the protections put in place by the Hogwarts teachers to guard the Philosopher's Stone. Harry used his broomstick-flying skills to capture the one hiding in the flock of others that would open a magically protected locked door.

They seized a broomstick each and kicked off into the air, soaring into the midst of the cloud of keys. They grabbed and snatched but the bewitched keys darted and dived so quickly it was almost impossible to catch one.

Harry Potter and the Philosopher's Stone

➤ STUDIES OF WINGED KEYS ▲
BY JIM KAY
Bloomsbury

OLGA HUNT'S BROOMSTICK

Few charmed objects are more closely associated with the Western image of the witch than the broomstick. Although the tradition has ancient roots in pagan fertility rights, the connection between witchcraft and broomsticks developed significantly in the art and popular superstitions that fed the witch hysteria of 16th- and 17th-century Europe. This colourful broomstick was once owned by a Devonshire woman called Olga Hunt. When there was a Full Moon, Olga could be spotted with her broomstick leaping around Haytor Rocks on Dartmoor, much to the alarm of courting couples and campers!

BROOMSTICK BELONGING TO OLGA HUNT
The Museum of Witchcraft and Magic, Boscastle

A WITCH AND HER FAMILIAR

In 1621, Anne Fairfax, the younger daughter of Edward Fairfax of Fewston, Yorkshire, died suddenly. Two of her sisters, together with a friend, accused some local women of practising witchcraft. The women were taken to trial at the local assizes, but the case collapsed when the friend confessed that the whole thing had been a hoax. Despite being chastised by the judge, Edward Fairfax remained resolute in his belief that Anne's death was caused by witches. This manuscript sets out the case for the prosecution. A later illustrator has added drawings of the 'witches' and their familiars, including 'Margaret Wait the elder, a widow, for that her husband died by the hand of the executioner. Her familiar is a deformed thing with many feet, rough with hair, the bigness of a cat, and the name of it is unknown.'

A DISCOURSE OF WITCHCRAFT AS IT WAS ACTED IN THE FAMILY OF MR. EDWARD FAIRFAX OF FUYSTONE (ENGLAND, 18TH CENTURY)
British Library

THE LANCASHIRE WITCHES

As the anonymous author of this book noted, the English county of Lancashire is 'famous for witches and the very strange pranks they have played'. Lancashire's popular association with witchery stems from the famous Pendle trials of 1612, when some nineteen people were accused of practising witchcraft. While the story of the Pendle witch craze is an unhappy one – the majority of the accused were hanged – the author of this text was eager to portray Lancashire witches in a more positive light. The book is illustrated with simple woodcuts, including this picture of a jolly witch mounting a broomstick.

THE HISTORY OF THE LANCASHIRE WITCHES (COVENTRY, 1825)
British Library

22

in destroying and laming of cattle, and drowning ships at sea, by raising storms. But it appears that the Lancashire witches chiefly divert themselves in merriment and sport; therefore they are found to be more sociable than any others.

CHAP. XI.
A short description of the famous Lapland Witches.

> *"The text accompanying this illustration states, 'Lancashire witches chiefly divert themselves in merriment and sport'. Perhaps it is little wonder, then, that* Quidditch Through the Ages *cites the first known account of a Quidditch match in 1385, as 'a game in Lancashire'."*
>
> ALEXANDER LOCK
> *Curator*

As every school-age wizard knows, the fact that we fly on broomsticks is probably our worst-kept secret. No Muggle illustration of a witch is complete without a broom [...] broomsticks and magic are inextricably linked in the Muggle mind.

Quidditch Through the Ages

HARRY AND DRACO

The world of magic was new and complicated for Harry when he arrived at Hogwarts, but in his very first flying lesson, having never previously touched a broom, he flew so naturally that Professor McGonagall instantly whisked him away to meet the Gryffindor Quidditch team captain. Harry became the youngest Seeker in a century to play in a Hogwarts Quidditch game. In this painting by Jim Kay, Harry is shown with his cape billowing and his hands firmly clasped around his broomstick, while a rain-blurred Draco Malfoy heads towards him in the background.

HARRY POTTER AND DRACO MALFOY PLAYING QUIDDITCH BY JIM KAY
Bloomsbury

> *"Kay's painting brings to life the opening Quidditch match against the Slytherin team in Harry's second year. In the match a Bludger went rogue and followed Harry relentlessly, eventually breaking his arm. Despite this, Harry caught the Snitch and won the game."*
>
> JOANNA NORLEDGE
> *Curator*

With a roar from the crowd to speed them upwards, the fourteen players rose towards the leaden sky. Harry flew higher than any of them, squinting around for the Snitch.

Harry Potter and the Chamber of Secrets

A MAGICAL RING

This 4th-century papyrus is part of an ancient Greek handbook for magic. As well as containing charms to discover thieves and to reveal the secret thoughts of men, the handbook describes how to prepare a magical ring. The owner was advised to inscribe the ring with a charm, according to the following formula: 'May something never happen as long as this remains buried'. It was intended that the ring be hidden in the ground, in order to prevent something from happening. By inscribing and burying the ring, the owner could specify, for example, that they did not want a rival to be lucky in love. With the exception of one added word, the inscription reads the same in either direction. This is a well known characteristic of magical charms.

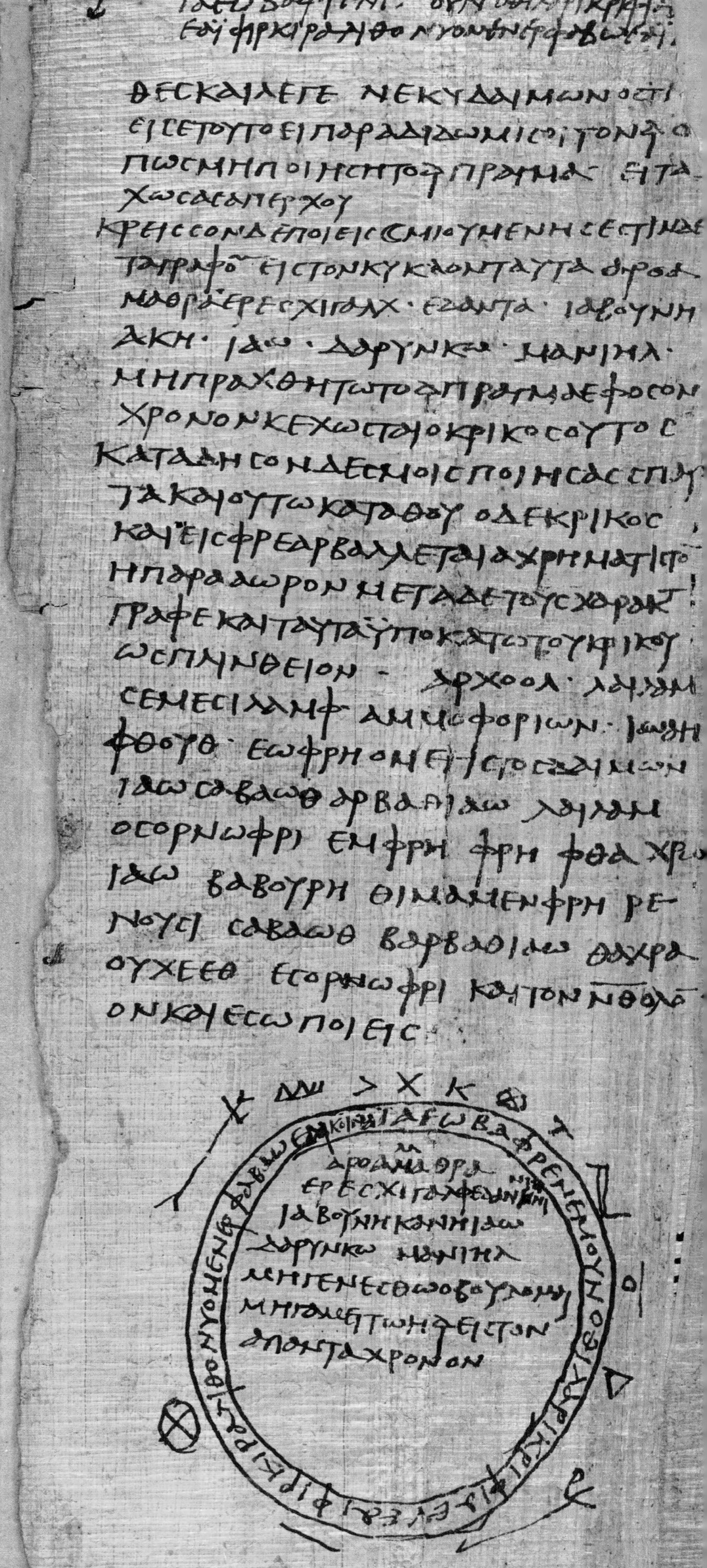

A RING CAPTIONED, 'MAY SOMETHING NEVER HAPPEN AS LONG AS THIS REMAINS BURIED', IN A GREEK HANDBOOK FOR MAGIC (THEBES, 4TH CENTURY)

British Library

ABRACADABRA

The 'Abracadabra' spell has been used by generations of magicians to conjure rabbits out of hats. In ancient times, however, the same word was held to be a charm with healing powers. Its first documented use appears in the *Liber Medicinalis* or 'Book of Medicine' written by Quintus Serenus Sammonicus. Serenus was a physician to the Emperor Caracalla, prescribing the charm 'Abracadabra' as a cure for malaria. Sufferers were instructed to write out the word again and again, leaving out one letter each time. This would produce a 'cone-shaped' text. The charm was then worn as an amulet around the neck in order to drive out the fever.

> *"The Abracadabra text is outlined in red ink in the margin of this manuscript. Serenus further recommended that flax, the fat of the lion or coral stones could be used to fix the charm around one's neck."*
>
> JULIAN HARRISON
> *Lead Curator*

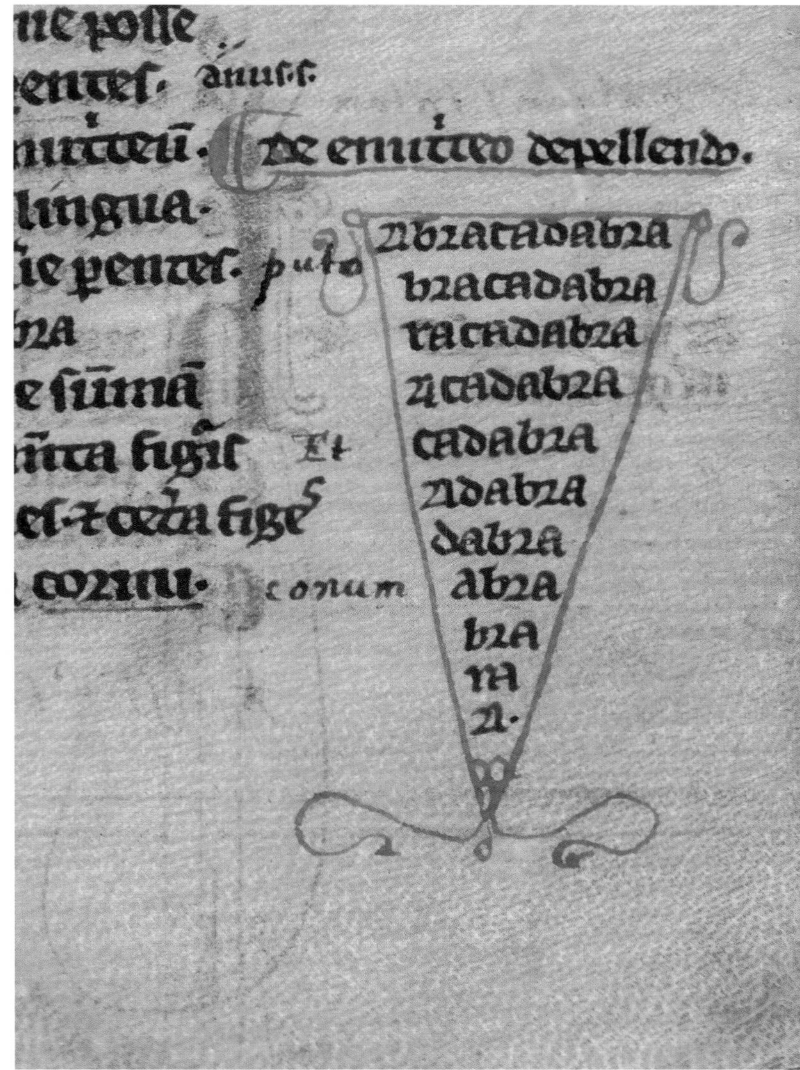

➢ *LIBER MEDICINALIS*
(CANTERBURY, 13TH CENTURY)
British Library

HOW TO TURN YOURSELF INTO A LION

In Ethiopia, magical practitioners commonly make collections of charms, spells and the names of plants and their properties, which are then copied into handbooks like this one. This page has been removed from a magical recipe book. It contains charms for reversing spells and for binding demons. One charm in particular supplies the formula for changing yourself into a lion or another beast: 'With red ink, write these secret names on a piece of white silk. To transform yourself into a lion, tie the silk to your head; to become a python, tie it on your arm; to turn into an eagle, tie it on your shoulder.'

➢ A CHARM TO TURN SOMEONE INTO A LION, A PYTHON OR AN EAGLE (ETHIOPIA, 18TH CENTURY)
British Library

'Transfiguration is some of the most complex and dangerous magic you will learn at Hogwarts,' she said. 'Anyone messing around in my class will leave and not come back. You have been warned.'

Professor McGonagall, Harry Potter and the Philosopher's Stone

A LOVE CHARM

Love potions and charms are still widely used across the world. Sometimes this type of magic even appeared at Hogwarts – from Professor Slughorn brewing Amortentia in class to Ron Weasley accidentally ingesting Romilda Vane's love potion. Made in the Netherlands, the love charm shown here is rich in symbolism that imbued the object with magical power. Painted onto an oyster shell to ensure fertility, the charm was produced for a couple whose first initials were 'J' and 'R'. Red thread binds the letters together while a pair of touching hearts represent their love. Above these letters are the couple's star signs – ♉ for Taurus and ♊ for Gemini.

➣ LOVE CHARM (NETHERLANDS, 20TH CENTURY)
The Museum of Witchcraft and Magic, Boscastle

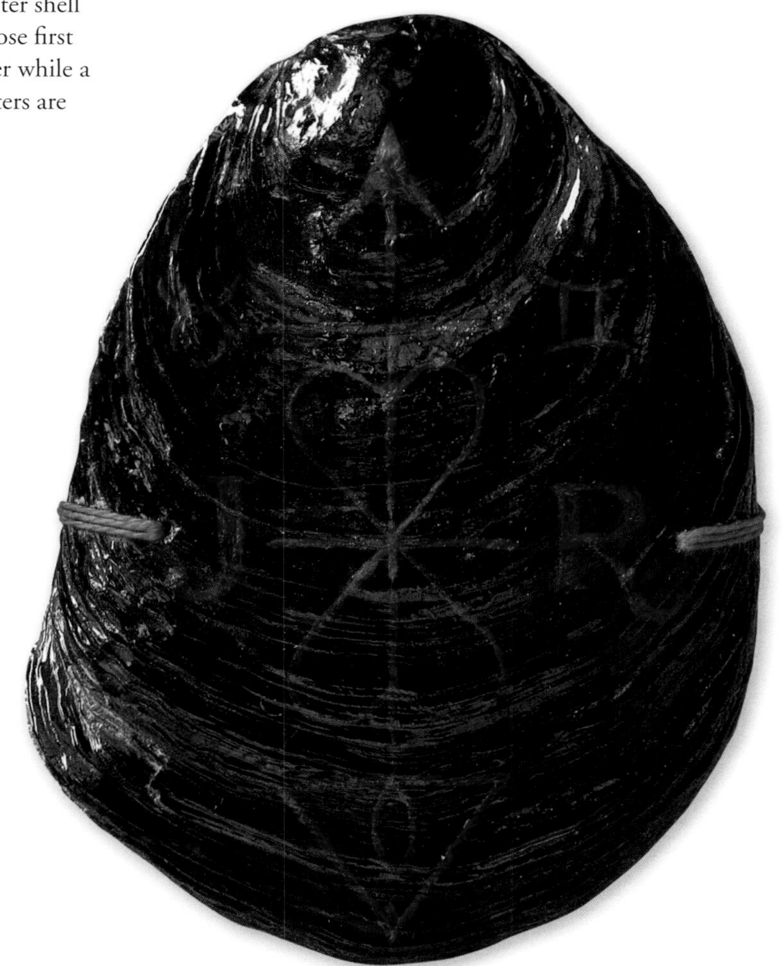

"The effectiveness of this love charm remains unknown. As Slughorn declared in his Potions class, 'It is impossible to manufacture or imitate love.'"

ALEXANDER LOCK
Curator

'Professor, I'm really sorry to disturb you,' said Harry as quietly as possible, while Ron stood on tiptoe, attempting to see past Slughorn into his room, 'but my friend Ron's swallowed a love potion by mistake. You couldn't make him an antidote, could you?'

Harry Potter and the Half-Blood Prince

CANCER
GEMINI
TAVRVS
LEO
LATITVDO LVNAE MERIDIONALIS
LATITVDO LVNAE SEPTENTRIO
CAPVT
CAVDA
M · A
M · D
S · D
AQVARIVS
CAPRICORNVS
SAGITTARIVS

Astronomy

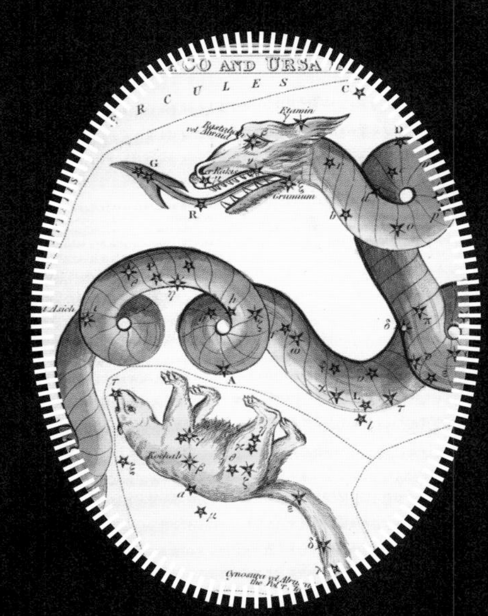

Astronomy

Tim Peake

British European Space Agency astronaut Tim Peake has had a lifelong passion for space. It started in his childhood, gazing at the stars and visiting airshows. A test pilot, he started training as an astronaut in 2009. From December 2015 he spent six months onboard the International Space Station, where he performed a spacewalk and hundreds of scientific experiments, ran a marathon and was part of the most successful education programme ever supported by an astronaut.

Shimmering curtains of vivid glowing green and red lights were dancing all around us, occasionally shooting off rays in an unexpected direction, as if we were flying through a giant cauldron brewing some mystical potion. But this was no magic spell – this hypnotic light show is a natural phenomenon, witnessed on many occasions from the International Space Station as we fly above and sometimes even through the 'aurora'. The effect arises when electrically charged particles from the Sun are channelled along Earth's magnetic field lines above the planet's polar regions. When they strike atoms in the upper atmosphere, such as oxygen and nitrogen, the interaction produces these characteristic colours. But despite the enchanting appearance, auroras have a dark side. In extreme events, the arrival of these particles can cause interference with satellites and radio transmissions, and create power blackouts on Earth. Fortunately, we have Sun-watching spacecraft looking out for us, giving us a forecast for the most unruly space weather.

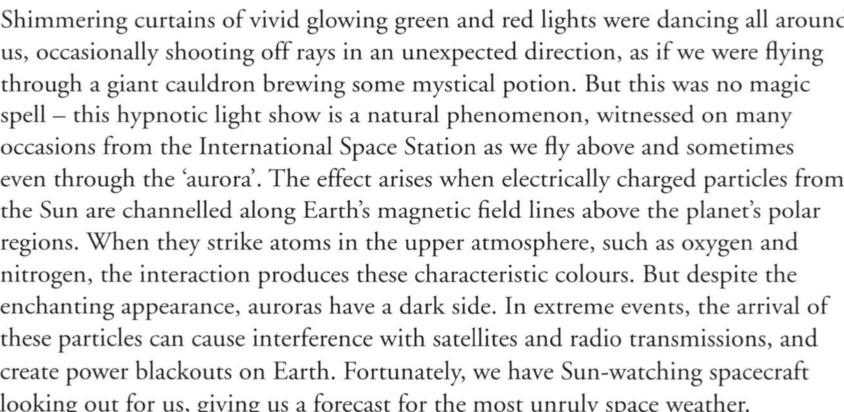

When we are not spellbound by the aurora, we can also appreciate the star-studded night sky from the Space Station, albeit in our very short nights. Our orbital outpost is travelling at over 17,000 mph (about 28,000 km/h), some 250 miles (400 km) above Earth, so it only takes about 90 minutes to circle the planet. That means we see as many as sixteen sunrises and sunsets a day. At night we can even see the grand sweep of stars and intervening dust clouds towards the centre of our own galaxy, the Milky Way. You can also see the Milky Way, aurora, stars and planets from the ground – although you may need a good spell to clear away the clouds! Astronomical phenomena and objects have inspired the names of many Harry Potter characters, including the Hogwarts Astronomy teacher herself, Professor Aurora Sinistra. There's also Andromeda, Bellatrix, Draco and Sirius, to mention a few. How many Harry Potter themed constellations and stars can you find in the evening sky?

20
10
80
70
60
50
40
ORBIS
CŒLESTIS
TYPUS

Learning the names of the stars and planets, and studying their movements during Astronomy lessons is not just an important subject for young wizards – Muggles throughout history have also been fascinated with the night sky. Ancient civilisations realised that objects in the sky appeared to move in a regular pattern, and they would use the positions of the stars and Moon to determine when to plant and harvest their crops, and for navigation.

One of the true pioneers of charting the sky was the ancient Greek astronomer Hipparchus. With only naked eye observations and simple geometry, he catalogued the relative brightness and positions of around 1,000 stars. More than two millennia later, the European Space Agency (ESA) launched a mission named in his honour. ESA's Hipparcos was the first satellite ever devoted to star mapping, revolutionising the field of precision astronomy with its catalogue of over two and a half million stars.

Today ESA has an even more powerful telescope in space – Gaia. It is cataloguing an unprecedented one billion stars at even greater precision, far greater than our ancient ancestors probably even dared to dream. With Gaia data, astronomers will be able to create a three-dimensional map of the Galaxy, not only showing accurate positions of the stars today, but also their past motions and even where they might be destined in the future. One can imagine it might be like looking into the 'perfect, moving model of the galaxy in a large glass ball' that Harry eyed up on his shopping trip to Diagon Alley. Owning one of these objects would apparently mean he would never need to take another Astronomy lesson. One can only assume there was a lot of knowledge contained within it, just like the catalogues Gaia is producing!

In their classes, Hogwarts students also had to learn something about the environments of our Solar System's planets and moons. In one memorable homework session Hermione corrects Harry and Ron on their knowledge of Jupiter's moons.

'Jupiter's biggest moon is Ganymede, not Callisto [...] and it's Io that's got the volcanoes [...] I think you must have misheard Professor Sinistra, Europa's covered in ice, not mice'

The students are discussing the four largest moons of Jupiter, collectively known as the Galilean satellites after the astronomer Galileo Galilei. He discovered them through one of the first simple telescopes in 1610. The astronomer noticed that when he looked on different nights, the positions of the four points of light changed – a sign that they were orbiting Jupiter. You can see the changing configuration for yourself using a pair of good binoculars or a simple telescope, and Jupiter can be seen with the naked eye.

The icy moons of Jupiter are the target of ESA's Jupiter Icy Moons Explorer that will launch in the 2020s. While Hermione was right that there are no mice on Europa, it is one of the best places to look for life beyond Earth – beneath its icy shell could be the biggest water ocean in the Solar System. On Earth, water and life go hand in hand. Could there be life on Europa, swimming in its ocean? Ganymede, which is indeed bigger than Callisto, is in fact the largest moon in the entire Solar System, comparable even to planet Mercury. Ganymede and Callisto might be hiding oceans under their rocky surfaces, too, and ESA's new mission is going to investigate the habitability potential of these planet-sized moons.

In the twenty years since *Harry Potter and the Philosopher's Stone* was published, we have seen extraordinary advances in the field of Astronomy and space exploration. We've sent missions to study the planets, and landed probes on other worlds. Our Huygens probe landed on Saturn's moon Titan in 2005, and Rosetta's Philae lander touched down on Comet 67P/Churyumov-Gerasimenko in 2014. We've also launched powerful space telescopes to study exotic phenomena like black holes and exploding stars, invisible dark matter and dark energy that influence our Universe in mysterious ways, and even the birth of the cosmos itself. Continuing the legacy of the pioneering first astronomers, we'll continue to look deeper and deeper into the sky for centuries more to come.

But remember, you don't need to be a professional astronomer, or even an astronaut or a wizard to enjoy the wonders of the night sky. Just look up, it's a magical experience.

LISTS OF HOGWARTS SUBJECTS AND TEACHERS

In this handwritten note, which was made as she was writing *The Philosopher's Stone*, J.K. Rowling has listed the subjects taught at Hogwarts alongside the prospective names of their teachers. Here you get a glimpse of some of the revisions and choices J.K. Rowling made as she developed Harry Potter's wizarding world. An early moniker for the Professor of Astronomy is recorded here as 'Aurelia Sinistra'. This later developed into 'Aurora Sinistra'. J.K. Rowling often uses Latin words for her names and spells. 'Aurora', which means 'the dawn', can also refer to the natural phenomenon that occurs near the magnetic poles, creating breathtaking light displays in the sky. As well as meaning 'left-hand side', 'Sinistra' is also the name of a star in the constellation of Ophiuchus, better known as the Serpent Bearer.

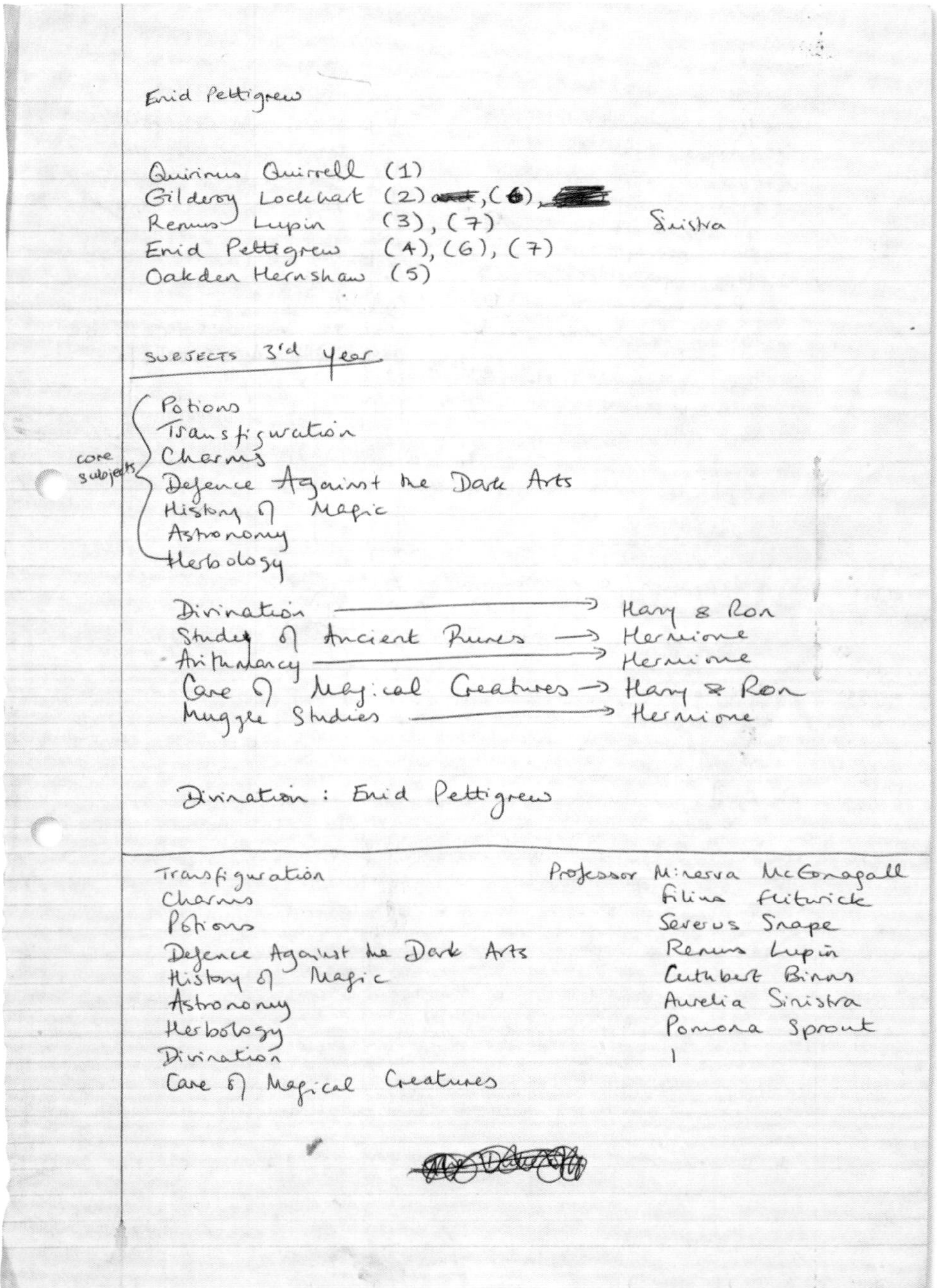

Enid Pettigrew

Quirinus Quirrell (1)
Gilderoy Lockhart (2), (6),
Remus Lupin (3), (7) Sinistra
Enid Pettigrew (4), (6), (7)
Oakden Hernshaw (5)

SUBJECTS 3'd year

core subjects:
Potions
Transfiguration
Charms
Defence Against the Dark Arts
History of Magic
Astronomy
Herbology

Divination → Harry & Ron
Study of Ancient Runes → Hermione
Arithmancy → Hermione
Care of Magical Creatures → Harry & Ron
Muggle Studies → Hermione

Divination: Enid Pettigrew

Transfiguration Professor Minerva McGonagall
Charms Filius Flitwick
Potions Severus Snape
Defence Against the Dark Arts Remus Lupin
History of Magic Cuthbert Binns
Astronomy Aurelia Sinistra
Herbology Pomona Sprout
Divination
Care of Magical Creatures

"The lists of Defence Against the Dark Arts teachers include unused characters with unfamiliar names like Enid Pettigrew, Oakden Hernshaw and Mylor Silvanus, none of whom appear in the published books."

JOANNA NORLEDGE
Curator

LIST OF THE HOGWARTS SUBJECTS AND TEACHERS BY J.K. ROWLING
J.K. Rowling

Transfiguration	♀	Prof. Minerva McGonagall
Charms	♂	Prof. Filius Flitwick
Potions	♂	Prof. Severus Snape
Herbology	♀	Prof. Pomona Sprout
D.A.D.A.	♂	Prof. Remus Lupin
Astronomy	♀	Prof. Aurora Sinistra
History of Magic	♂	Prof. Cutubert Binns
Divination	♂	Prof. Mopsus etc
Study of Ancient Runes	♀	Prof. Batusheda ~~Vector~~ Babbling
Arithmancy	♀	Prof. Septima Vector
Care of Magical Creatures	♂ →	~~Hagrid~~ Rubeus Hagrid
Muggle Studies	♀	Prof.

igit

i

ctor

ptima
Vector

<u>Hippogriffs</u> Stormswift
Hothoof
Fleetwing

Gibberish
Gobbledegook
also check tongues/languages Greek etc

Mylor Silvanus

ata

e fates

e furies
½

Rosmerta "Good purveyor"
village woman?

---

1) Quirrell
2) Lockhart
3) Lupin
4) Pettigrew
5) <u>Mylor</u> person. Oakden Hobday

THE OLDEST ATLAS OF THE NIGHT SKY

In 1907, a Hungarian-British archaeologist called Aurel Stein was searching for artefacts in the desert on the southern Silk Road. He entered a cave in Dunhuang, Central China, that had been sealed for thousands of years. At that moment Aurel Stein stumbled upon an amazing discovery – the cave was a treasure trove containing 40,000 ancient Buddhist manuscripts, paintings and documents. This paper scroll was among them, the oldest preserved star atlas from any civilisation. At the time that the atlas was made, it was believed that the movement of the stars reflected the actions of the emperor and his court on Earth. A solar eclipse, for example, might be interpreted as a sign of a forthcoming coup. The scroll shows more than 1,300 stars visible to the naked eye in the Northern Hemisphere. It is staggering to think that a chart of such accuracy was created by observation alone – the Dunhuang Star Atlas is the oldest map of the night sky, yet it stands up well compared to modern charts today.

"This star atlas is a remarkable survival. It is astonishing to think that it was created centuries before the invention of the telescope. The scroll dates back to approximately AD 700, and its detail and accuracy are extraordinary."

JULIAN HARRISON
Lead Curator

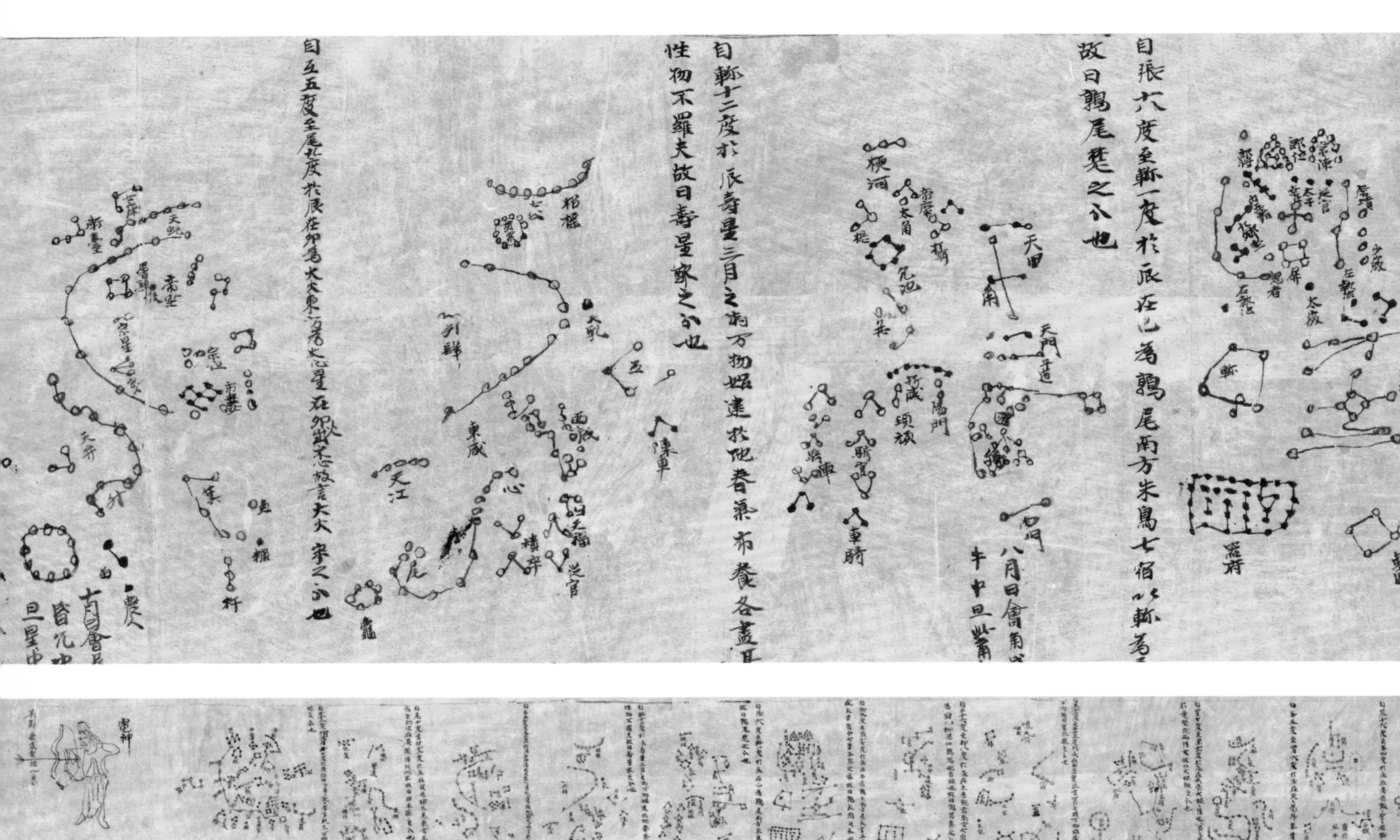

'Lie back on the floor,' said Firenze in his calm voice, 'and observe the heavens. Here is written, for those who can see, the fortune of our races.'

Harry Potter and the Order of the Phoenix

THE DUNHUANG STAR ATLAS (CHINA, C. AD 700)
British Library

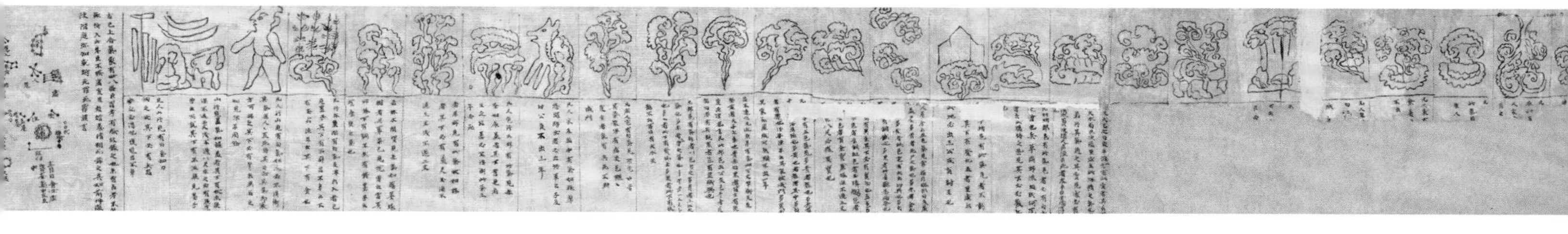

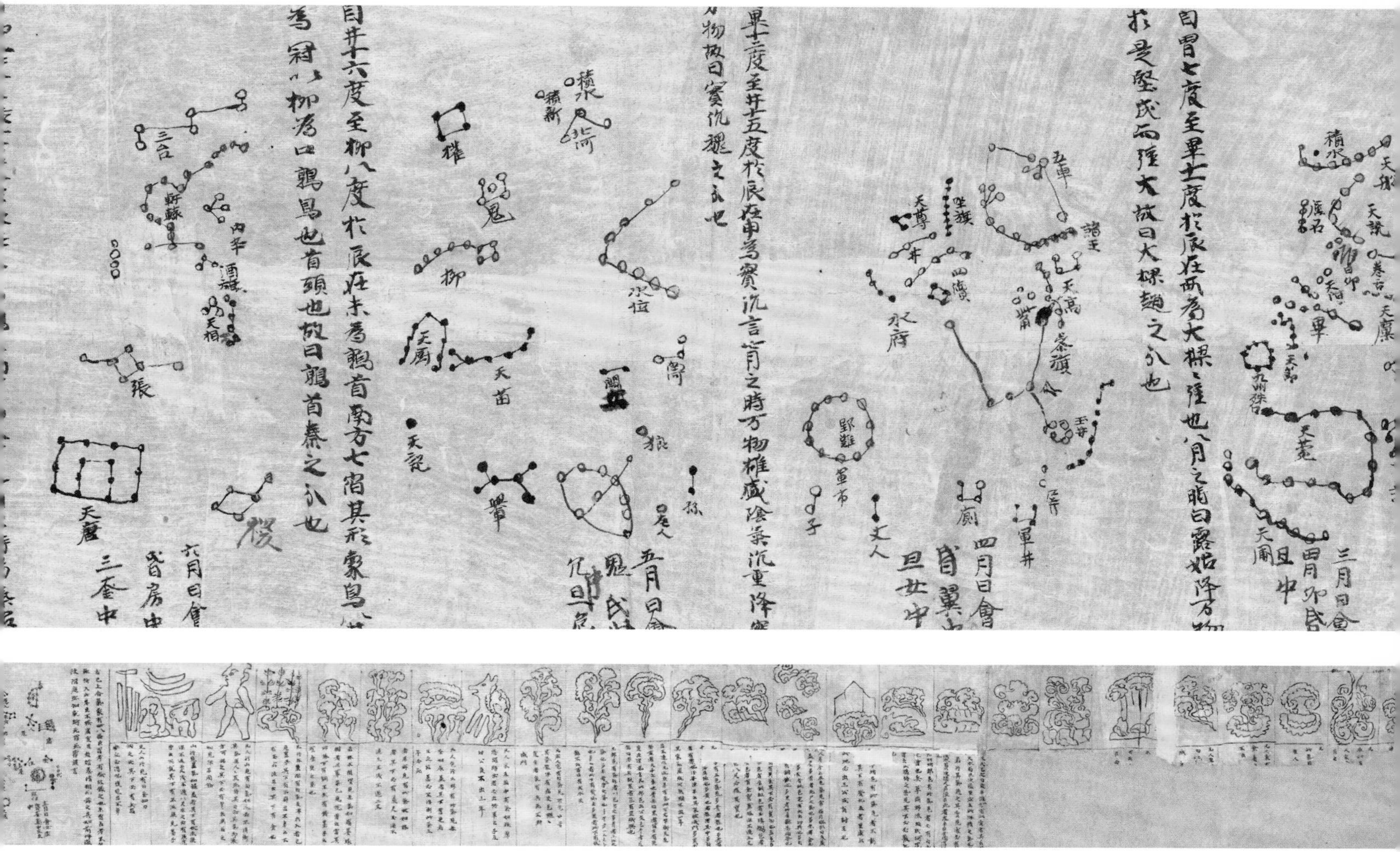

WRITTEN IN THE STARS

The creators of this Anglo-Saxon manuscript have skilfully used illustration to bring the constellations to life. The centaur on the right-hand page is shown with his cloak flowing as he draws back his bow, as if ready to fire an arrow at Capricorn, the goat-fish, struggling to flee on the left. The centaur represents the constellation Sagittarius, taking its name from the Latin for 'archer'. The images in the book are so vivid, it is hard to believe that they were painted over a thousand years ago. This manuscript was completed shortly before the Norman invasion of England, perhaps at Winchester or Canterbury. A book with this level of detail and artistry would have been made by a team of people, whose names we will never know. Each picture would have been painted onto the page first, with a scribe carefully adding the text around it afterwards.

'Never,' said Hagrid irritably, 'try an' get a straight answer out of a centaur. Ruddy star-gazers. Not interested in anythin' closer'n the moon.'

Harry Potter and the Philosopher's Stone

AN ANGLO-SAXON MISCELLANY (ENGLAND, 11TH CENTURY)

British Library

"The Anglo-Saxon Miscellany is a stunningly beautiful manuscript. Each star is represented by an orange orb, showing its relative position in the night sky. The artist has then painted around the orbs to form the namesake creature of the constellation."

JULIAN HARRISON

Lead Curator

PORRO SAGITTARIUS SCORPIONE ORIENTE ASCENDIT QUO ASCENDENTE OCCIDIT ORION ET CEPHEI
manus in cuius signi regione zodiacus circulus humillimus .e. ppter
dequinda crura. Quidam negant dicentes. Numquam centauros sagittis
usus fuisse. Sositheus autem illum adfirmat filium illu' musarum fuisse.
Habet stellas in capite .ii. in acumine sagittae .ii. in
dextro cubito .i. in manu .i. in uentre .i. claram in dorso .ii.
in cauda .i. in genu priori .i. in summo pede .i.
in posteriori genu .i. fiunt .xiii.

89

Atque etiam sup hoc nauis pelagoq: uagatur
Mense sagitti potens solis cū sustinet orbem
Hac iam iam cumminus exiguo lux tempore presto est
hoc signu ueniens poterunt prenoscere nautae.
Iam ppe pcipitante. licebit uisere nocti
Ut se se ostendens ostendat scorpius alte
Posteriore trahens flexum ui corporis arcum
Iam sup hunc cernes arti caput esse minoris
Et magis erectu adsummu uersarier orbem
Tum se se orion toto iam corpore condet
Extrema ppe nocte et cepheus conditor alte
Lumboru tenus aprima depulsus aduumbras.

SAGITTARIUS

For one brief moment, the great black dog reared on to its hind legs and placed its front paws on Harry's shoulders, but Mrs Weasley shoved Harry away towards the train door, hissing, 'For heaven's sake, act more like a dog, Sirius!'

Harry Potter and the Order of the Phoenix

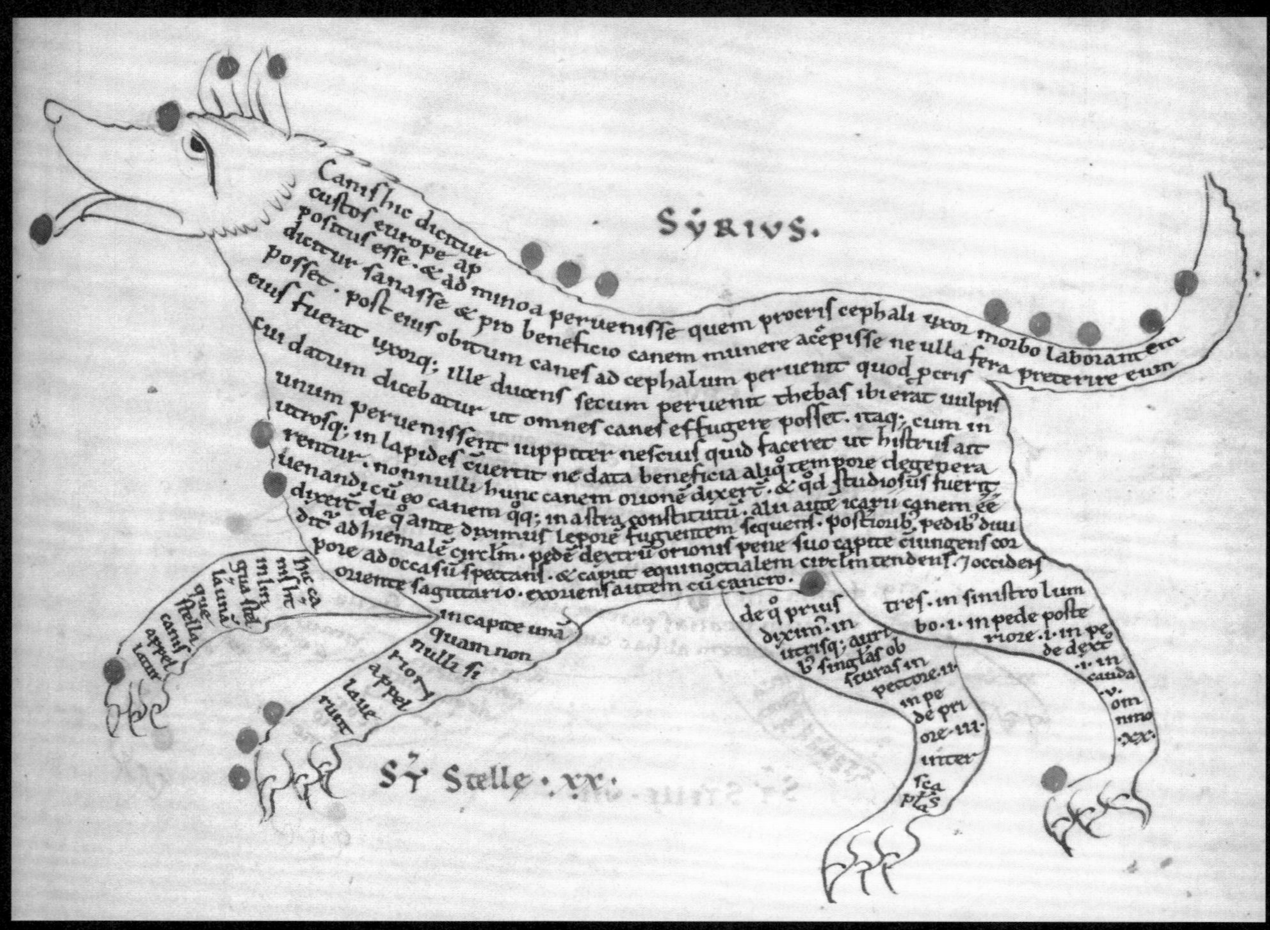

SIRIUS BLACK

The wonders of the night sky have inspired many of the character names in the Harry Potter series. Hogwarts alumni include Andromeda Tonks, Bellatrix Lestrange and of course their cousin, Sirius Black. This medieval manuscript shows the constellation of Canis Major. The most famous star in that constellation and also the brightest light that can be seen from Earth is Sirius, the Dog Star. The shape of the dog in this manuscript is infilled with a pattern poem in Latin, derived from the writings of the Roman author Hyginus.

A AN ASTRONOMICAL MISCELLANY (PETERBOROUGH, 12TH CENTURY)
British Library

EYES TO THE SKIES

Astronomers of the past used a range of equipment to help them plot the movement of the stars. This exquisite brass instrument is called an astrolabe. It could be used to create a two-dimensional map of the heavens, similar to the star charts that Harry and his classmates were expected to plot in their Astronomy exams. An astrolabe was also able to determine latitude, and was employed by many in the Islamic world to find the direction of Mecca. This finely decorated astrolabe has been inlaid with silver.

AN ASTROLABE FOUND IN SYRIA (13TH CENTURY)
British Museum

Sir John Mandeville was a celebrated, but fictitious, medieval English traveller. The story goes that Mandeville served the Sultan of Cairo and met the Great Khan, before settling down in 1357 to write about his experiences. The travelogue proved highly popular, and was translated into several European languages. This illustration accompanied the Czech translation of *Mandeville's Travels*. It shows a group of astronomers standing on Mount Athos in Greece, studying the stars with astrolabes and quadrants, special instruments that measure the angle of an object in the night sky. Others below are shown writing a series of strange characters in the dust with their sticks.

MINIATURE OF ASTRONOMERS ON MOUNT ATHOS (BOHEMIA, 15TH CENTURY)
British Library

TURNING CIRCLES

Celestial globes show the position of stars in the sky as perceived from the Earth. The art dates back thousands of years – the first celestial globes were created in ancient Greece. This majestic example was designed by a Franciscan monk called Vincenzo Coronelli, considered to be one of the greatest globe makers in the world. Although most of his work was produced in Venice, this one was actually made in Paris. Here Coronelli collaborated with Jean Baptist Nolin, engraver to the French Crown. Working with draft maps provided by Coronelli, Nolin engraved the beautiful constellation figures that appear across the surface of the globe.

VINCENZO CORONELLI & JEAN BAPTIST NOLIN,
ORBIS COELESTIS TYPUS (PARIS, 1693)
British Library

"This impressive globe measures 108 centimetres in diameter, making it the largest of Coronelli's commercially produced globes. Nolin's work is full of detail and action – animals, men and mythical creatures are shown in constant dialogue as they move together across the night sky."

ALEXANDER LOCK
Curator

He was sorely tempted, too, by the perfect, moving model of the galaxy in a large glass ball, which would have meant he never had to take another Astronomy lesson.

Harry Potter and the Prisoner of Azkaban

A MINIATURE ORRERY MADE BY JOHN TROUGHTON (LONDON, 18TH CENTURY)

Science Museum

MECHANICAL MAGIC

An orrery is a model of the Solar System. This mechanical marvel was made in London by the mathematical instrument maker, John Troughton. It displays the movement of Earth in relation to the Moon and two other planets. The model rests on an octagonal wooden base, above which curves a series of bands marking celestial longitude and latitude. Orreries have long been used in teaching and were even available for purchase in Diagon Alley. At Hogwarts they are not only used for Astronomy, but also for 'planetary divination'. Professor Sybill Trelawney's orrery holds 'the moons […] the nine planets and the fiery sun, all of them hanging in thin air beneath the glass'.

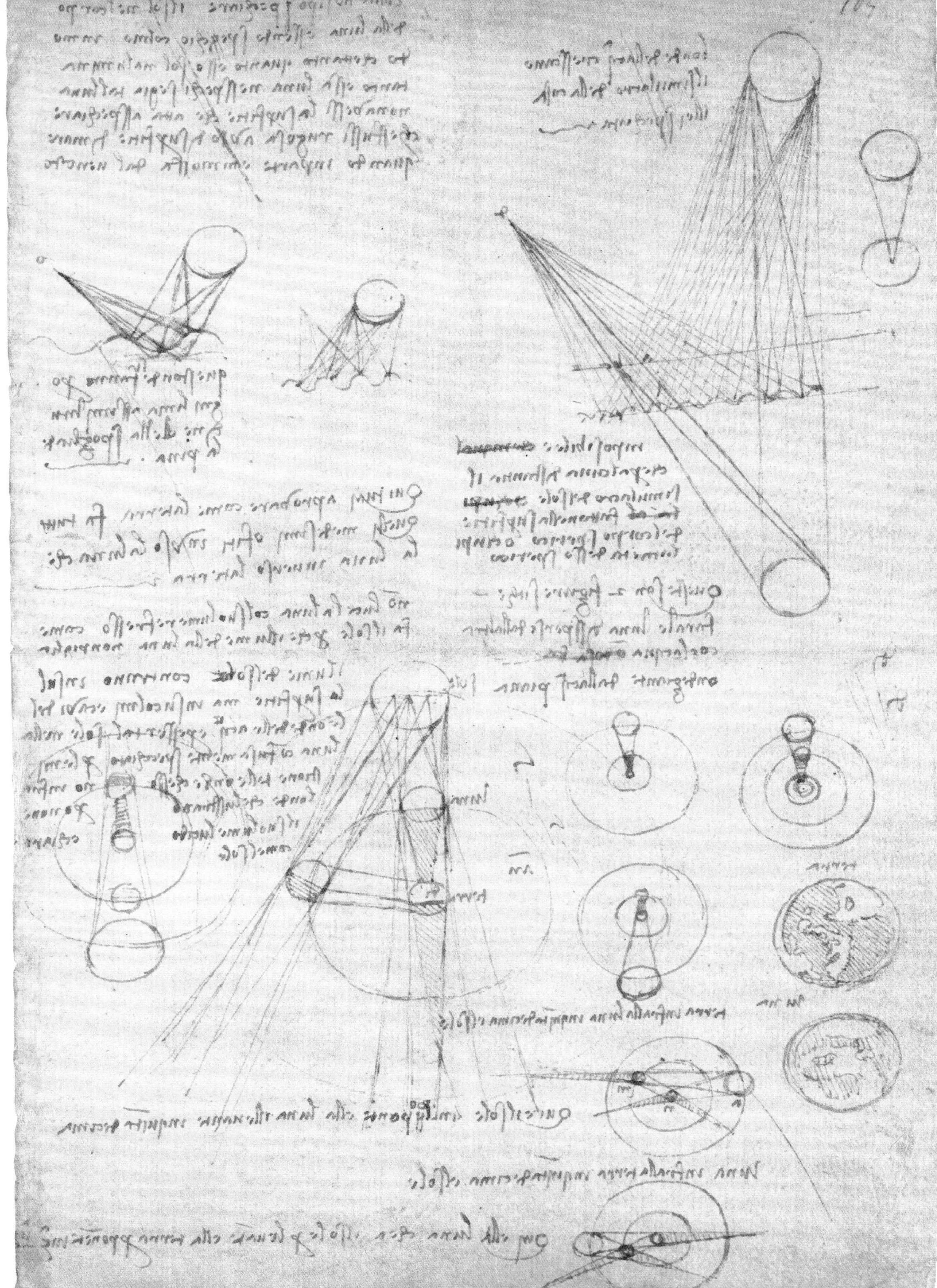

LEONARDO ON THE MOON

Leonardo da Vinci – inventor, scientist, artist – was centuries ahead of his time. Throughout his career Leonardo made notes written in curious mirrored handwriting that reads from right to left. Some of these pages were later gathered into a notebook known as the 'Codex Arundel', named after a former owner, the Earl of Arundel. The shaded diagram in the centre left describes the reflection of light, according to the alignments of the Sun, Moon and Earth. Leonardo's drawing shows the Sun and Moon revolving round the Earth, accepting the theory by the Greek astronomer Ptolemy that the Earth was the centre of the universe. Leonardo also believed that the Moon was covered with water and that its surface would reflect light like a convex mirror.

LEONARDO DA VINCI'S NOTEBOOK (ITALY, C. 1506–8)

British Library

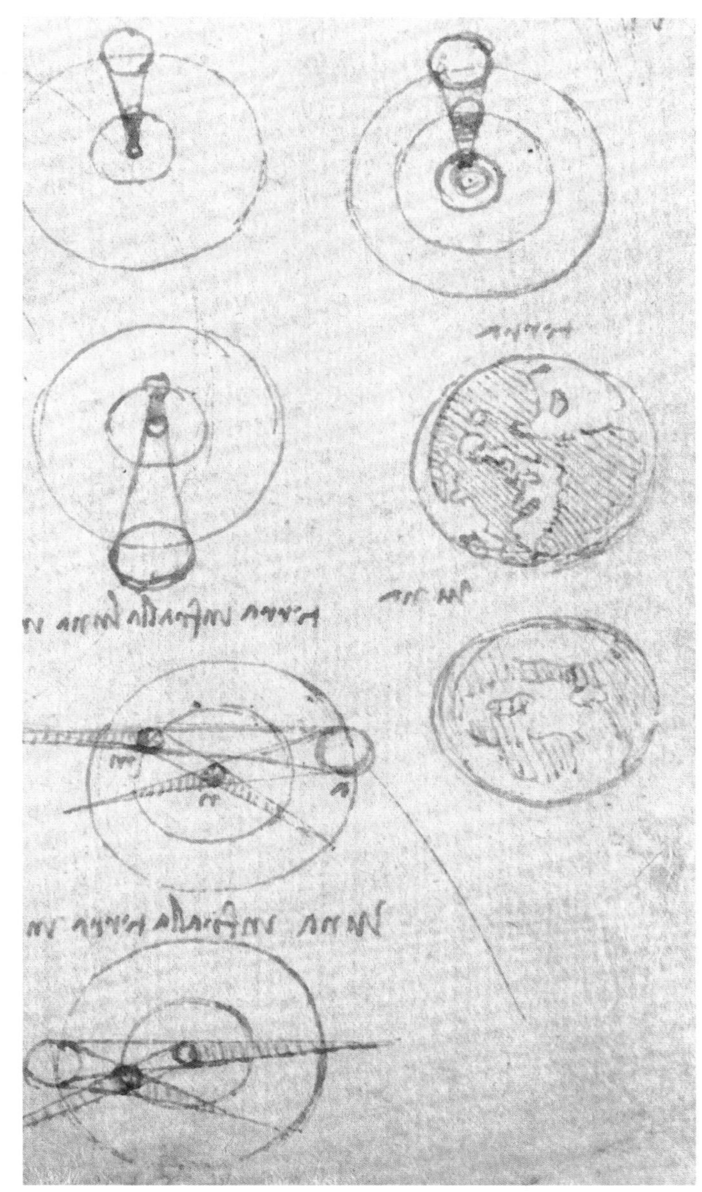

Harry watched the cloudy sky, curves of smoke-grey and silver sliding over the face of the white moon. He felt light-headed with amazement at his discoveries.

Harry Potter and the Deathly Hallows

KEPLER ON THE STARS

Written by the imperial astronomer Johannes Kepler, the *Rudolphine Tables* helped its readers to locate the planets in relation to the stars. It was a massive achievement, containing the position of 1,005 stars, and is the most accurate catalogue of the pre-telescope era. The elaborate illustrated frontispiece of the book shows a temple of Urania, the Muse of Astronomy. The temple is filled with great star-gazers – Hipparchus of Nicaea, Ptolemy, Nicolaus Copernicus, Kepler's predecessor Tycho Brahe and an unnamed Chaldean, an ancient people renowned for their astronomical skills. In a panel underneath the temple there is also a picture of Kepler himself.

JOHANNES KEPLER, *TABULÆ RUDOLPHINÆ* (ULM, 1627)
British Library

They bought Harry's school books in a shop called Flourish and Blotts where the shelves were stacked to the ceiling with books as large as paving stones bound in leather

Harry Potter and the Philosopher's Stone

"In 1617, Kepler's mother was suspected of witchcraft, a crime punishable by death. The accused spent over a year in prison, but was eventually released when her son intervened. Kepler was an official astronomer to the Holy Roman Emperor – this family intrigue must have been very difficult for him."

ALEXANDER LOCK
Curator

SPINNING DRAGON

Petrus Apianus, the son of a shoemaker, went on to become an acclaimed German astronomer, mathematician and printer. His most famous work, *Astronomicum Cæsareum*, is a beautifully produced book that contains a series of rotating paper models known as volvelles. The movement of the discs pinned at their centre mimics the movement of the planets. In this example, Apianus describes how to determine the latitude of the Moon. A dragon sits in the middle, which can be spun round to point at the various signs of the zodiac. The volvelles could be used in turn to cast horoscopes, showing how blurred the distinction between astrology and astronomy was in the 16th century.

▲ PETRUS APIANUS, *ASTRONOMICUM CÆSAREUM* (INGOLSTADT, 1540)
British Library

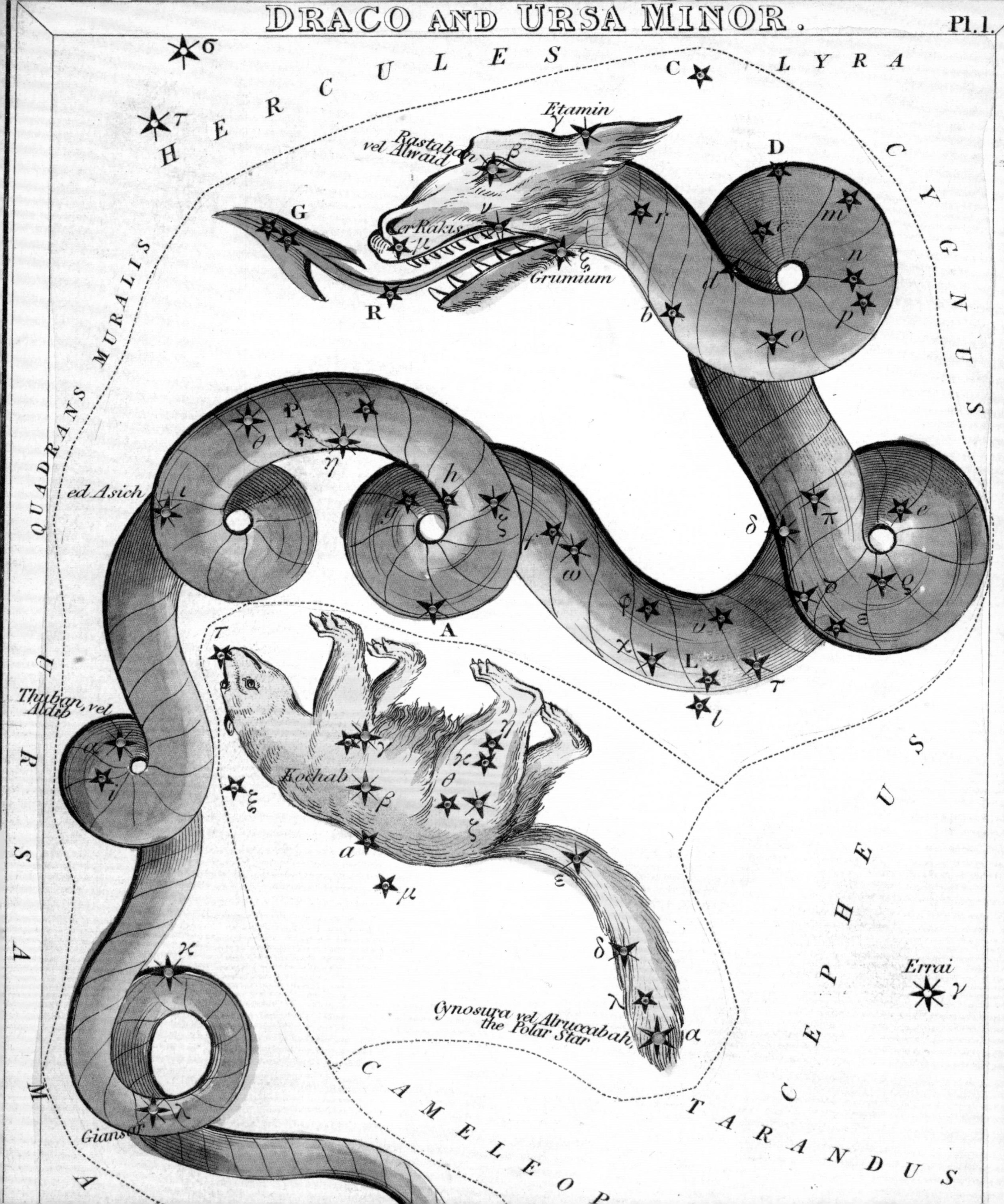

DRACO AND URSA MINOR.
Pl. I.
HERCULES
LYRA
CYGNUS
CEPHEUS
CAMELEOP
TARANDUS
QUADRANS MURALIS
URSA MA
Etamin
Rastaban vel Alwaid
Er Rakis
Grumium
ed Asich
Thuban, vel Adib
Kochab
Giansar
Errai
Cynosura vel Alruccabah, the Polar Star

URANIA'S MIRROR; OR A VIEW OF THE HEAVENS
(LONDON, 1834)
British Library

A VIEW OF THE HEAVENS

Just the thing for Hogwarts First Years, *Urania's Mirror* is a set of 32 star charts, printed on card and sold for astronomical self-instruction. Each card is pierced with holes that correspond to the size of the brightest stars, giving a realistic impression of a constellation when held up to the light. The images were engraved by the mapmaker Sidney Hall and then painted by hand. Hall worked to the designs of an anonymous 'Lady', who has since been identified as the Reverend Richard Bloxam, an Assistant Master at Rugby School. It is unclear why Bloxam hid his connection with these cards. Perhaps, like other authors, he felt that his gender might affect sales in a market that, at the time, wanted to attract custom from the opposite sex.

[...] Harry looked upwards and saw a velvety black ceiling dotted with stars. He heard Hermione whisper, 'It's bewitched to look like the sky outside, I read about it in **Hogwarts: A History.***'*

Harry Potter and the Philosopher's Stone

The Signification of LINES and other Marks in the HANDS.

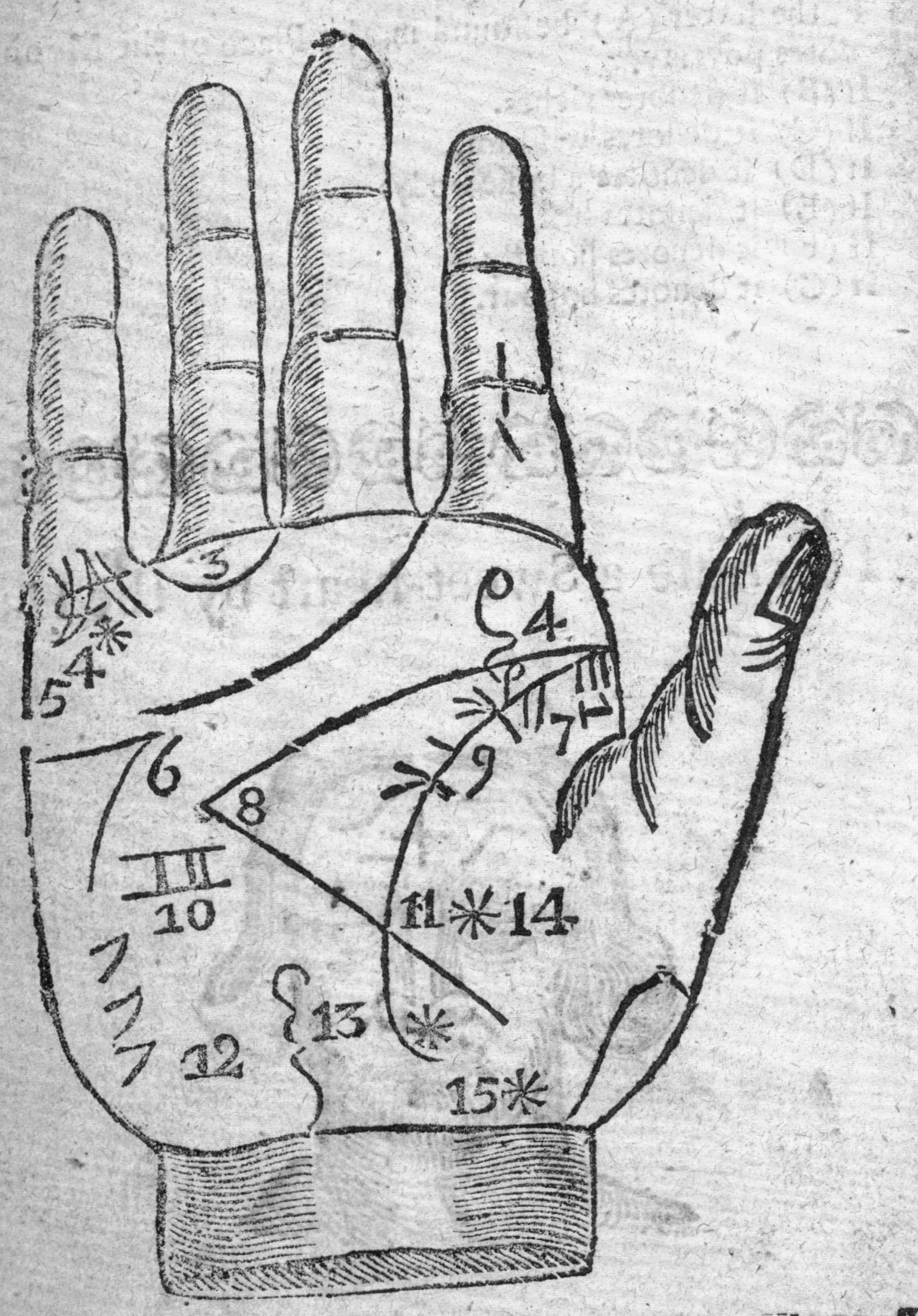

1 A Star in this place ſignifies riches and honour. 2 The party will heir an eſtate. 3 Denotes increaſe of goods and ſubſtance. 4 Signifies a truſty and faithful perſon. 5 Predicts a woman to be a ſtrumpet. 6 So many ſtright lines, ſo many ſons, ſo many crooked lines, ſo many daughters. 7 Theſe points denote a whore-maſter. 8 Denotes a ſharp wit.

Chapter Six

Divination

DIVINATION

Owen Davies

Owen Davies is Professor of Social History at the University of Hertfordshire. He has published widely on the history of witchcraft, magic, ghosts and popular medicine from the ancient world to the present. He recently edited the Oxford Illustrated History of Witchcraft and Magic, and is the author of numerous books, including Grimoires: A History of Magic Books. His academic interest in magic stems from reading fantasy novels and folklore.

The desire to divine the secrets of the future has preoccupied people from the dawn of history. The earliest written records on clay tablets from the Middle East show that in the civilisations of Mesopotamia, some four thousand years ago, divination was a valuable science that guided the lives of the humblest and shaped the nature of society. To know the future was to be in control of one's destiny. Harry Potter and his friends might not have enjoyed Sybill Trelawney's lessons, but divination has always been at the very heart of magic.

In ancient times, divining the future meant dealing with the gods that held sway over human destiny. What did they have in store for us mere mortals? If there was a drought, how long did they intend it to last? If there was a plague, who was destined to die or survive? Kings and emperors wanted to know if they would be successful in battle. Would their wives bear male heirs? The poor had their own perennial concerns about who they would marry, whether the weather would be good next week, and would their farms or occupations prosper? In ancient Greece, oracles and temples were created dedicated to the gods Zeus and Apollo in order to cater for the popular desire for such knowledge. At the same time, across the globe in China, emperors and servants were guided by the calendar of auspicious and inauspicious times to do things. What day would be best to begin construction of a new palace? When was the ideal moment to plant seeds?

Myriad forms of divination developed in different cultures over time. Oneiromancy, or the interpretation of dreams, is one of the most widespread and venerable divinatory arts. In the ancient world sleep was seen as a state in which

God, the gods, and spirits, liked to communicate with mortals, and provide intimations of the future. During the early 20th century, the psychiatric theories of Sigmund Freud would give modern scientific credence to the idea that dreams were full of messages waiting to be decoded. Equally ancient, if not more so, is the interpretation of the stars, or astrology. This is a 'science' close to the heart of the centaur, Professor Firenze, who was dismissive of some of Professor Trelawney's other techniques. There are two main forms. Natural astrology concerns the interpretation of visible movements in the sky, such as the appearance of comets and the phases of the Moon. Judicial astrology involves complex calculations as to the position of the stars at certain moments. Horoscopes are drawn up to examine the destinies of individuals based on the constellations at the moment of their birth. What are called 'horary' calculations predict events based on the position of the planets at the moment a question is asked.

The main divinatory techniques that Harry Potter was taught at Hogwarts were crystal-ball scrying, reading tea leaves, palmistry and cartomancy. While the power of divination was often thought to be divinely inspired, there is no point holding lessons in a subject if it cannot be learned. Crystal balls only became widely used for fortune-telling in the late 19th century, when they could be mass-produced cheaply. Before then, other reflective surfaces had long been used, such as oil on water, mirrors and even thumbnails. In *The Prisoner of Azkaban*, Professor Trelawney sets great store by tea leaves. Well before tea became a popular drink in Europe, however, in the ancient Mediterranean world the shapes left by the dregs of wine in a goblet had similarly been interpreted. And when coffee became a popular drink in the 18th century, the grounds remaining in a cup were also consulted in the same way. Palmistry or chiromancy was a branch of physiognomy, a term that derives from the Greek meaning 'interpreter of nature'. It could merely be seen as an indication of a person's character, but in popular culture came to be a divinatory art. Other forms of physiognomy that were popular in 17th- and 18th-century fortune-telling manuals were metoposcopy or the reading of lines on the forehead, and also the interpretation of the patterns of moles on the body. Most fortune-tellers in the past used a normal deck of familiar playing cards, but, by the late 18th century, the mysterious Tarot became increasingly popular among occultists, with its Hanged Man denoting trial and sacrifice, and the Magician card being a good omen when laid upright.

From the ancient world to the present, there have always been certain people who were thought to have special knowledge or powers to divine the future. In the earliest days, these would be male priests, though in ancient Greece the Pythia, or high priestess, at the Temple of Apollo at Delphi, became the model for female prophetesses down the subsequent centuries. Over time, the diviner or fortune-teller became less of a religious figure. Certain groups of people, such as the gypsies, developed reputations for their abilities to predict the future. Divination also came to be seen as a hereditary ability. Professor Trelawney's own reputation depended, in part, on that of her great-great-grandmother Cassandra Trelawney. In the Muggle world, the seventh daughter of a seventh daughter was widely thought to have the natural power of foresight or clairvoyance. In Scotland, the home of Hogwarts, there was also the tradition of Second Sight, whereby certain seers were gifted a third eye, so to speak, to dream or see visions of the future.

Harry Potter's miserable early childhood with the Dursleys gave little indication of the destiny that was waiting for him at Hogwarts. It was only through various divinatory techniques that he and others could piece together what was to come and prepare for the final reckoning. In the wizarding world, to be forewarned is to be forearmed!

'My name is Professor Trelawney. You may not have seen me before. I find that descending too often into the hustle and bustle of the main school clouds my Inner Eye.'

Harry Potter and the Prisoner of Azkaban

A TRUE SEER

Here is the completed portrait of Professor Sybill Trelawney, Harry Potter's Divination teacher at Hogwarts, wrapped in a shawl and dressed in her bangles and beads. To create this image Jim Kay painted an initial version in which Trelawney was not wearing her thick spectacles – the glasses and other elements were designed separately and added digitally later. The professor's fervent upward gaze captures how swept up she could become in the theatrics of her subject, in her view 'the most difficult of all magical arts'. The red glow of the Divination tower classroom behind her is visually evocative of a grand theatre set.

PORTRAIT OF SYBILL TRELAWNEY BY JIM KAY

Bloomsbury

CHINESE ORACLE BONES

Oracle bones were used in ancient divination rituals. Questions relating to subjects such as warfare, agriculture and natural disasters would be engraved on the bone before heat was applied with metal sticks, causing it to crack. The diviners interpreted the patterns of the fractures to determine the answer to the question posed. The bones are carved with the Shang Dynasty script, the oldest known form of Chinese writing. This shoulder bone bears an inscription that there will be no misfortune in the coming ten-day period. The character for 'Moon' (*yue* 月 in modern Chinese) is visible at the top centre. On the reverse is a record of a lunar eclipse that is precisely datable to 27th December, 1192 BC – an event that actually happened. The darkness caused by an eclipse was seen as a negative omen, indicating that an ancestral spirit needed to be pacified.

ORACLE BONE (CHINA, 1192 BC)
British Library

"This oracle bone is the oldest precisely datable item in the British Library's collections. As well as being an early example of Chinese literacy, it shows that the art of divination goes back for millennia."

JULIAN HARRISON
Lead Curator

'… the omens were never good, Harry … but why have you not returned to Divination? For you, of all people, the subject is of the utmost importance!'

Professor Trelawney, Harry Potter and the Half-Blood Prince

WONDERS!!! PAST, PRESENT, AND TO COME; BEING THE STRANGE PROPHECIES AND UNCOMMON PREDICTIONS OF THE FAMOUS MOTHER SHIPTON (LONDON, 1797)

British Library

MOTHER SHIPTON

Mother Shipton, known as the Yorkshire Prophetess, is the subject of this little book. Little is known about her life, and we cannot even be sure that she existed. She was supposedly incredibly ugly, and in addition to her powers of prophecy she was able to levitate. Most of the 'strange prophecies' in this book relate to the succession of the monarchy, although Mother Shipton also predicted the day and time of her own death. Today, the prophetess is best known for her birthplace, which was said to be near the 'Dropping Well' in Knaresborough, Yorkshire. For centuries the well was believed to have magical properties, and the capacity to turn objects into stone. The waters actually have a high mineral content, enabling them to petrify objects within a few weeks.

"Mother Shipton made her most famous prophecy in 1530, when she foretold that Cardinal Wolsey, who had been made Archbishop of York, would see the city but never reach it. According to this book, Wolsey saw the city from the top of a nearby castle, but was immediately arrested and taken to London."

TANYA KIRK
Curator

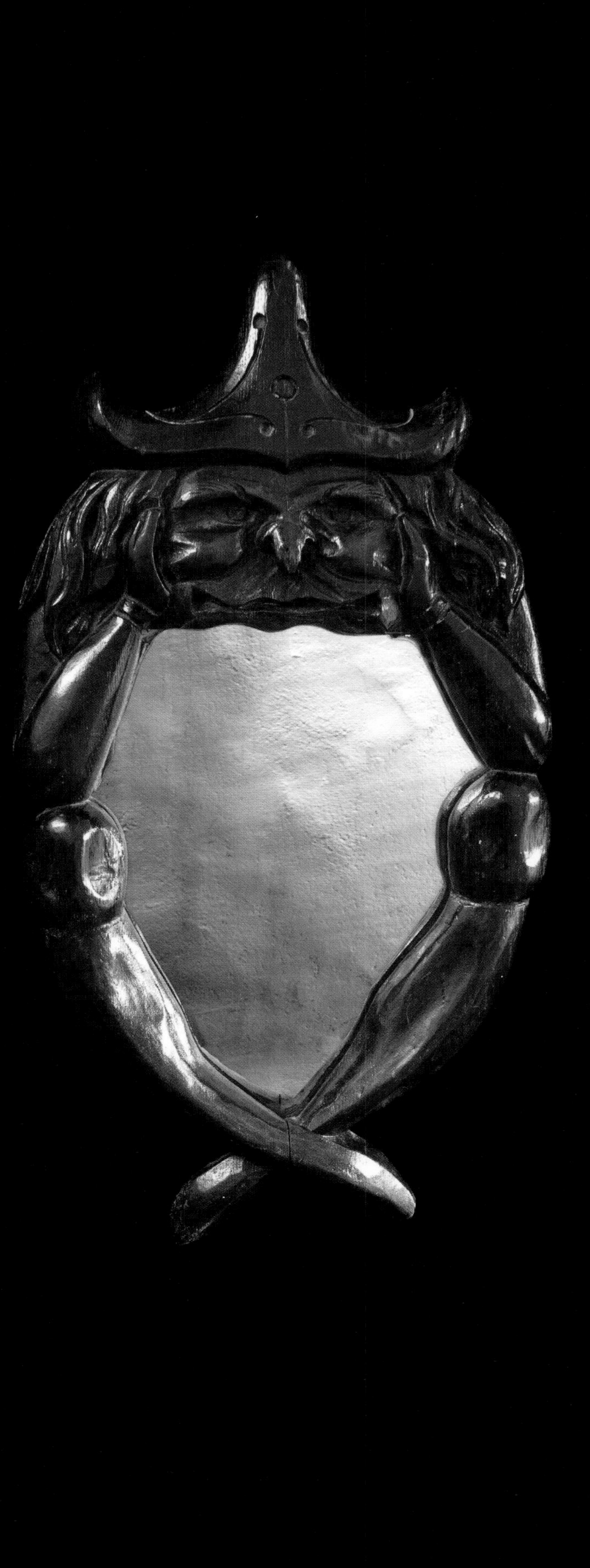

A WITCH'S SCRYING MIRROR

Divination with a mirror or another reflective surface is an ancient practice known as scrying. The term originates from the word 'descry', meaning 'to catch sight of'. Despite being carved in the shape of an ugly, old hag, the design of this mirror was very popular among early 20th-century English witches, who would have used it for divination. This item once belonged to the witch Cecil Williamson. He warned that if you gaze into it, 'and suddenly see someone standing behind you, whatever you do, do not turn around'. The Mirror of Erised appears to act like a scrying mirror. It is equally dangerous, too, as 'It shows us nothing more or less than the deepest, most desperate desire of our hearts.'

A WOODEN WITCH'S MIRROR
The Museum of Witchcraft and Magic, Boscastle

He whirled around. His heart was pounding far more furiously than when the book had screamed – for he had seen not only himself in the mirror, but a whole crowd of people standing right behind him.

Harry Potter and the Philosopher's Stone

THE ART OF CARTOMANCY

Cartomancy is a form of divination that uses cards to predict the future. Although playing cards have long been used in fortune-telling, this pack is reputedly the earliest set designed specifically for divination. The 52 cards follow an unusual procedure. The kings prompt questions that are answered in the form of enigmatic rhyming phrases. Each card was inscribed with the name of a famous astronomer, seer or magician, such as Merlin, Doctor Faustus and Nostradamus. It was hoped that each figure's association with astrology and divination would enhance confidence in the card's predictions.

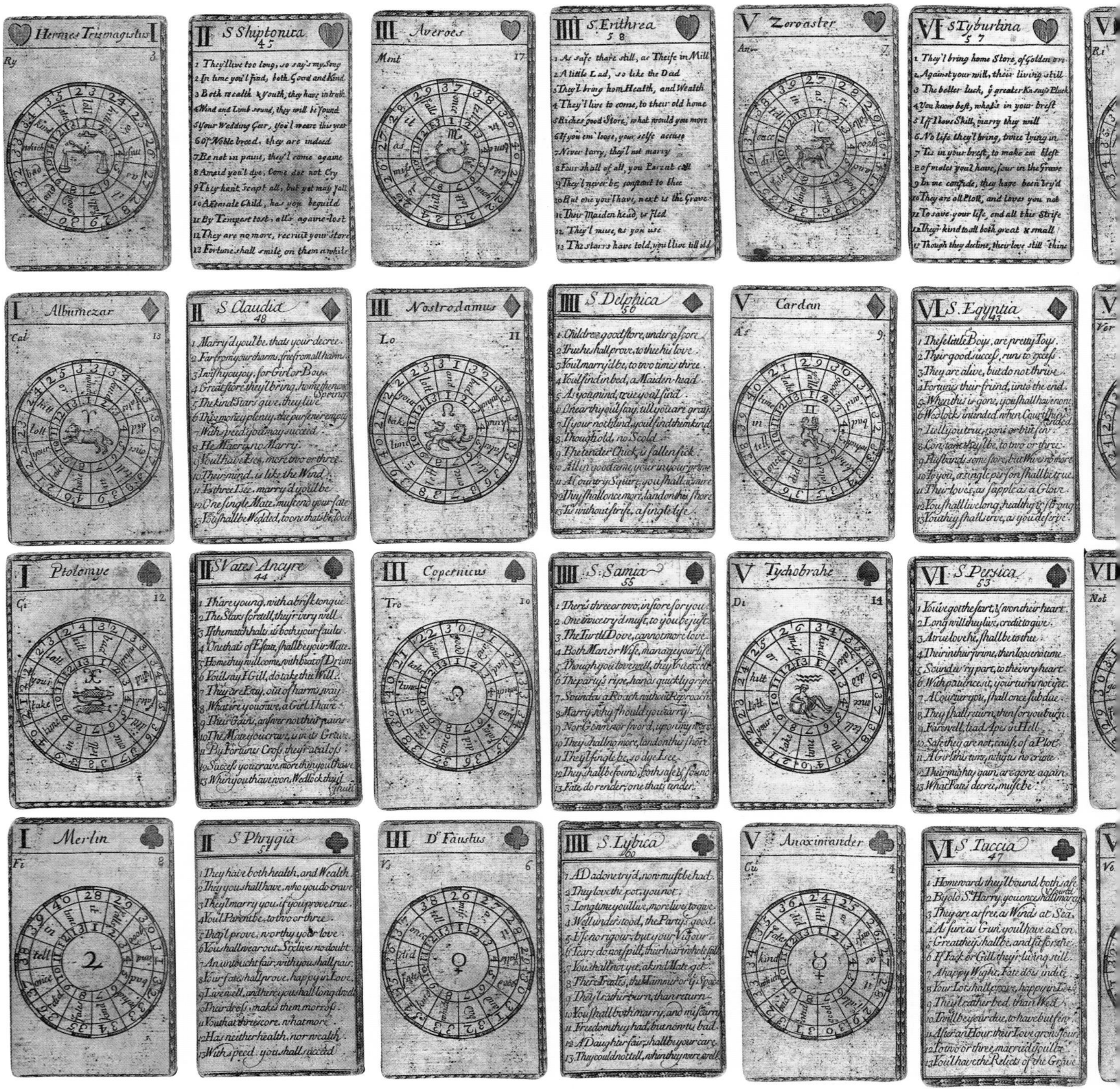

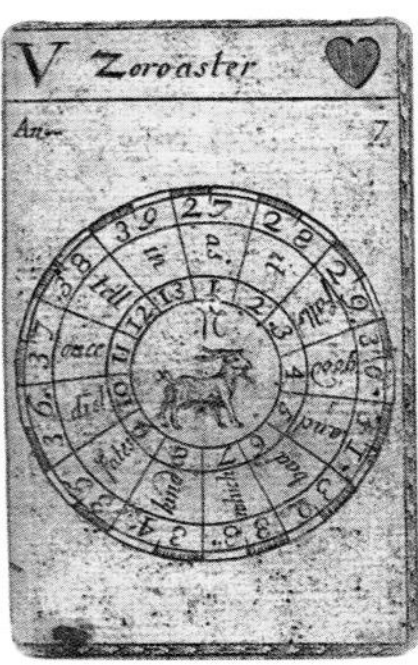

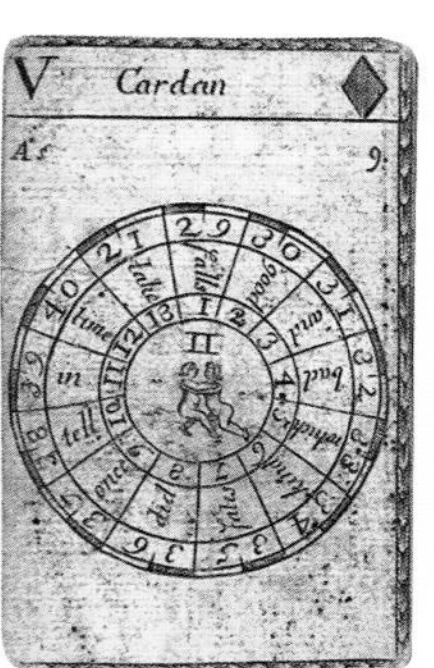

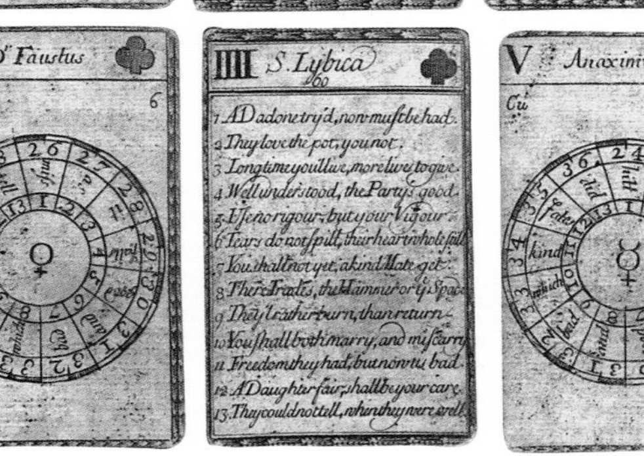

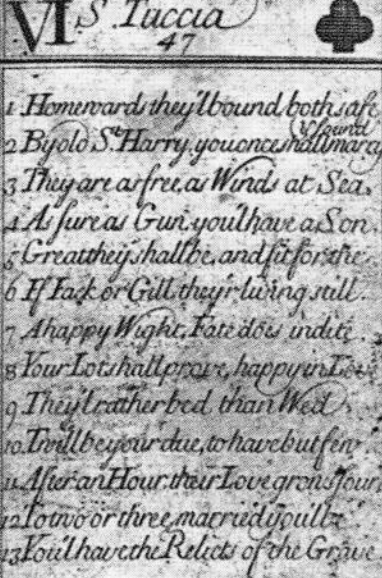

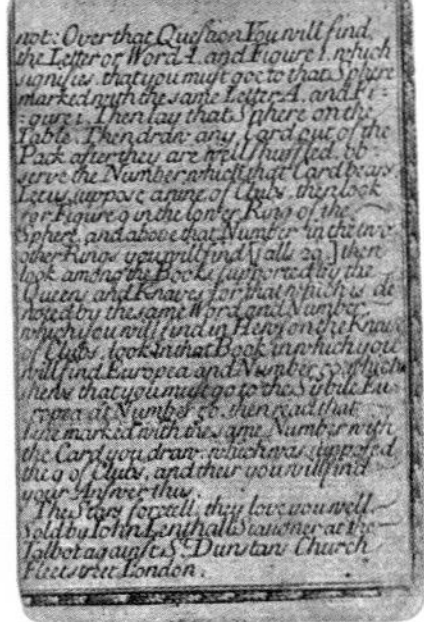

▼ A PACK OF DIVINATION PLAYING CARDS (LONDON, C. 1745–56)
British Museum

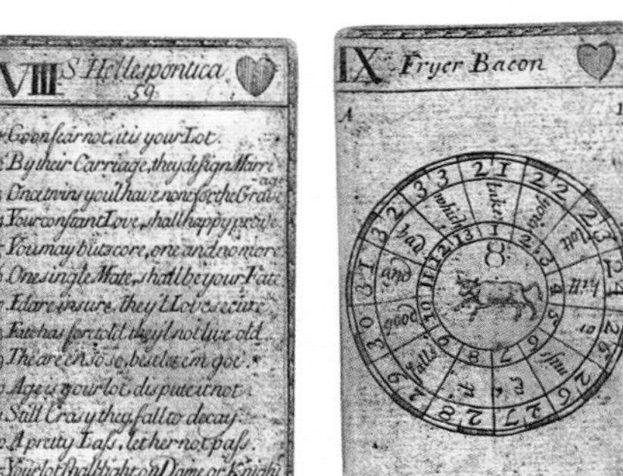

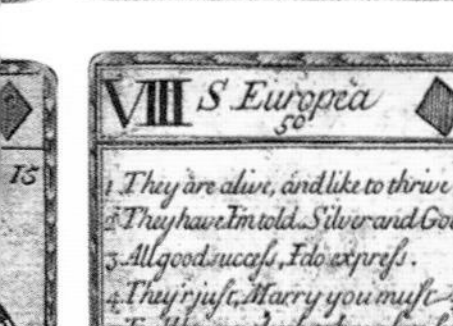

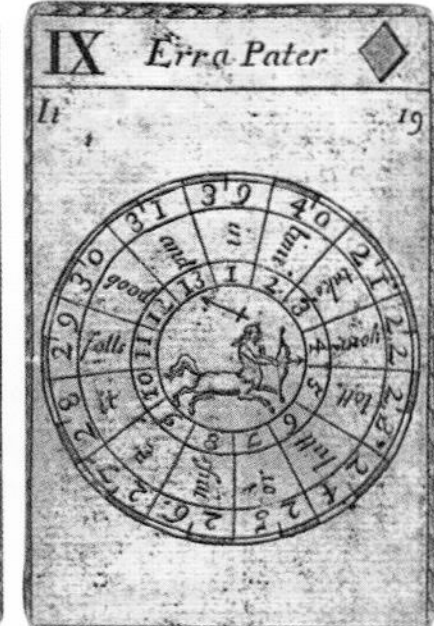

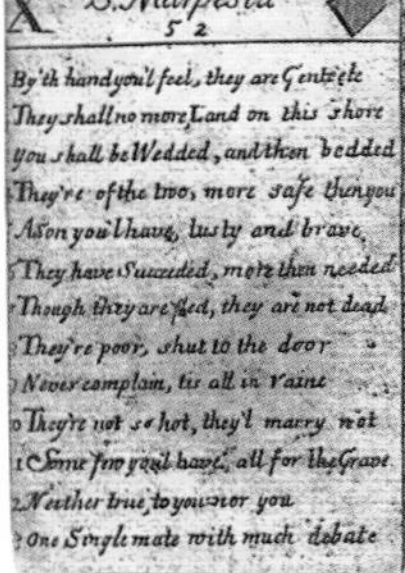

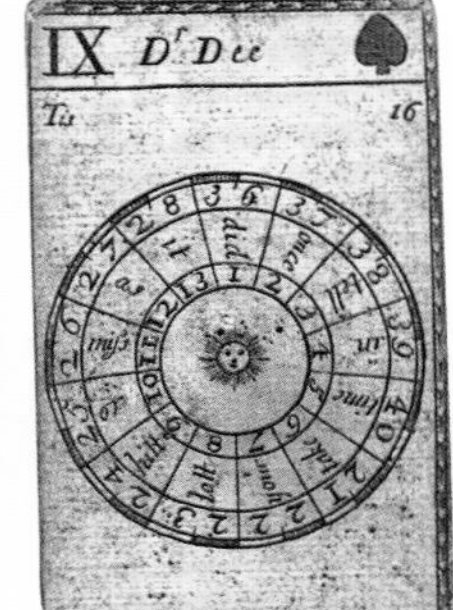

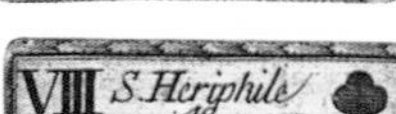

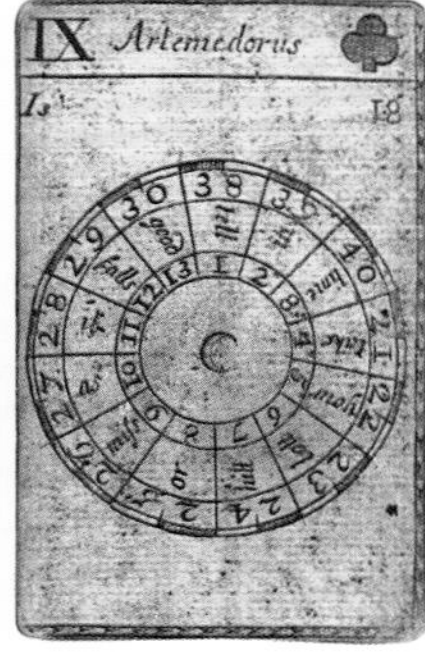

LUCKY IN LOVE?

In 19th-century Siam, people would have consulted a divination specialist on matters of love and relationships. This divination manual (*phrommachat*) contains horoscopes based on the Chinese zodiac, including drawings of the animals of the twelve-year cycle and their reputed attributes – earth, wood, fire, iron and water. Each zodiac page is followed by a series of paintings, which symbolise the fate of a person under certain circumstances. The illustrations are of outstanding quality. The unnamed artist paid great attention to every single detail. The facial expressions, hand gestures and body language are beautifully observed, along with the elaborate designs of clothes and jewellery.

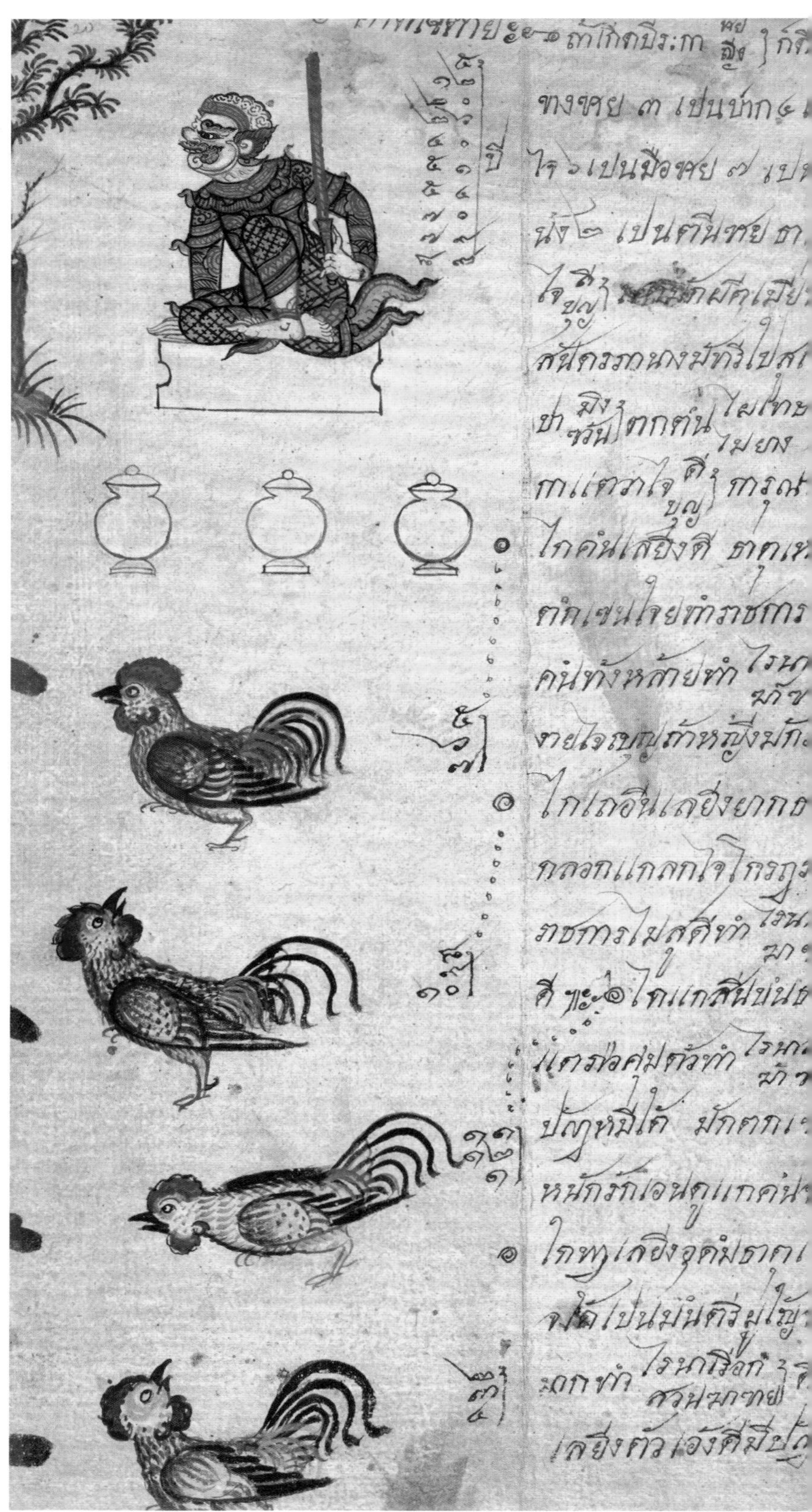

A THAI DIVINATION MANUAL (*PHROMMACHAT*) (SIAM, 19TH CENTURY)
British Library

> *"This manuscript describes both lucky and unlucky constellations for couples, taking into consideration their characters as well as their horoscopes. Indeed, it would appear that a hot-tempered couple would have a better chance of living happily together than a demonic male and an angelic female."*
>
> JANA IGUNMA
> *Curator*

SEEING THE FUTURE

Early in their Divination classes, the Hogwarts students were taught to divine using crystal balls. As Professor Trelawney recognised, 'Crystal-gazing is a particularly refined art'. It was also an art that many of her students struggled to master. Harry 'felt extremely foolish, staring blankly at the crystal ball', while Ron simply 'made some stuff up'. Crystallomancy has its roots in the Middle Ages, but this large ball is typical of the orbs consulted in the 19th and 20th centuries. It sits on an elaborate stand formed of three griffins at the base of an Egyptian-style column.

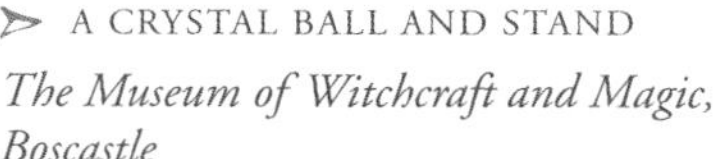

A CRYSTAL BALL AND STAND

The Museum of Witchcraft and Magic, Boscastle

SMELLY NELLY'S CRYSTAL BALL

In their third year, Ron, Hermione and Harry chose to study Divination. Lessons took place in a heavily scented classroom, filled with a 'sickly sort of perfume'. 'Smelly Nelly', the 20th-century Paignton witch who owned this black crystal ball, also had a taste for strong aromas. One witness who saw her using it reported how, 'You caught her scent a mile off downwind.' Smelly Nelly believed that the fragrance appealed to the spirits who helped her to divine the future. Known as a Moon crystal, this black globe had to be consulted at night, so that the seer could read the Moon's reflection in the glass.

A BLACK MOON CRYSTAL BALL

The Museum of Witchcraft and Magic, Boscastle

'I do not expect any of you to See when first you peer into the Orb's infinite depths. We shall start by practising relaxing the conscious mind and external eyes [...] Perhaps, if we are lucky, some of you will See before the end of the class.'

Harry Potter and the Prisoner of Azkaban

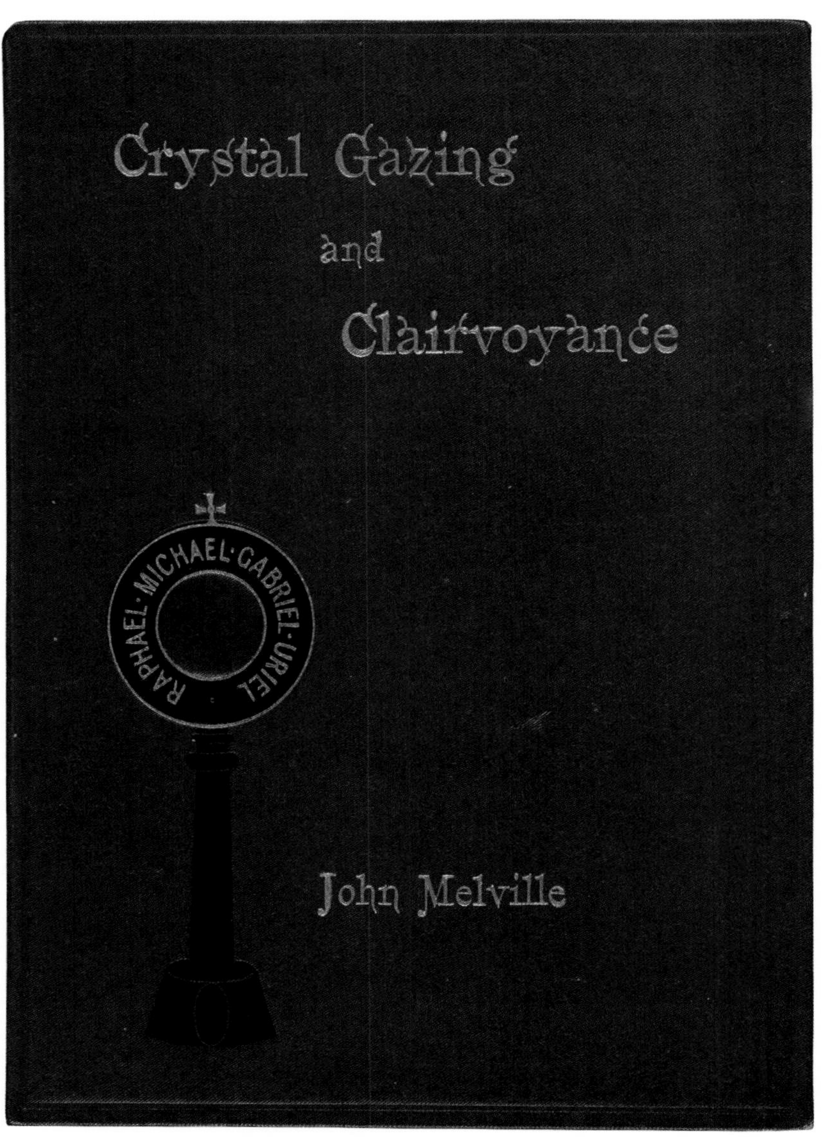

A PRACTICAL GUIDE TO CRYSTAL GAZING

In the late 19th century, as interest in crystal divination increased, the clairvoyant John Melville wrote this popular guide to help those struggling with the ancient art. Melville recommended taking 'an infusion of the herb *Mugwort* … or of the herb *Succory*', which, 'if taken occasionally during the Moon's increase … [would] constitute an *aid* to the attainment of the most desirable *physical conditions* of the experimenter's body.' It is unclear how far Melville's instructions helped those not gifted with Second Sight.

◄ JOHN MELVILLE, *CRYSTAL-GAZING AND THE WONDERS OF CLAIRVOYANCE, EMBRACING PRACTICAL INSTRUCTIONS IN THE ART, HISTORY, AND PHILOSOPHY OF THIS ANCIENT SCIENCE*, 2ND EDN (LONDON, 1910)
British Library

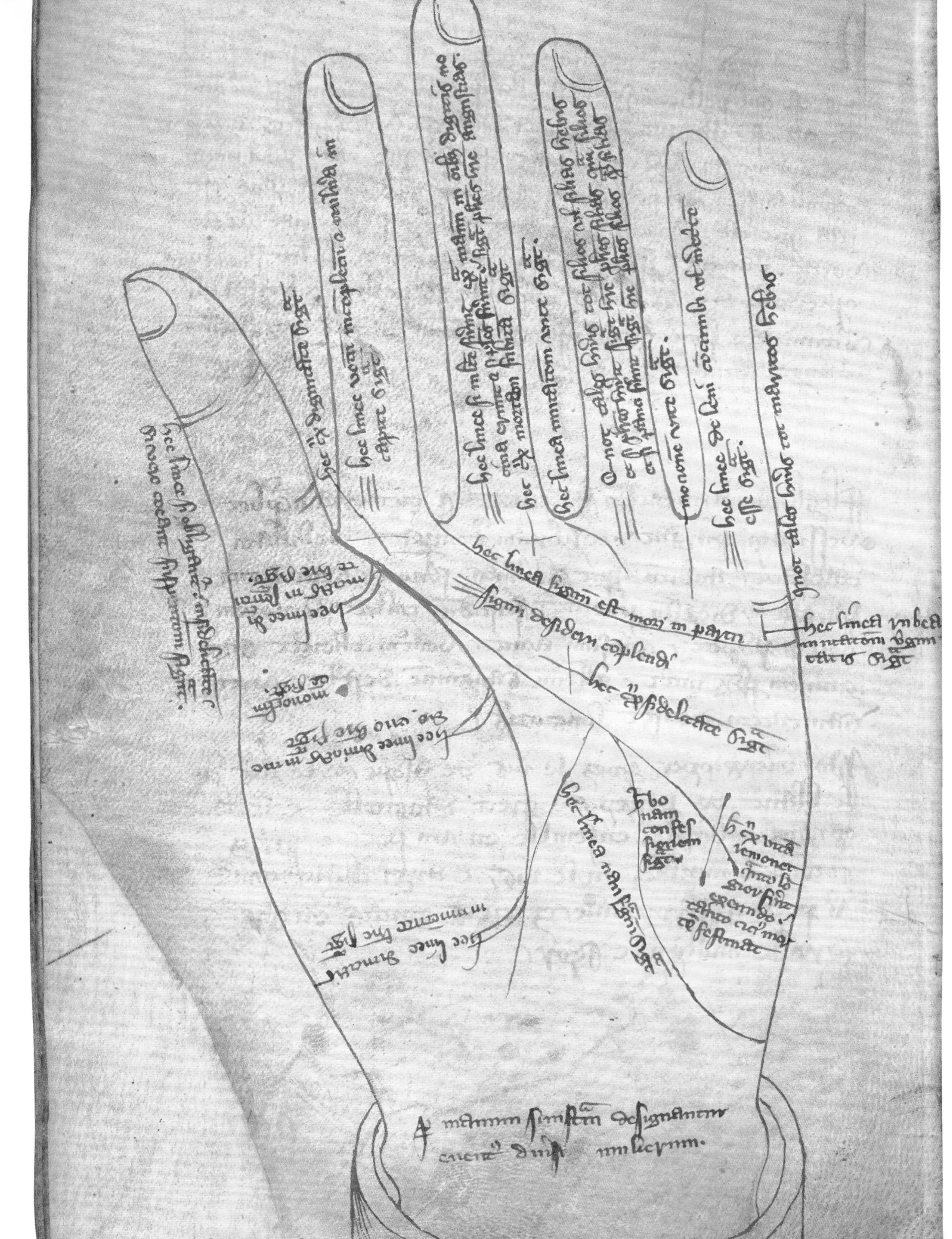

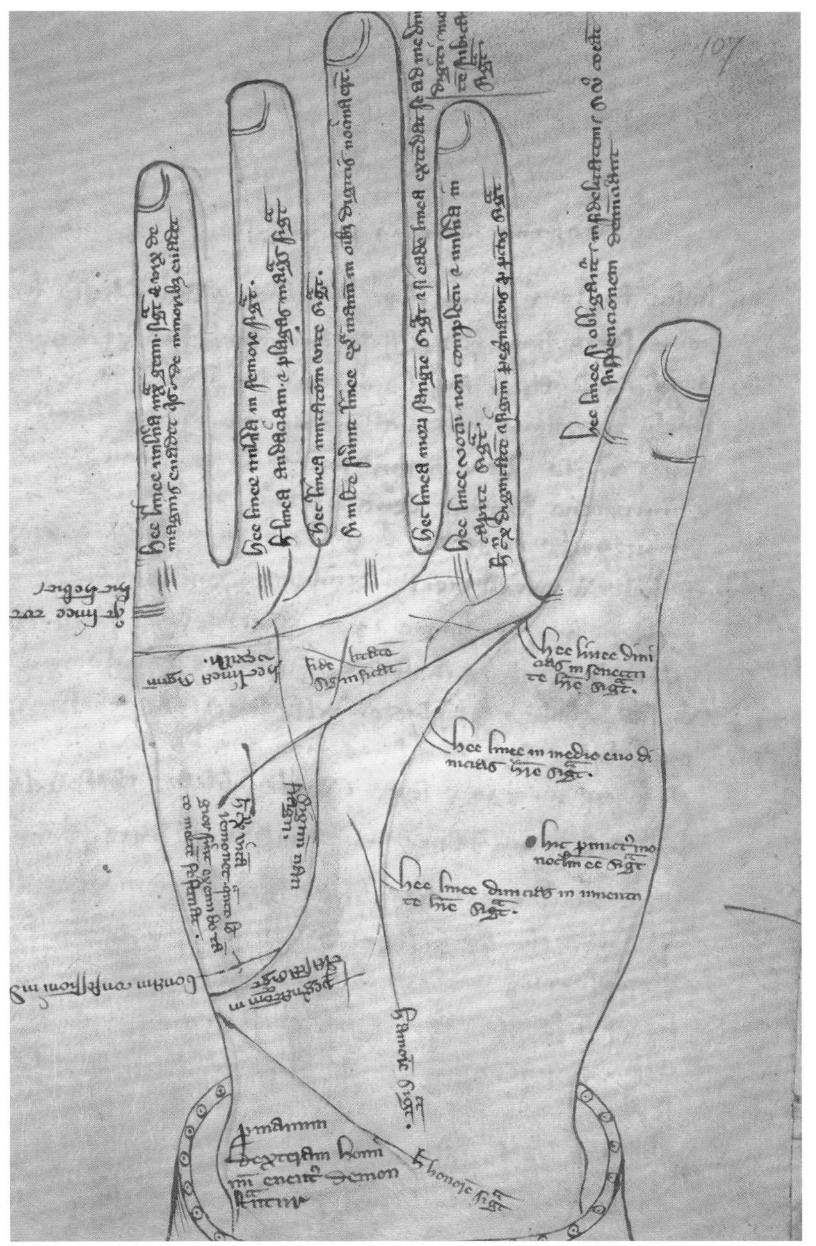

READING THE PALMS

Making a prediction based on the shape and lines of the hand is known as palmistry or chiromancy. This medieval manuscript contains a collection of prophecies and treatises on fortune-telling. Every hand contains three natural lines, forming a 'triangle'. These diagrams show a right and a left hand, onto which are mapped the natural lines and other accidental lines. On the right hand, a vertical stroke running down the palm reads, 'this line represents love'. A vertical line running between the middle and index finger has a less fortunate meaning: 'This line signifies a bloody death and if the line reaches unto the middle of the finger it signifies a sudden death.'

READING THE HANDS, IN A FORTUNE-TELLING MANUSCRIPT (ENGLAND, 14TH CENTURY)
British Library

The first Divination lesson of the new term was much less fun; Professor Trelawney was now teaching them palmistry, and she lost no time in informing Harry that he had the shortest life-lines she had ever seen.

Harry Potter and the Prisoner of Azkaban

A PALMISTRY HAND

This ceramic palmistry hand would have been used for teaching. It shows the various lines and mounts on the palm and wrist, along with some of their significant meanings. Hands like this were first manufactured in Britain in the 1880s, following the growing popularity of palmistry inspired by the celebrated astrologer William John Warner, also known as Cheiro or Count Louis Hamon. Harry Potter did not do well in palmistry. During his exams he mixed up 'the life and head lines' of his examiner, 'informing her that she ought to have died the previous Tuesday'.

"We love the practicality of this palmistry hand. The art of chiromancy first became popular in Western Europe in the 12th century, under Arabic influence."

ALEXANDER LOCK
Curator

A PALMISTRY HAND
The Museum of Witchcraft and Magic, Boscastle

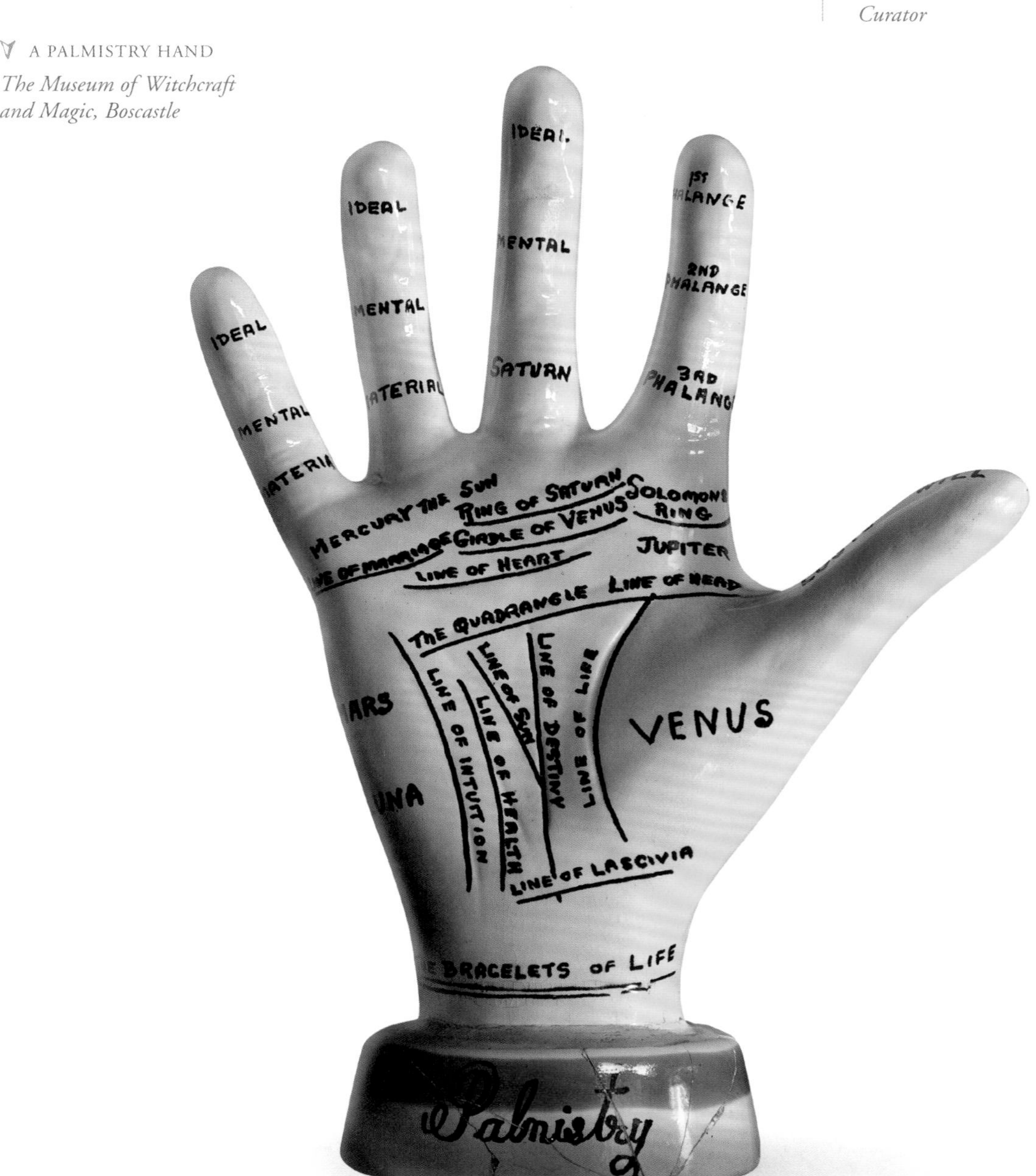

THE OLD EGYPTIAN FORTUNE-TELLER'S LAST LEGACY

This fascinating 18th-century pamphlet explores, and perhaps exploits, Egypt's mystical reputation. Supposedly a collection of Egyptian divination techniques, it was compiled by an anonymous British writer. *The Old Egyptian Fortune-Teller's Last Legacy* was printed cheaply and then sold on to the lower middle classes. In addition to palmistry, it explains how to prick an image with a pin to decide who to marry and how to divine the future by interpreting the moles on your face and body. Even the position and number of your wrinkles are deemed to hold secrets to the future.

THE OLD EGYPTIAN FORTUNE-TELLER'S LAST LEGACY (LONDON, 1775)
British Library

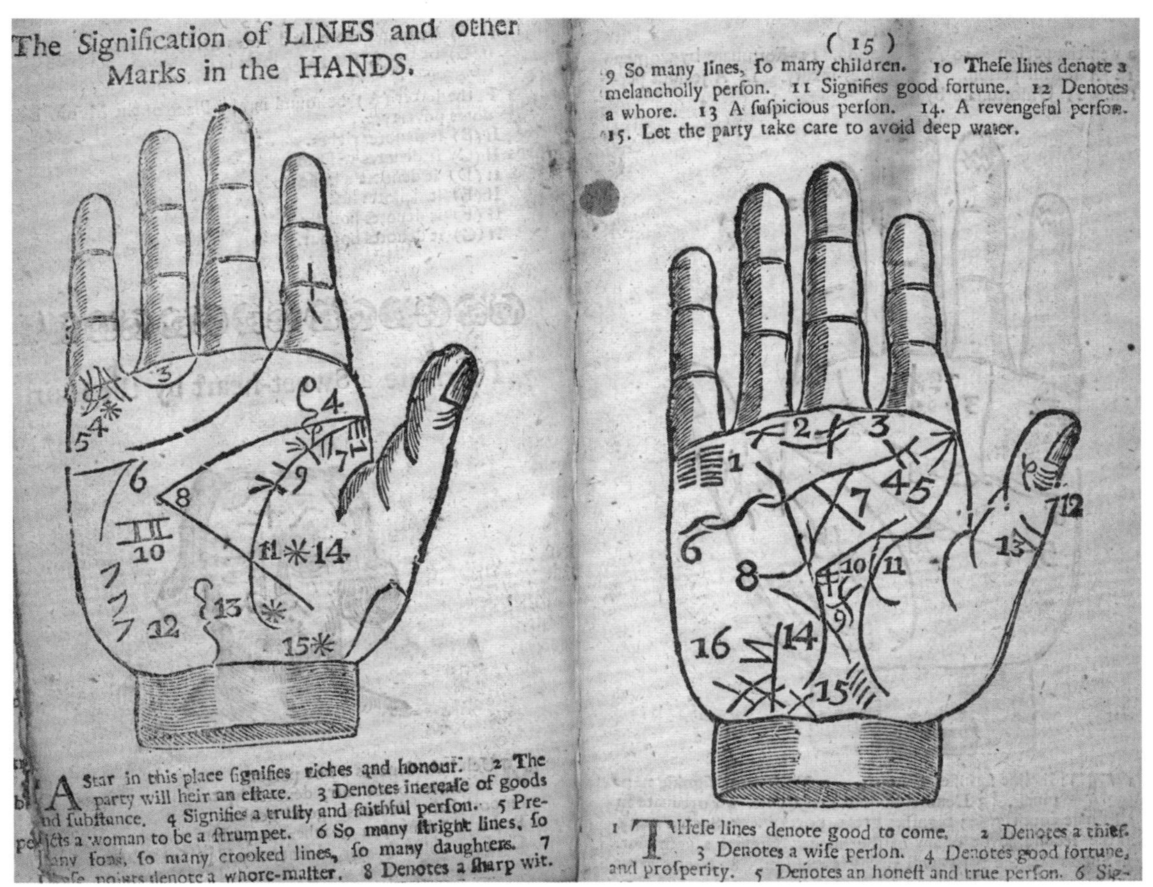

The Signification of LINES and other Marks in the HANDS.

A Star in this place ſignifies riches and honour. 2 The party will heir an eſtate. 3 Denotes increaſe of goods and ſubſtance. 4 Signifies a truſty and faithful perſon. 5 Predicts a woman to be a ſtrumpet. 6 So many ſtright lines, ſo many ſons, ſo many crooked lines, ſo many daughters. 7 These points denote a whore-maſter. 8 Denotes a ſharp wit.

(15)

9 So many lines, ſo many children. 10 Theſe lines denote a melancholly perſon. 11 Signifies good fortune. 12 Denotes a whore. 13 A ſuſpicious perſon. 14. A revengeful perſon. 15. Let the party take care to avoid deep water.

1 THeſe lines denote good to come. 2 Denotes a thief. 3 Denotes a wiſe perſon. 4 Denotes good fortune, and proſperity. 5 Denotes an honeſt and true perſon. 6 Sig-

*'Here you are,' said the manager, who had climbed a set of steps to take down a thick, black-bound book. '**Unfogging the Future.** Very good guide to all your basic fortune-telling methods – palmistry, crystal balls, bird entrails ...'*

Harry Potter and the Prisoner of Azkaban

A FORTUNE-TELLING TEACUP

Tasseography – from the French *tasse* (cup) and Greek *graph* (writing) – is a form of divination that interprets the sediment in cups, usually left by tea leaves. The first European accounts of this method of divination appeared in the 17th century, following the introduction of tea from China. The location and shape of the tea leaves in the cup have different symbolism. This delicate pink divination cup was made in the 1930s by Paragon, a Staffordshire manufacturer of bone china. The inside of the cup has been decorated with symbols to help interpret the leaves. A legend runs around the rim: 'Many curious things I see when telling fortunes in your tea'.

A FORTUNE-TELLING CUP AND SAUCER MADE BY PARAGON (STOKE-ON-TRENT, C. 1932–39)
The Museum of Witchcraft and Magic, Boscastle

The shelves running around the circular walls were crammed with dusty-looking feathers, stubs of candles, many packs of tattered playing cards, countless silvery crystal balls and a huge array of teacups.

Harry Potter and the Prisoner of Azkaban

A SCOTTISH DIVINATION MANUAL

This detailed manual on tea leaf divination was written by an unnamed author, described on the cover as 'a Highland Seer'. It provides instructions not only on interpreting the various shapes made by the leaves, but also on the ideal size and shape of cup and the type of tea to use.

➢ *TEA CUP READING: HOW TO TELL FORTUNES BY TEA LEAVES* BY A HIGHLAND SEER (TORONTO, C. 1920)
British Library

> *"In this book, the position of each tea leaf symbol is also significant. The author advises that the nearer an image appears to the handle of the cup, the sooner the predicted event will occur."*
>
> TANYA KIRK
> *Curator*

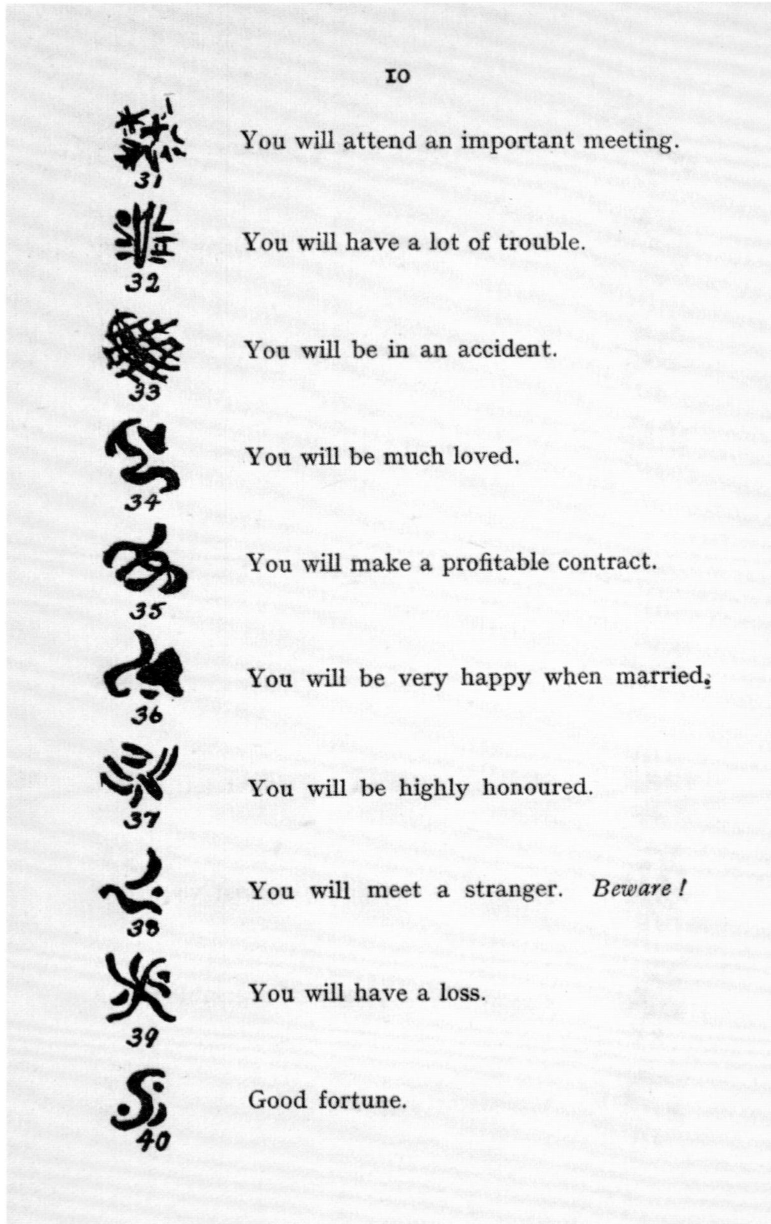

10

31 You will attend an important meeting.

32 You will have a lot of trouble.

33 You will be in an accident.

34 You will be much loved.

35 You will make a profitable contract.

36 You will be very happy when married.

37 You will be highly honoured.

38 You will meet a stranger. *Beware !*

39 You will have a loss.

40 Good fortune.

READING TEA LEAVES

This slim volume on tea leaf divination traces the first use of tasseography all the way back to 229 BC. In that year, a Chinese princess rejected astrological predictions in favour of a new technique proposed by a student, using a popular beverage. The prophecies she obtained using tea leaves were so accurate that she 'raised the fortunate cup reader to the dignity of a Mandarin'. Most of the pamphlet comprises a handy guide to decoding a range of shapes formed by leaves in the bottom of the cup. Many of the predictions are quite general; others are bizarrely specific. Number 44, for instance, indicates, 'You will be interested in the Navy.' Readers struggling to get to grips with this volume might sympathise with Harry Potter, who could only see 'A load of soggy brown stuff'.

◄ *HOW TO READ THE FUTURE WITH TEA LEAVES*, TRANSLATED FROM THE CHINESE BY MANDRA (STAMFORD, C. 1925) ►
British Library

"Some of the shapes in this book are remarkably difficult to tell apart. Numbers 38 and 42 are tantalisingly similar, but while the first means 'You will meet a stranger', the other warns that 'You will make an enemy.'"

TANYA KIRK
Curator

'[...] drink until only the dregs remain. Swill these around the cup three times with the left hand, then turn the cup upside-down on its saucer; wait for the last of the tea to drain away, then give your cup to your partner to read.'

Harry Potter and the Prisoner of Azkaban

You will have a large family.

You will make an enemy.

If you ask a favour now it will be granted.

You will be interested in the Navy.

You will be prosperous and happy.

You have found a new love.

You will have bad news.

You will attend a wedding.

You will make a good bargain.

You will meet your beloved soon.

A

Chapter Seven

Defence Against the Dark Arts

Defence Against the Dark Arts

The Reverend Richard Coles

The Reverend Richard Coles is a priest of the Church of England and Vicar of Finedon in Northamptonshire, where two of his ancestors were vicars in the 17th century (the latter sequestered for malignancy). He has a parallel career in broadcasting and currently co-presents Saturday Live on BBC Radio 4. He appears regularly on television, and is the author of Fathomless Riches and Bringing in the Sheaves. Richard is also known for partnering Jimmy Somerville in the 1980s band The Communards.

When I was a boy my grandparents had a holiday home in Norfolk, two tiny cottages made into one, built two hundred years ago on the ancient Roman road, Peddars Way. My grandfather liked to frighten us by saying that at midnight when the Moon was full you could hear the ghostly tramp of legions marching from their battles with Boadicea, Queen of the Iceni, and if you listened carefully you could hear even the lopsided march of those who had lost a leg to the whirling blades fixed to her chariot's wheels.

We later discovered that my grandfather was not the only resident of the cottages to have had a lively sense of the supernatural. During renovations we found a witch's bottle plastered in the wall, a crudely blown article that rattled when shaken with the bones of bats and the teeth of dragons – according to Grandpa. I am not sure that this list of contents was quite right, but I never got to hear the lopsided marching of those one-legged legionaries, so I suppose it was effective at least at deterring Roman spooks. I later found out that these bottles were very common in houses in East Anglia, left in walls, or laid under the threshold, to keep witches and their conjuring at bay. It was an ancient custom, unlikely to meet the strictures of modern building regulations, but you still see horseshoes nailed over doors to bring good luck to those who live beyond them.

Defending people and places against the dark arts is still common in the lives of many parish priests. I was once a curate in rural Lincolnshire at a famous medieval church often visited by Travellers. Visitors from that community liked to fill bottles with water from the font to keep as protection at home, and to buy fridge magnets of the Virgin Mary from our shop, which they would ask the clergy to bless.

物産
十八

They were charms to keep the lively protection of the Holy Mother active in their caravans, I guess, although that was not strictly what we thought we were doing.

It is also not unusual to be asked to visit a house or flat that the residents believe to be haunted or affected by an evil spirit. Often a sense of déjà vu is explained when you recognise what they describe from a film or something on television. I have not heard of anyone encountering a basilisk or a kappa, but I did have someone once describe to me what sounded like a plague of Dementors, because we pattern our mysterious and anxiety-provoking experiences using the resources to hand. I too use the resources to hand – holy water, a crucifix, a printed psalm from the Bible (not unlike the Ethiopian *Ketab* in the exhibition) – to allay their fears, fortunately, with only one exception. On this occasion I was summoned to a flat where a teenage boy lived, but he and his parents were so frightened at something nameless inside they would not even step over the threshold when I arrived with my kit. I went in alone and found exactly what I expected to find, an untidy rather squalid scene with full ashtrays and empty pizza boxes … until I opened the door to the kitchen. I found it, with a shock that I can still recall, pristine, gleaming, and with all the contents of the drawers and cupboards arranged in intricate patterns on the floor and counters. I experienced, in that moment, intense dread and a sense of icy cold – classic symptoms – but there was nothing supernatural about it. I think what disturbed me was feeling that this patterning was meant to tell me something, something of urgent importance, and yet I could not understand it.

Mysterious symbols, unsolved puzzles, spells half-understood – it would have been helpful to call upon the teaching staff at Hogwarts, but actually each diocese in the Church does have its own Exorcist. These folk are C of E Aurors really, although they are more commonly called Ministers of Deliverance (which to me unfortunately sounds like the bloke on a moped who brings your takeaway). These are the real Professor Lupins, experienced at dealing with those troubled by deeds of darkness. The one or two that I have known are not fanciful or self-dramatising, and many difficult cases are referred to the relevant therapeutic professional, but not all of them. I have been told of ashtrays flying across the room unaided, a pinch and a punch from an invisible hand, the inexplicable identification of a long dead relative by a child – not as a tale told by firelight, but as a debrief.

What is going on when these things happen? I don't know, but I have no embarrassment leaving a crucifix, a printed prayer, a sprinkle of holy water in places where people are frightened and anxious. I suppose what's different is that I do not think of them as lucky charms, magical protections against Dark Lords, but as tokens of a victory already won. Because good has triumphed, once and for all, and in spite of the darkness and horrors that the world will sometimes throw at us, we all live as children of the light.

Richard Coles

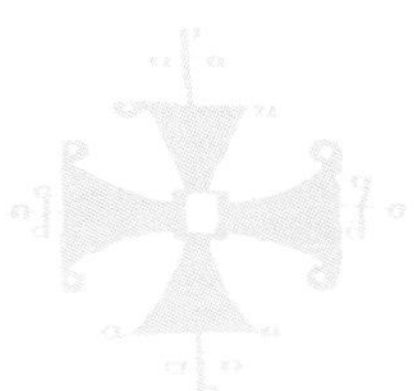

A PORTRAIT OF PROFESSOR REMUS LUPIN BY JIM KAY
Bloomsbury

A MYSTERIOUS MAN

This portrait shows Professor Lupin, Harry Potter's Defence Against the Dark Arts teacher. Remus Lupin only educated Harry during his third year at Hogwarts, resigning after Snape informed the students' parents about the professor's 'furry little problem'. Lupin, of course, was a werewolf. Lupin's lessons offered instruction on shape-shifting Boggarts and demonic Grindylows, and it was he who taught Harry to cast a Patronus for the first time. In this portrait, Lupin stands with his hands in his pockets, averting his gaze from the reader. The dark rings under his eyes and greying hair perhaps make him look older than he really is. The professor stands in his office, a bookcase behind him loaded with bottles, books and bones. A poster of the Full Moon hangs on the shelves, the thing he fears the most.

"The greyscale colouring lends a solemn air to this beguiling picture. Despite being persecuted by the wizarding community, Lupin was one of Harry's closest links to his deceased father."

JOANNA NORLEDGE
Curator

He pushed his greying hair out of his eyes, thought for a moment, then said, 'That's where all of this starts – with my becoming a werewolf. None of this could have happened if I hadn't been bitten ... and if I hadn't been so foolhardy ...'

Harry Potter and the Prisoner of Azkaban

For a full minute the three of them stood and looked at the little bundle; Hagrid's shoulders shook, Professor McGonagall blinked furiously and the twinkling light that usually shone from Dumbledore's eyes seemed to have gone out.

Harry Potter and the Philosopher's Stone

HARRY ARRIVES AT PRIVET DRIVE

This original drawing by J.K. Rowling depicts the black night when Harry Potter was delivered to the Dursleys. With only the Moon and stars to light the way, since Dumbledore had put out the street lamps with his Deluminator, Privet Drive is not visible. The giant Hagrid, still wearing his motorcycle goggles, stoops down to show baby Harry Potter to Dumbledore and Minerva McGonagall. Harry is the central focus of this image, wrapped in a white blanket, shining as brightly as the Moon. As the group contemplates the baby, Dumbledore's forehead is creased with concern. Professor McGonagall clasps her hands together, her hair drawn back in a severe bun. This quiet, dark moment was the beginning of Harry's story, fresh from his first encounter with Lord Voldemort.

➢ DRAWING OF HARRY POTTER, DUMBLEDORE, McGONAGALL AND HAGRID BY J.K. ROWLING
J.K. Rowling

'Dinner, Nagini,' said Voldemort softly, and the great snake swayed and slithered from his shoulders on to the polished wood.

Harry Potter and the Deathly Hallows

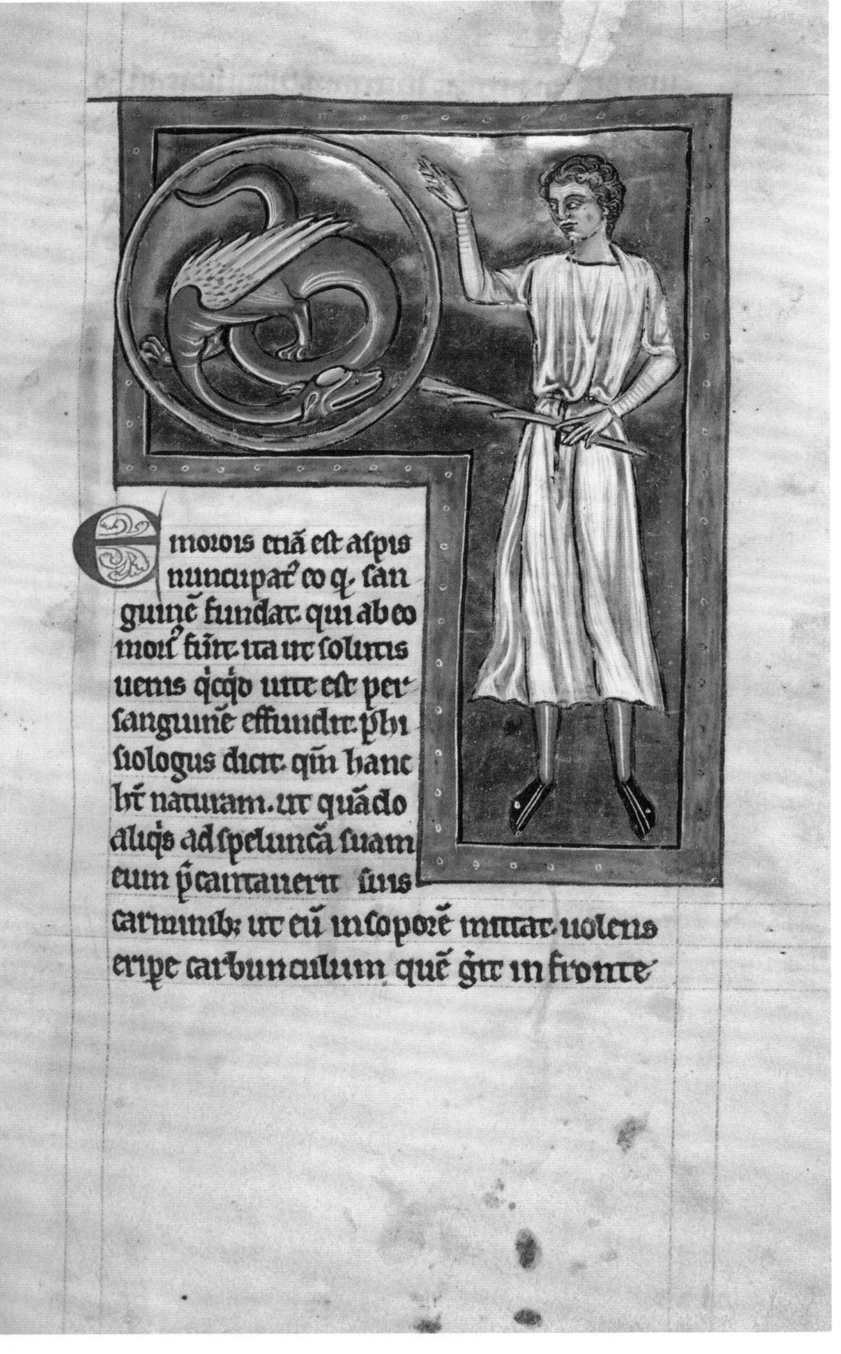

A SNAKE CHARMER

This image of a 'wizard' charming a serpent is found in a beautifully illustrated bestiary. The accompanying text describes several mythological snakes, including the *cerastes* (a horned serpent) and the *scitalis* (a creature with incredible markings on its back). It then focuses on the *emorroris*, a type of asp so called because its bite causes haemorrhages of such disastrous proportions a victim will sweat out their own blood until they die. Fortunately, the manuscript does explain one way to avoid such a horrible demise. The asp can be trapped if a conjurer sings to it in its cave, lulling it into sleep. Once the serpent is slumbering, the snake charmer would be free to remove the precious stone that grows on the asp's forehead. Without the stone, the snake is rendered powerless.

IMAGE OF A SNAKE CHARMER, IN A BESTIARY (ENGLAND, 13TH CENTURY)
British Library

"The thick gold leaf in this bestiary bathes the page in light. The manuscript contains a further 80 illustrations of various real and mythical creatures, such as the phoenix, the unicorn and the centaur."

JULIAN HARRISON
Lead Curator

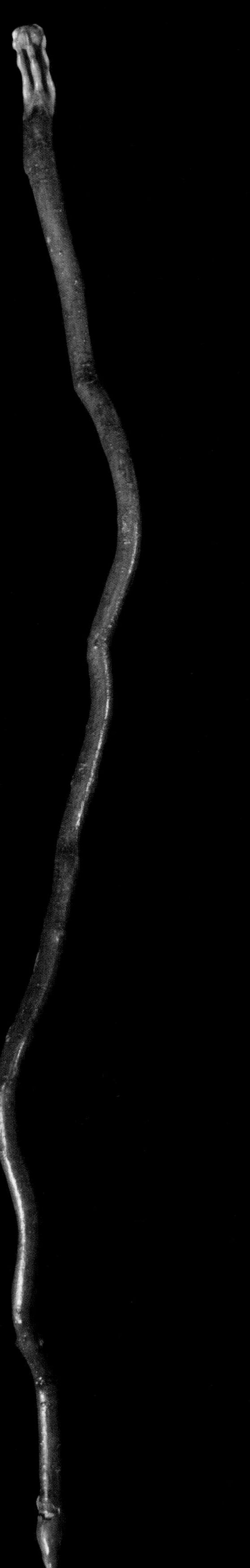

A SERPENTINE WAND

Snakes have long been considered magical creatures with great symbolic power. The ability of snakes to shed and regrow their skin is integral to their association with renewal, rebirth and healing. In many cultures, snakes also represent good and evil, a dualism that has importance for their connection with magic. As Professor Dumbledore recognised in the Harry Potter books, anyone who associates with snakes is 'supposedly connected with the Dark Arts, although as we know, there are Parselmouths among the great and the good too.' This slender, serpentine wand was a tool for channelling magical forces – its dark colour and snake-like shape force us to question whether it was used for good or for evil.

A WAND SHAPED LIKE A SNAKE
The Museum of Witchcraft and Magic, Boscastle

A SERPENT STAFF

This magic staff was carved from timber that had been buried for centuries in peat known as bog oak. The low oxygen levels, acidity and tannins of the peat preserved the wood, hardening and blackening it in the process. It was carved by the Neopagan Stephen Hobbs and given to a Wiccan priest called Stewart Farrar during the late 20th century. The staff has been decorated with a serpent in order to enhance its power. Not only do snakes represent a capacity for change, renewal and transformation, but their coils symbolise the dual cycles of light and dark, life and death, reason and passion, healing and poison, protection and destruction.

A SERPENT STAFF
The Museum of Witchcraft and Magic, Boscastle

SSSSSNAKES ALIVE!

Albertus Seba was a Dutch apothecary and collector, based in Amsterdam. From this centre of maritime trade, Seba supplied drugs to the Russian Tsar, Peter the Great. He also provided the port's ships with medicines, which he often traded for exotic animal specimens. After selling his first collection of snakes, birds and lizards to the Tsar in 1717, Seba began a second, larger collection, which he kept in his own house. In 1731, he commissioned artists to draw every single item in precise detail. This was such a huge undertaking the project did not get completed until 30 years after Seba's death. Many of the specimens Seba collected were used for medical research. He took a keen interest in the potential of snakes for life-saving cures – his collection contained many serpents such as this reticulated python, native to South-East Asia.

ALBERTUS SEBA, *LOCUPLETISSIMI RERUM NATURALIUM THESAURI ACCURATA DESCRIPTIO, ET INCONIBUS ARTIFICIOSISSIMIS EXPRESSIO, PER UNIVERSAM PHYSICES HISTORIAM,* 4 VOLS (AMSTERDAM, 1734–65)
British Library

BEWARE THE WEREWOLF

Johann Geiler von Kaysersberg was a theologian who preached at Strasbourg Cathedral in France. In 1508, he gave a series of sermons for Lent, which were transcribed and decorated with woodcut illustrations. The collection was later posthumously published as *Die Emeis (The Ants).* On the third Sunday of Lent ('Oculi'), Geiler delivered a sermon on werewolves. While Professor Snape may not have wished 'to fathom the way a werewolf's mind works', Geiler listed seven reasons why such beasts could attack. He also advised that the likelihood of being bitten was affected by a werewolf's age and its experience of eating human flesh.

➣ JOHANN GEILER VON KAYSERSBERG, *DIE EMEIS* (STRASBOURG, 1516)
British Library

"If he were in charge, Geiler would never have allowed a werewolf like Professor Lupin anywhere near Hogwarts School. According to his sermon, werewolves were dangerous beasts that especially liked to eat children."

ALEXANDER LOCK
Curator

Von dem wüteden Heer XLI

vnd von den ſelbigen eyer ſchalelē vñ vō den federn machen ſie inen hüſſer vnd be cleibens mit kot vnd mit ertreich vñ ſprechen etlich das ſie nit geware menſchē ſeient aber thier/ſie ſeint aber die aller nechſten thier bei der vernunfft vnd glidmoß des menſchen vnd neher den kein aff aber es ſeint thier. Es ſeint manſcherlei leutt in dē inſulē fundē wordē da ſelbeſten vm̄ her zů vnſeren zeiten. Die v wildenmā ſeint böſe geiſt.

Du fragſt künnen die zaubrer geware vnd rechte thier machen/das iſt der teufſel an irer ſtat vnd ſie wenen ſie haben es gethon wie man den daruon redt. Jch gib antwurt wie Auguſtinus vnd Rabanus vnd ſprich ia/daz ſie mögen machen vnd wol künnen dir als da ſein fröſch ſchlangen vnd ſoliches wan ſagen die lerer/das der böß geiſt kan wol in kurtzer zeit dē ſomen bringen/wen der ſomen da iſt vnd den die zaubrer ir in cantaciones vnnd beſchwerung vnd wort die darzů ghören vñ bruchen/ſo kan er es wol machē durch krüter oder wie e r im thůt dz vnď dem ſomē die thier werdē vñ er macht die thier wie du das feur macheſt du macheſt das feur dz feur nit/du bloßt es wol vff du leiſt holtz daran ꝛc. Vnd diſe ding kan der teufel thůn in kurtzer zeit aber nit in eim augē blick aber bald. Aber es iſt kein gewar wunder vnd ein recht zeichen wan es beſchicht zů betriegen den menſchen darum̄ ſo iſt ein falſch zeichen.

Am dritten ſontag in der faſten Occuli prediget Doctor Keiſerſperg von den werwölffen.

As wiltu vns von den werwöffen ſagē ſeint alſo werwölff die in die dörffen lauffen vnnd kind vnnd menſchen eſſen. Als man etwan daruon ſagt das ſie alſo mit verhengtem zorn die menſchen ſchedigen vnd heiſſen berwölff oder werwölff. Du weiſt mee daruon den ich. Jch ſprich ia. Es

There was a terrible snarling noise. Lupin's head was lengthening. So was his body. His shoulders were hunching. Hair was sprouting visibly on his face and hands, which were curling into clawed paws.

Harry Potter and the Prisoner of Azkaban

THE 'RED-EYED DWARF'

These typed pages are part of an early draft of *Harry Potter and the Philosopher's Stone.* In this scene, Hagrid comes to the office of Fudge, a Muggle minister, and warns him about You-Know-Who (even in this early draft Hagrid refuses to say the name). In turn, Fudge warns the public about this 'red-eyed dwarf'. The red eyes remain in the final incarnation of Lord Voldemort, but the character took time to develop fully into the terrifying figure we now know from the published stories. This scene is reminiscent of Cornelius Fudge visiting the Prime Minister of the Muggles in the first chapter of *The Half-Blood Prince.* As J.K. Rowling has said, 'I often cut ideas and put them into later books. Never waste a good scene!'

"Your kind?"

"Yeah... our kind. We're the ones who've bin disappearin'. We're all in hidin' now./ But I can't tell yeh much abou' us. Can't 'ave Muggles knowin' our business. But this is gettin' outta hand, an' all you Muggles are gettin' involved - them on the train, fer instance - they shouldn'ta bin hurt like that. That's why Dumbledore sent me. Says it's your business too, now."

"You've come to tell me why all these houses are disappearing?" Fudge said, "And why all these people are being killed?"

"Ah, well now, we're not sure they 'ave bin killed," said the giant. "He's jus' taken them. Needs 'em, see. 'E's picked on the best. Dedalus Diggle, Elsie Bones, Angus an' Elspeth McKinnon ... yeah, 'e wants 'em on 'is side."

"You're talking about this little red-eyed -?"

"Shh!" hissed the giant. "Not so loud! 'E could be 'ere now, fer all we know!"

Fudge ~~shivered~~ shuddered and looked wildly aroudn them. "C - could he?"

"S'alright, I don' reckon I was followed," said the giant in a gravelly whisper.

"But who is this person? What is he? One of - um - your kind?"

The giant snorted.

"Was once, I s'pose," he said. "But I don' think 'e's anything yeh could put a name to any more. 'E's not a 'uman. ~~'E's not an animal. - 'E's not properly~~ Wish 'e was. 'E could be killed if 'e was still 'uman enough."

"He can't be <u>killed</u>?" whispered Fudge in terror.

"Well, we don' think so. But Dumbledore's workin' on it. 'E's gotta be stopped, see?"

"Well, yes of course," said Fudge. "We can't have this sort of thing going on..."

"This is nothin'," said the giant, "'E's just gettin' started. Once 'e's got the power, once 'e's got the followers, no-one'll be safe. Not even Muggles. I 'eard 'e'll keep yeh alive, though. Fer slaves."

Fudge's eyes bulged with terror.

~~"But who is this - this person?~~

"This Bumblebore - Dunderbore -"

"Albus Dumbledore," said the the giant severely.

"Yes, yes, him - you say he has a plan?"

"Oh, yeah. So it's not hopeless yet. Reckon Dumbledore's the only one He's still afraid of. But 'e needs your 'elp. I'm 'ere teh ask yeh."

""Oh dear," said Fudge breathlessly, "The thing is, I~~'d be~~ was planning to retire early. Tomorrow, as a matter of fact. Mrs. Fudge and I were thinking of moving to Portugal. We have a villa-"

The giant lent forward, his beetle brows low over his glinting eyes.

"Yeh won' be safe in Portugal if 'e ain' stopped, Fudge."

"Won't I?" said Fudge weakly, "Oh, very well then... what is it Mr. Dumblething wants?"

"Dumble<u>dore</u>," said the giant. "Three things. First, yeh gotta put out a message. On television, an' radio, an' in the newspapers. Warn people not teh give 'im directions. 'Cause that's 'ow 'e's gettin' us, see? 'E 'as ter be told. Feeds on betrayal. I don' blame the Muggles, mind, they didn' know what they were doin'.

"Second, ~~yeh gotta make sure~~ ye're not teh tell anyone abou' us. If Dumbledore manages ter get rid of 'im, yeh gotta swear not ter go spreadin' it about what yeh know, abou' us. We keeps ourselves quiet, see? Let it stay that way.

An' third, yeh gotta give me a drink before I go. I gotta long journey back."

The giant's face creased into a grin behind his wild beard.

"Oh - yes, of course," said Fudge shakily, "Help yourself - there's brandy up there - and - not that I suppose it will happen - I mean, I'm a Muddle - a Muffle - no, a Muggle - but if this person - this thing - comes looking for me -?"

"Yeh'll be dead," said the giant flatly over the top of a large glass of brandy. "No-one can survive if 'e attacks them, Ain' never been a survivor. But like yeh say, yer a Muggle. 'E's not interested in you."

The giant drained his glass and stood up. He pulled out an umbrealla. It was pink and had flowers on it.

"I'll be off, then," he said.

"Just one thing," said Fudge, watching curiously as the giant opened the umbrella, "What is this - person's - name."

The giant looked suddenly scared.

"Can' tell yeh that," he said, "We never say it. Never."

He raised the pink umbrella over his head, Fudge blinked - and the giant was gone.

* * * * *

AN EARLY DRAFT OF HARRY POTTER AND THE PHILOSOPHER'S STONE
J.K. Rowling

Fudge wondered, of course, if he was going mad. He seriously considerd the possibility that the giant had been a hallucination. But the brandy glass the giant had drunk from was real enough, left standing on his desk.

Fudge wouldn't let his secretary remove the glass next day. It reassured him he wasn't a lunatic to do what he knew he had to do. He telephoned all the journalists he knew, and all the television stations, chose his favourite tie and gave a press conference. He told the world there was a ~~maniac madman-about~~ a strange little man going about. A little man with red eyes. he told the public to be very careful not to tell this little man where anyone lived. Once he had given out this strange message, he said "Any questions?" But the room was completely silent. Clearly, they all thought he was off his rocker. Fudge went back to his office and sat staring at the giant's empty brandy glass. ~~This-was-the-end-of-his-career.~~-

The very last person he wanted to see was Vernone Dursley. Dursley woudl be delighted. Dursley would be happily counting the days until he was made Minister, now that Fudge was so clearly nuttier than a bag of salted peanuts.

But Fudge had another surprise in store. Dursley knocked quietly, came into his office, sat opposite him and said flatly,

You've had a visit from One of Them, haven't you?"

"~~One-of-~~ Fudge looked at Dursley in amazement.

"You - know?"

"Yes," said Dursley bitterly, "I've known from the start. I - happened to know there were people like that. Of course, I never told anyone.

* * * * *

~~Most-peop-~~
Perhaps ~~people-did-~~ most people did think Fudge

Whether or not nearly everyone thought Fudge had gone very strange, the fact was that he seemed to have stopped the odd accidents. Three whole weeks passed, and still the empty brandy glass stood on Fudge's desk to give him courage, and not one bus flew, the houses of Britain stayed where they were, the trains stopped going swimming. Fudge, who hadn't even told Mrs. Fudge about the giant with the pink umbrella, waited and prayed and slept with his fingers crossed. Surely this Dumbledore would send a message if they'd managed to get rid of the red eyed dwarf? Or did this horrible silence mean that the dwarf had in fact got everyone he wanted, that he was even now planning to appear in Fudge's office and vanish him for trying to help the other side - whoever they were?

And then - one Tuesday -

Later that evening, when everyone else had gone home, Dursley sneaked up to Fudge's office carrying a crib., which he laid on Fudge's desk.

The child was asleep. Fudge peered nervously into the crib. The boy had a cut on his forehead. It was a very strangely shaped cut. It looked like a bolt of lightening.

"Going to leave a scar, I expect," said Fudge.

"Never mind the ruddy scar, what are we going to do with him?" said Dursley.

"Do with him? Why, you 'll have to take him home, of course," said Fudge in surprise. "He's your nephew. His parents have vanished. What else can we do? I thought you didn't want anyone to know you had relatives involved in all these odd doings?"

"Take him home!" said Dursley in horror. "My son Didsbury is just this age, I don't want him coming in contact with one of these."

"Very well, then, Dursley, we shall just have to try and fin someone who does want to take him. Of course, it will be difficult to keep the story out of the press. Noone else has lived after one of these vanishments. There'll be a lot of interest -"

"Oh, very <u>well</u>," snapped Dursley. "I'll take him."

He picked up the crib and stumped angrily from the room.

Fudge closed his briefcase. It was time he was getting home too. He had just put his hand on the doorhandle when a ~~low~~ cough behind him made him clap his hand to his heart.

"Don't hurt me! I'm a Muggle! I'm a Muggle!"

"I know yeh are," said a ~~low,~~ growling voice.

It was the giant.

"You!" said Fudge. "What is it? Oh, Good Lord, don't tell me-" For the giant, he saw, was crying. Sniffing into a large spotted handkerchief.

"It's all over," said the giant.

"Over?" said Fudge faintly, "It didn't work? Has he killed Dunderbore? Are we all going to be turned into slaves?"

"No, no," sobbed the giant. "He's gone. Everyone's come back. Diggle, the Bones, the McKinnons... they're all back. Safe. Everyone 'e took is back on our side an' He's disappeared 'imself."

"Good Heavens! This is wonderful news! You mean Mr. Dunderbumble's plan worked?"

"Never 'ad a chance to try it," said the giant, mopping his eyes.

"While many details of the world described in this chapter are familiar from the published books, such as the concept of Muggles, these scenes provide a very different account of the beginning of the story."

JOANNA NORLEDGE
Curator

HARRY AND THE BASILISK

Salazar Slytherin's monster, the giant basilisk, is shown coiling past Harry in this striking image from *The Chamber of Secrets*. The beast is so huge, it is hard to tell where its body begins or ends, and the dark colours of its scales are oppressive and intimidating. Harry is clutching the ruby-decorated sword of Godric Gryffindor in his hands, frozen in the air mid-swing. The bright white tip of the sword mirrors the sharp teeth of the basilisk. The monster's terrible yellow eyes are streaming with blood after Fawkes the phoenix has pierced them with its beak. This is an intense picture full of action and danger.

HARRY POTTER AND THE BASILISK BY JIM KAY
Bloomsbury

The Basilisk's head was falling, its body coiling around, hitting pillars as it twisted to face him. He could see the vast, bloody eye sockets, see the mouth stretching wide, wide enough to swallow him whole, lined with fangs long as his sword, thin, glittering, venomous ...

Harry Potter and the Chamber of Secrets

KING OF SERPENTS

This Italian manuscript contains 245 drawings of different animals, executed by an individual known as Idonius. Many of these creatures are mythical in nature, including the jaculus (a flying serpent), the onocentaur (half man, half donkey) and the basilisk, shown here. The accompanying description is based on the works of Claudius Aelianus and Pliny the Elder. According to Aelianus, the basilisk was only the width of a palm, but it could kill someone instantly with its stare. In Africa, the creature was said to make a whistling sound to scare away snakes that were feeding on the cadavers of mules.

A BASILISK, IN *HISTORIA ANIMALIUM* (ITALY, 1595)
British Library

"Pliny reported that, although the basilisk was only twelve inches long, both its touch and breath were deadly. Intriguingly, the basilisk could be killed using the scent of a weasel. If weasels were let loose in their lairs, they were able to slay the basilisk with their odour."

JULIAN HARRISON
Lead Curator

A brief
DESCRIPTION of the NATURE
OF THE
Basilisk, or Cockatrice.

Quos viuens vidi, necui, nunc mortuus, Vni
Do Vitam; dum me gens numerosa videt.

All men I kill'd that I did see,
But now I am Dead one lives by mee.

A BRIEF DESCRIPTION OF THE BASILISK

This very *Brief Description*, comprising only a title page and two pages of text, was written by Jacobus Salgado. Salgado was a refugee from Spain and a convert to Protestantism, who came to settle in England. Around 1680, in need of cash, Salgado displayed a basilisk given to him by a Dutch doctor who had recently returned from Ethiopia. The creature presumably had been stuffed or preserved in some way. Salgado wrote this pamphlet to accompany the spectacle, describing the beast as yellow, with a crown-like crest and the body of a cockerel attached to a serpent's tail. The pamphlet also spells out the danger of the basilisk's glare. Salgado declares that 'In the time of Alexander the Great, there was one of them which, lying hid in a wall, killed a great troop of his soldiers by the poisonous glances of his eyes upon them.'

JACOBUS SALGADO, *A BRIEF DESCRIPTION OF THE NATURE OF THE BASILISK, OR COCKATRICE* (LONDON, C. 1680)
British Library

"Despite Salgado's terrifying description of the basilisk, the creature on the title page looks rather benign, even though it has just killed the person in the foreground."

TANYA KIRK
Curator

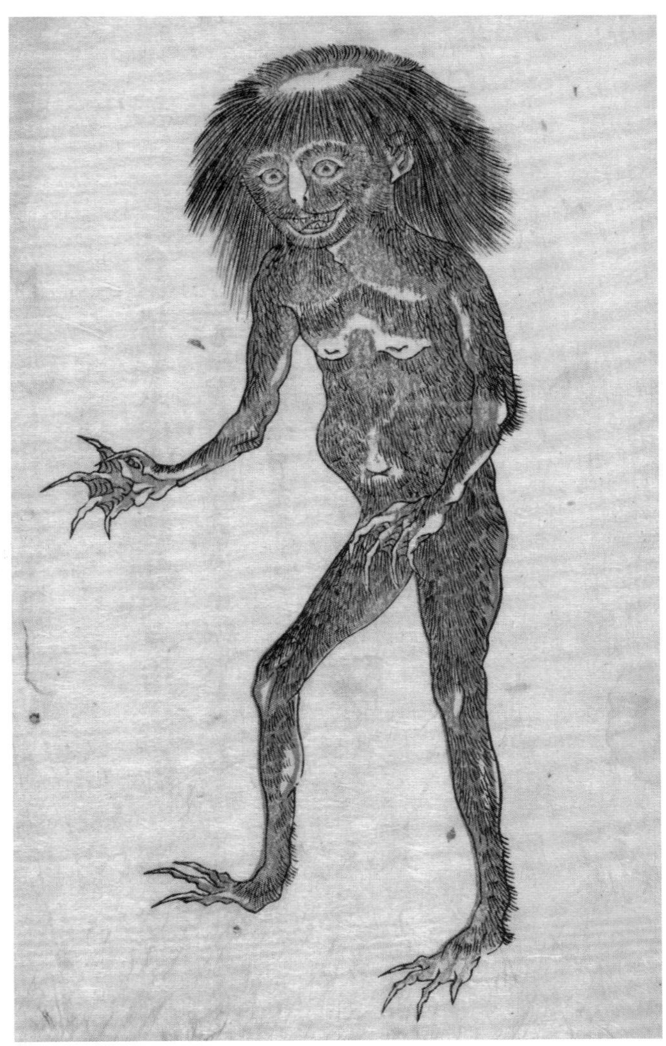

THE KAPPA

The kappa takes its name from the Japanese words for 'river' and 'child'. These were mischievous creatures, with the power to pull people into the lakes or rivers in which they dwelt. The wizarding world's famous Magizoologist Newt Scamander recognised this danger, noting that 'The Kappa feeds on human blood but may be persuaded not to harm a person if it is thrown a cucumber with that person's name carved into it.' The seated kappa below is in the form of a *netsuke* – a small sculptural object that is part of traditional Japanese dress. *Netsuke* frequently took the shape of mythical beasts and could function as talismans. The *neneko* kappa, illustrated on the left, moved to a new location every year, causing destruction wherever it went.

> *"The kappa's head has a distinctive hollow to contain its vital fluid. In* Fantastic Beasts and Where to Find Them, *Scamander advised that the wizard should trick the kappa into bowing, so that the water in its head would run out, depriving it of its strength."*
>
> JULIAN HARRISON
> *Lead Curator*

A *NENEKO* KAPPA (1855) AND A *NETSUKE* IN THE SHAPE OF A KAPPA (JAPAN, 19TH CENTURY)
British Library, British Museum

The Kappa is a Japanese water demon that inhabits shallow ponds and rivers. Often said to look like a monkey with fish scales instead of fur, it has a hollow in the top of its head in which it carries water.

Fantastic Beasts and Where to Find Them

OF THE SPHINGA

Or SPHINX.

HE *Sphinx* or *Sphinga* is of the kinde of Apes, hauing his body rough like Apes, but his breaſt vp to his necke, pilde and ſmooth without hayre: the face is very round yet ſharp and piked, hauing the breaſts of women, and their fauor or viſage much like them: In that part of their body which is bare without haire, there is a certaine red thing riſing in a round circle like Millet ſeed, which giueth great grace & comelineſſe to their coulour, which in the middle parte is humaine: Their voice is very like a mans but not articulat, ſounding as if one did ſpeake haſtily with indignation or ſorow. Their haire browne or ſwarthy coulour. They are bred in *India* and *Ethyopia*. In the promontory of the fartheſt *Arabia* neere *Dira*, are *Sphinges* and certaine Lyons called *Formicæ*, ſo likewiſe they are to be found amongeſt the *Trogladitæ*. As the *Babouns* & *Cynocephals* are more wilde than other Apes, ſo the Satyres and *Sphynges* are more meeke and gentle, for they are not ſo wilde that they will not bee tamed, nor yet ſo tame but they will reuenge their own harmes: as appeared by that which was ſlayne in a publike ſpectacle among the *Thebanes*. They carrye their meat in the ſtorehouſes of their own chaps or cheeks, taking it forth when they are hungry, and ſo eat it: not being like the *Formicæ*, for that which is annuall in them, is daily and hourely amongeſt theſe.

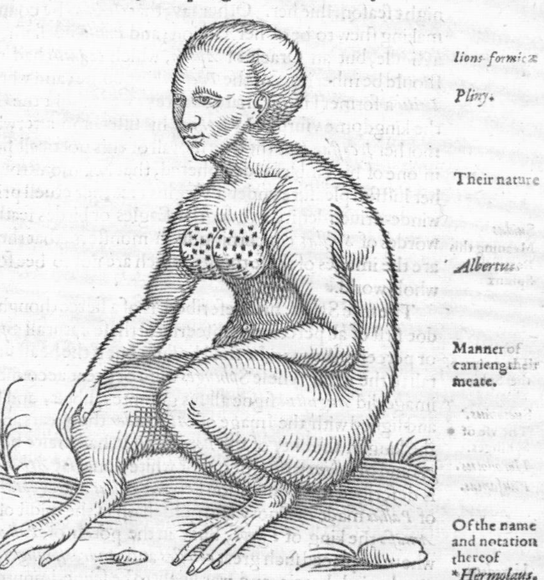

The name of this *Sphynx* is taken from * binding, as appeareth by the Greek notation, or elſe of delicacie and dainty nice * looſneſſe, (wherefore there were certain common ſtrumpets called *Sphinctæ*, and the *Megarian Sphingas*, was a very popular phraſe for notorious harlots) hath giuen occaſion to the Poets, to faigne a certaine monſter called *Sphynx*, which they ſay was thus deriued. *Hydra* brought foorth the *Chimæra*, *Chimæra* by *Orthus* the *Sphinx*, and the *Nemæan* Lyon: now this *Orthus* was one of *Geryons* Dogges. This *Sphinx* they make a treble-formed monſter, a Maydens face, a Lyons legs, and the wings of a fowle, or as *Anſonius* and *Varinus* ſay, the face and hand of a mayde, the body of a Dogge, the winges of a byrd, the voice of a man, the clawes of a Lyon, and the tayle of a Dragon: and that ſhe kept continually in the *Sphincian* mountaine; propounding to all trauailers that came that way an *Ænigma* or Riddle, which was this: *What was the creature that first of all goeth on foure legges; afterwards on two, and laſtly on three*: and all of them that could

Pliny.
Caliſthius.
The deſcription.
Ælianus.
Countrey of breed.
lions formicæ
Pliny.
Their nature
Albertus.
Manner of carrieng their meate.
Of the name and notation thereof
**Hermolaus.*
**Varrianus*
Heſiod.
Auſonius.
The deſcription of the Poets Phinx.
The Riddle of the Sphinx

THE SPHINX

The Historie of Foure-Footed Beastes was the first major book about animals to be published in English. It features a variety of animals, from the common (rabbits, sheep, goats) to the exotic (lions, elephants, rhinoceroses) and the legendary. This chapter focuses on the sphinx. The woodcut illustration shows a creature with a woman's head and a lion's body. Edward Topsell described the sphinx as 'of a fierce but tameable nature'. Less well known is its ability to store food in its cheeks until it is ready to eat – just like a guinea pig! Sphinxes are famous for their enigmatic powers. In *The Goblet of Fire*, Harry had to answer the sphinx's riddle to proceed through the maze during the Triwizard Tournament.

EDWARD TOPSELL, *THE HISTORIE OF FOURE-FOOTED BEASTES* (LONDON, 1607)
British Library

It had the body of an overlarge lion; great clawed paws, and a long yellowish tail ending in a brown tuft. Its head, however, was that of a woman. She turned her long, almond-shaped eyes upon Harry as he approached.

Harry Potter and the Goblet of Fire

AMULET SCROLLS

Amulets, written on leather or metal, have been worn by Ethiopians and other peoples in the Horn of Africa for thousands of years. This practice remains strongest in the northern Highlands of Ethiopia, where amulets are believed to bring health, to protect babies and to ward off the evil eye. The parchment scrolls themselves are known as *Ketab*, and they vary considerably in length. They are kept in leather cases, or in cylindrical silver containers like those shown here. The *Ketab* can then be hung up at home or worn around the neck, depending on their size. This particular scroll was created to protect its owner from harm. It contains prayers for undoing spells (*maftehé seray*), after which the talismanic drawings were added, giving effect to its powers.

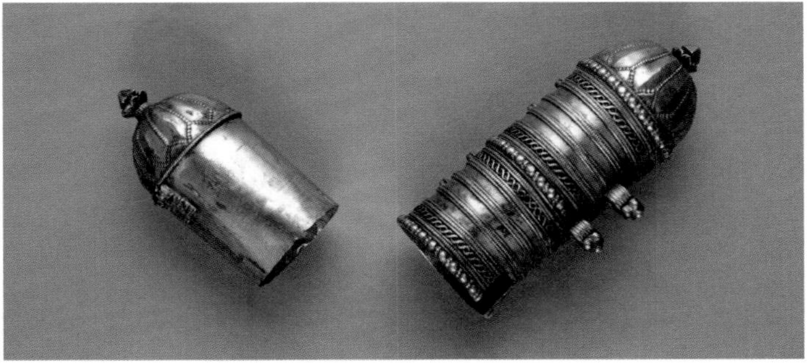

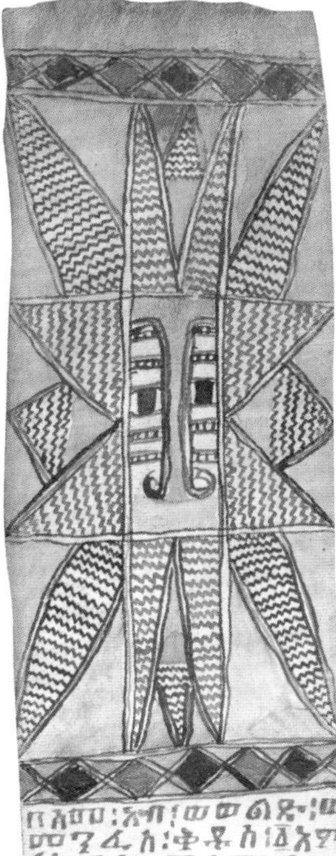

TWO AMULET SCROLLS, ONE WITH A PROTECTIVE CYLINDRICAL CASE (ETHIOPIA, 18TH CENTURY)

British Library

> *"The drawings in this scroll have a specific purpose. They are intended to cure sickness, to exorcise demons and to protect those taking long and difficult journeys."*
>
> EYOB DERILLO
>
> *Curator*

ለገብረ፡እግዚአብሔር፡
ወለአመተ፡እግዚአብሔር፡

ETHIOPIAN TALISMANS

This personally annotated, magical recipe book was made in Ethiopia. Written in Ge'ez, also known as classic Ethiopic, it contains a rich collection of protective amulets, talismans, charms and incantations. This manuscript would have belonged to an exorcist or a Debtera, ደብተራ (Däbtära), a highly educated, ordained layman. Däbtäras typically study for several years or come from families of clergy. On these pages are talismans and geometric images, used for making amulet scrolls, and accompanied by prayers for undoing spells and charms. Talismanic drawing focuses on the image of the eye, providing a defence against the evil eye and the dark arts.

> *"Since medieval times, Däbtäras have worked in the courts or have taught in small parish schools, supplementing their income by producing amulet scrolls and practising traditional medicine. From the marginal notes in this recipe book, we can deduce with some certainty that it belonged to a practitioner of magic."*
>
> EYOB DERILLO
> *Curator*

AN ETHIOPIAN MAGICAL RECIPE BOOK (1750)
British Library

Unfortunately, you needed a specially signed note from one of the teachers to look in any of the restricted books and he knew he'd never get one. These were the books containing powerful Dark Magic never taught at Hogwarts and only read by older students studying advanced Defence Against the Dark Arts.

Harry Potter and the Philosopher's Stone

J.W.Waterhouse

THE MAGIC CIRCLE

John William Waterhouse, the renowned Pre-Raphaelite artist, often returned to the subject of magic and witches. He painted Circe, the Greek goddess of magic, several times, as well as sirens, water nymphs, and a sorceress gazing into a crystal ball. Although witches have often been presented throughout history as ugly and unnatural women, this was not the image Waterhouse decided to portray. Here he shows an enchantress drawing a protective circle around herself with a wand. Outside the magic circle, in a strange, barren landscape, are foreboding-looking creatures such as ravens and toads, and a skull half-buried in the ground. In direct contrast, within the circle we can see a warm fire, flowers growing and the witch herself, dressed in a beautifully vibrant gown. This positive depiction of defensive magic echoes Hermione Granger's use of protective enchantments to create a safe camp in *Harry Potter and the Deathly Hallows.*

JOHN WILLIAM WATERHOUSE, *THE MAGIC CIRCLE* (1886)
Tate Britain

'If we're staying, we should put some protective enchantments around the place,' she replied, and raising her wand, she began to walk in a wide circle around Harry and Ron, murmuring incantations as she went.

Harry Potter and the Deathly Hallows

A LEAKY CAULDRON

Cauldrons are one of the most ancient and widely recognised symbols of magic in Western culture. Indeed, to be a *strioportius* (witch's cauldron carrier) was a punishable offence in 6th-century Salic law. All First Year students at Hogwarts were required to pack their own cauldron when attending school. This enchanted cooking pot is coated in a black tarry substance. It exploded when some Cornish witches were concocting a powerful potion by the sea. The group had gathered to invoke a spirit. One account describes how, when 'it was realised that the volume of the smoke was reaching unprecedented proportions … they lost their nerve and panicked and fled the spot as best they could'.

AN EXPLODED CAULDRON
The Museum of Witchcraft and Magic, Boscastle

De la Licorne.

CARE OF MAGICAL CREATURES

Care of Magical Creatures

Steve Backshall

Steve Backshall is one of TV's busiest wildlife experts. He is especially popular with younger viewers, who are both terrified and delighted to watch his encounters with extraordinary and inspiring predators. As well as writing numerous books, hosting sell-out live events and filming extreme adventures for the BBC, Steve is also the proud Ambassador for Cubs and the Get Outside champion for Ordnance Survey.

Deep inside the crater of an extinct volcano, nestled amid the dense jungles of New Guinea, tree-dwelling kangaroos clamber from branch to branch and neon butterflies the size of paperback novels flutter among the foliage. It was in this lush, lost paradise that I held in my arms a silky cuscus – a dark-furred marsupial that occurs nowhere else on Earth. My team and I were the first human beings ever to see this mammal, and although in my career as a naturalist I have had countless amazing encounters with majestic, unique, and at times terrifying creatures, this was among the most magical. The sensation that overtakes you during such an experience is almost indescribable – that tingle like an electrical charge up the back of the neck … It's exactly this heady mix of excitement, awe and incredulity that I imagine Harry Potter felt when he first set eyes on Buckbeak the hippogriff.

Harry's attitude to Buckbeak is one that any experienced animal handler would applaud. The first rule of working with wild animals is respect – for their personal space, their safety and their wellbeing. With intelligent animals it is vital to let them take the lead, just as Harry was advised to do with Buckbeak, only approaching once the hippogriff had returned his bow. If I'm diving with an adult male sea lion for example, I understand he has the ability to tear me limb from limb. Therefore, if we are to be friends, it must be on his terms. I keep my distance, swim around trying to look like an interesting plaything, and hope that his curiosity gets the better of him!

When navigating new environments in the wild I regularly call on the expertise of local guides and trackers. For Harry, guidance comes in the form of Rubeus Hagrid, gamekeeper and animal enthusiast. Hagrid reminds me of the Scottish ghillie. While ghillies are inextricably connected to hunting, they also have an almost superhuman perception of the natural world. They are phenomenal trackers, able to

look at a simple footprint and know everything from the age and sex of the animal to its health and behaviour. Hagrid shares this innate affinity with wild creatures. It is Hagrid who, having won an egg in a card game, gives Harry his first glimpse of a real-life dragon. The study of newt and salamander eggs was part of my Masters thesis, and so I was inevitably drawn to the connections between animal eggs in our world and those of dragons in the Potter universe. Like birds' eggs, dragons' eggs have hard shells and rely on heat from the parent to incubate them. However, dragons are probably closer to our reptiles, such as crocodiles, turtles or Komodo dragons. Such animals have leathery soft-shelled eggs, and the mother plays no part in incubating them. Instead they are often buried in nests of vegetation. As the mulch decomposes, the nest generates heat, warming the eggs. After many weeks, the young animal breaks out. Unlike Harry and his friends, I've never had the privilege of watching a dragon egg hatch. However, I have been lucky enough to hold a crocodile egg up to the sunlight, to look through the translucent shell and see a baby croc wriggle inside, to marvel as it breaks its way out of the shell with the aid of its temporary egg tooth. The spectacle of the tiny hatchling emerging, its cuteness belying the lethal beast it will soon become, is a spectacle that beams you back tens of millions of years.

Hagrid is at home in the harshest environments and is by Harry's side when he first enters the Forbidden Forest – akin, in my experience, to the Boreal forests of the far north and home to wolves, bears and wolverine. Here, the cloak of moss over everything deadens sounds, and gives the air a peculiar kind of silence. As dusk falls, light fades far faster than in the world beyond, and before you know it you're stumbling around in darkness, under the unseen gaze of a thousand eyes. The Forbidden Forest is home to Aragog the Acromantula and his colony. On coming face-to-face with this gigantic, flesh-eating spider, Harry and Ron were quite understandably dumbstruck. Throughout history pioneering naturalists have faced similar disbelief at their incredible discoveries. When Maria Merian first brought back paintings of bird-eating spiders from the jungles of Surinam, people in Europe didn't believe they truly existed. As someone who has kept bird-eating tarantulas as pets, I find these huge, hairy and very real horrors to be utterly fascinating. In the wild, I've sat in wonder watching them hunt. They sit motionless in the entrance to their burrows, with tripwires of silk alerting them to the passing of possible prey. When a hapless insect, frog, lizard or small mammal tangles the silk, the spider will leap out and devour them, tearing them apart with mighty fangs that can be long as a panther's claws. Generally, though, tarantulas are docile and gentle towards things they can't eat.

Pet-keeping helps teach our children to care for and respect animals. At Hogwarts the students are allowed to bring a cat, an owl or a toad to school with them. Toads (such as Neville Longbottom's much maligned Trevor) may be the least popular choice among wizards, but in my experience they are intriguing and not to be sneered at. Many of them have virulent toxins or poisons – some strong enough to kill a small animal. The largest toads are basketball-sized, and will eat any living thing they can fit into their massive mouths. Harry has a fine animal compatriot in Hedwig. Snowy owls make their home in the frozen north, where their speckled white plumage is sublime camouflage. They can fly over featureless landscapes and use their phenomenal hearing to locate rodents scuttling around beneath the surface,

before punching down with their talons to catch them. Their one weakness is that as they live in Arctic landscapes where there are no trees, they are used to standing on frozen ground, and are very uncomfortable on perches. Small wonder then that Hedwig does not care for being cooped up in a cage.

Among the most magical and sacred of creatures in Harry's world is the unicorn. Every part of them, from their horns to their tails, contains valuable properties. In our world, too, the unicorn is legendary. The myth of this unique beast was spread after explorers discovered long, twisted helical horns swept up on Arctic beaches. As it turns out, these are actually an extended canine tooth protruding from the upper jaw of the narwhal whale. Very occasionally females grow them; even more unusually two tusks may grow. Originally, the horns were thought to be used for fighting, but we now know that they are packed with nerves, so may be used for passing on sensory information, as a thermometer and even for gentle physical contact. Recently narwhals have even been recorded carefully swiping their horns through the water in order to stun small fish. When it comes to wildlife, it seems, the truth is frequently stranger than fiction.

"Hagrid [is] the earthy, warm and physical man, lord of the forest; Dumbledore the spiritual theoretician, brilliant, idealised and somewhat detached. Each is a necessary counterpoint to the other as Harry seeks father figures in his new world."

J.K. Rowling on Pottermore

HAGRID

Rubeus Hagrid, the half-giant, introduced Harry to many of the wonderful creatures that stride, scuttle and soar around the wizarding world. Jim Kay's artwork brings to life Hagrid's mane of black hair and 'wild, tangled beard'. 'Hagrid is a relief to draw,' says Jim Kay, 'because drawing children you can't put a line wrong, a misplaced scribble can age a child by ten years. There are no such problems with Hagrid; he's a mass of scribbles with eyes.' In the Harry Potter books, the gamekeeper was a reliable and trustworthy presence, despite his blind spot towards dangerous beasts. Hagrid became the Professor for Care of Magical Creatures in Harry's third year, and in *The Order of the Phoenix* he went on a mission to gain the giants' support against Lord Voldemort. Hagrid subsequently brought his half-brother, Grawp, to the Forbidden Forest in order to domesticate him.

PORTRAIT OF RUBEUS HAGRID BY JIM KAY
Bloomsbury

56 LIBER OCTAVUS, SECT. II.

ſolito altius agellum foderet, lapideum tumulum inſcriptione ornatum, & in ſepulchro viri mortui corpus proceræ adeò ſtaturæ, ut muros urbis excederet; cadaver integrum erat, ac ſi paulo ante ſepulturæ datum fuiſſet, in pectore vulnus latiſſimum geſtabat; ſupra caput autem corporis defuncti reperta eſt lucerna perpetuo igne ardens, quæ nec flatu, nec aquæ alteriuſve liquoris ullius ſuperinjectione extingui potuit: ſed in fundo perforata & rupta ſtatim evanuit; iſtud autem fuiſſe corpus magni *Pallantis* Arcadis, qui filius *Euandri* Regis, comes *Æneæ* bello ſingularique certamine dudum interfectus fuit à *Turno* Rutilorum rege, multo prius antequam Roma conderetur. Quæ omnia à *Volaterrano* confirmantur.

Pallantis corpus.

Atque hæc ſunt, quæ de Gigantibus eorumque immenſa vaſtitate adducenda duximus; reſtat tandem hoc loco, num verè tam prodigioſæ ſtaturæ homines unquam in Mundo fuerint, hoc loco demonſtrare.

DISQUISITIO PRIMA.

Num verè Natura tam monſtruoſæ magnitudinis homines, quam Authores allegati referunt, unquam protulerit.

IN ſepulchris lociſque ſubterraneis ſubinde oſſa reperiri, quæ oſſa gigantum eſſe dicuntur, non abnuo; nam ut ſuprà annotavimus, Gigantes vaſti corporis homines fuiſſe, vel ipſa Sacra Scriptura teſtatur, *Gen:* 7. & *lib.* 1. *Reg. c.* 17. *Maximiliano* Cæſari anno 1511. teſte *Surio*, giganteæ magnitudinis vir ex Polonia oriundus, oblatus fuit, qui &

pro magnitudine corporis, proportionato cibo ſingulis prandiis vitulum & ovem abſumebat. Similis noſtris temporibus *Ferdinando* II. in comitiis Ratiſponenſibus, *anno* 1623. exhibitus fuit, ut proinde de inuſitatæ magnitudinis hominibus utriuſque ſexus minimè dubitem, cum tales nullum non ſeculum protulerit.

Ho-

THE SKELETON OF A GIANT, IN ATHANASIUS KIRCHER, *MUNDUS SUBTERRANEUS* (AMSTERDAM, 1665)

British Library

A GIANT FROM UNDERGROUND

Were there skeletons of 90 metre-tall giants found on Mount Erice in Sicily, Italy? This reconstructed image of what they may have looked like is taken from *Mundus Subterraneus* ('The Underground World'), by the German author Athanasius Kircher. While travelling in Italy, Kircher became fascinated with what might lie beneath the Earth. He even climbed inside the volcano Mount Vesuvius, which had last erupted seven years earlier. Kircher claimed that an enormous skeleton had been discovered sitting in a Sicilian cave in the 14th century. Here he shows the scale of it in comparison to a normal human, the Biblical giant Goliath, a Swiss giant and a Mauritanian giant.

"Throughout history, there have been records of both dangerous and friendly giants. An example of the latter is the Cornish giant Holiburn, who died of grief after accidentally killing a youth by tapping him playfully on the head. This anecdote shows that, despite their lethal size and phenomenal strength, giants are often big of heart."

JOANNA NORLEDGE
Curator

HAGRID AND HARRY AT GRINGOTTS

In this original drawing by J.K. Rowling, Hagrid is shown taking Harry on his first trip to his vault at Gringotts, located in the caverns deep beneath the wizarding bank. Hagrid covers his eyes with his hands during the ride. Harry, on the other hand, keeps his eyes 'wide open' for the whole journey. This image shows visually Hagrid's discomfort at being cramped up inside the Gringotts cart. J.K. Rowling uses the giant's streaming hair and the torch flame bending in the wind to convey a sense of rattling speed.

➢ DRAWING OF HARRY AND HAGRID AT GRINGOTTS BY J.K. ROWLING
J.K. Rowling

At first they just hurtled through a maze of twisting passages. Harry tried to remember, left, right, right, left, middle fork, right, left, but it was impossible. The rattling cart seemed to know its own way, because Griphook wasn't steering.

Harry Potter and the Philosopher's Stone

A DRAFT OF THE PHILOSOPHER'S STONE

This typed draft represents an unedited version of *Harry Potter and the Philosopher's Stone*. As part of the editorial process, a literary draft may be amended in order to improve the pacing. For a scene like this, full of action and drama, some passages were subsequently shortened to move the story along more quickly. Some scenes, in turn, may be completely cut, such as the encounter with a preoccupied Nearly Headless Nick, and Hermione reciting the textbook definition of trolls, both shown on page 167.

➣ A TYPED DRAFT OF *HARRY POTTER AND THE PHILOSOPHER'S STONE*
BY J.K. ROWLING
J.K. Rowling

"Hello, hello," he said absently, "Just pondering a little problem, don't take any notice of me..."

"What's Peeves done this time?" asked Harry.

"No, no, it's not Peeves I'm worried about," said Nearly Headless Nick, looking thoughtfully at Harry. "Tell me, Mr. Potter, if you were

167

worried that someone was up to something they shouldn't be, would you tell someone else, who might be able to stop it, even if you didn't think much of the person who might be able to help?"

"Er - you mean - would I go to Snape about Malfoy, for instance?"

"Something like that, something like that...."

"I don't think Snape would help me, but it'd be worth a try, I suppose," said Harry curiously.

"Yes... yes... thank you, Mr. Potter..."

Nearly Headless Nick glided away. Harry and Ron watched him go, puzzled looks on their faces.

"I suppose you're bound not to make much sense if you've been beheaded," said Ron.

Quirrell was late for class. He rushed in looking pale and anxious and told them to turn to "p-page fifty four" at once, to look at "t-t-trolls."

"N-now, who c-c-can tell me the three types of t-troll? Yes, Miss G-

167

Granger?"

"Mountain-dwelling, river-dwelling and sea-dwelling," said Hermione promptly. "Mountain-dwelling trolls are the biggest, they're pale grey, bald, have skin tougher than a rhinoceros and are stronger than ten men. However, their brains are only the size of a pea, so they're easy to confuse -"

"Very g-good, thank you, Miss Gr -"

"River trolls are light green and have stringy hair -"

"Y-y-yes, thank you, that's excell -"

" - and sea trolls are purplish grey and -"

"Oh, someone shut her up," said Seamus loudly. A few people laughed.

There was a loud clatter as Hermione jumped to her feet, knocking her chair over, and ran out of the room with her face in her hands. A very awkward silence followed.

"Oh d-d-dear," said Professor Quirrell.

*

When Harry woke up next day, the first thing he noticed was a delicious smell in the air.

"It's pumpkin, of course!" said Ron, "Today's Hallowe'en!"

Harry soon realised that Hallowe'en at Hogwarts was a sort of mini-Christmas. When they got down to the Great Hall for breakfast, they found that it had been decorated with thousands of real bats, which were hanging off the ceiling and window-sills, fast asleep. Hagrid was putting hollow pumpkins on all the tables.

"Big feast tonight," he grinned at them, "See yeh there!"

There was a holiday feeling in the air because lessons would be finishing early. No-one was in much of a mood for work, which annoyed Professor McGonagall.

168

"Unless you settle down, you won't be going to the feast at all," she said, a few minutes into Transfiguration. She stared at them until they had all fallen silent. Then she raised her eyebrows.

"And where is Hermione Granger?"

They all looked at each other.

"Miss Patil, have you seen Miss Granger?"

Parvati shook her head.

A TYPED DRAFT OF *HARRY POTTER AND THE PHILOSOPHER'S STONE*
BY J.K. ROWLING
J.K. Rowling

cupboard doors, but not a hint of a troll did they find.

They'd just decided to try the dungeons when they heard footsteps.

"If it's Snape, he'll send us back - quick, behind here!"

They squeezed into an alcove behind a statue of Godfrey the Gormless.

Sure enough, a moment later they caught a glimpse of Snape's hook nose rushing past. Then they heard him whisper "Alohomora!" and a click.

"Where's he gone?" Ron whispered.

"No idea - quick, before he gets back -"

They dashed down the stairs, three at a time, and rushed headlong into the cold darkness of the dungeons. They passed the room where they usually had Potions and were soon walking through passages they'd never seen before. They slowed down, looking around. The walls were wet and slimey and the air was dank.

"I never realised they were so big," Harry whispered as they turned yet another corner and saw three more passageways to choose from. "It's like Gringotts down here..."

173

Ron sniffed the damp air.

"Can you smell something?"

Harry sniffed too. Ron was right. Above the generally musty smell of the dungeons was another smell, which was rapidly becoming a foul stench, a mixture of old socks and public toilets, the concrete kind that no-one seems to clean.

And then they heard it. A low grunting - heavy breathing - and the shuffling footfalls of gigantic feet.

They froze - they couldn't tell where the sound was coming from amid all the echoes -

Ron suddenly pointed; at the end of one of the passageways,

something huge was moving. It hadn't seen them... it ambled out of sight...

"Merlin's beard," said Ron softly, "It's enormous..."

They looked at each other. Now that they had seen the troll, their ideas of fighting it seemed a bit - stupid. But neither of them wanted to be the one to say this. Harry tried to look brave and unconcerned.

"Did you see if it had a club?" Trolls, he knew, often carried clubs.

Ron shook his head, also trying to look as though he wasn't bothered.

"You know what we should do?" said Harry, "Follow it. Try and lock it in one of the dungeons - trap it, you know..."

If Ron had been hoping Harry was going to say, "Let's go back to the feast", he didn't show it. Locking up the troll was better than trying to fight it.

"Good idea," he said.

They crept down the passageway. The stench grew stronger as they reached the end. Very slowly, they peered around the corner.

174

There it was. It was shuffling away from them. Even from the back, it was a horrible sight. Twelve feet tall, its skin was a dull, granite grey, its great lumpy body like a boulder with its small bald head perched on top like a coconut. It had short legs thick as tree trunks with flat, horny feet. The smell coming from it was incredible. It was holding a huge wooden club, which dragged along the floor because its arms were so long.

They pulled their heads back out of sight.

"Did you see the size of that club?" Ron whispered. Neither of them could have lifted it.

"We'll wait for it to go into one of the chambers and then barricade the door," said Harry. He looked back around the corner.

The troll had stopped next to a doorway and was peering inside. Harry could see its face now; it had tiny red eyes, a great squashed nose and a gaping mouth. It also had long, dangling ears which waggled as it shook its head, making up its tiny mind where to go next. Then it slouched slowly into the chamber.

Harry looked around, searching -

"There!" he whispered to Ron, "See? On the wall there!"

A long, rusty chain was suspended about half way down the passageway. Harry and Ron darted forward and pulled it off its nail. Trying to stop it clinking, they tiptoed towards the open door, praying the troll wasn't about to come out of it -

Harry seized the door handle and pulled it shut: with trembling hands, they looped the chain around the handle, hooked it onto a bolt sticking out of the wall and pulled it tight.

"It'll take it a while to get out of that," Harry panted, as they pulled the chain back across the door and tied it firmly to a torch bracket, "Come

175

on, let's go and tell them we've caught it!"

Flushed with their victory they started to run back up the passage, but as they reached the corner they heard something that made their hearts stop - a high, petrified scream - and it was coming from the chamber they'd just chained up -

"Oh, no," said Ron, pale as the Bloody Baron.

"There's someone in there!" Harry gasped.

"*Hermione!*" they said together.

It was the last thing they wanted to do, but what choice did they have? Wheeling around they sprinted back to the door and ripped the chain off, fumbling in their panic - Harry pulled the door open - they ran inside.

"Here you can read a slightly different account of Ron and Harry coming face-to-face with a troll in the girls' bathroom. For example, the paragraph at the top of page 175 is reduced to two sentences in the published text. This draft also preserves the idea of securing the door with a chain, rather than locking the door with a key, as occurs in the published version."

JOANNA NORLEDGE
Curator

A MOUNTAIN TROLL

This is a preparatory study of a mountain troll or, to use the scientific name, *Troglodytarum alpinum*. In J.K. Rowling's wizarding world trolls can grow to twelve feet tall, and are extremely strong and thick-skinned. Due to the very small size of their brains, they are easily confused and quick to flare into a temper. A violent disposition, alongside a taste for human flesh, meant that these creatures were classed as dangerous by the Ministry of Magic. This troll, covered in growths and with a perplexed look in his eye, is typical of his species.

DRAWING OF A MOUNTAIN TROLL BY JIM KAY
Bloomsbury

It was a horrible sight. Twelve feet tall, its skin was a dull, granite grey, its great lumpy body like a boulder with its small bald head perched on top like a coconut. It had short legs thick as tree trunks with flat, horny feet.

Harry Potter and the Philosopher's Stone

PEEVES THE POLTERGEIST

Peeves is shown here in his visible form, but he was able to become invisible at will. A *poltergeist* (meaning 'noisy ghost' in German) is generally understood to be a malevolent spirit. In this drawing, Peeves almost resembles a court jester, with his curly-toed shoes, bow tie and spotty hat. J.K. Rowling has captured his glinting, wicked eyes, emphasising them with a pair of slanted eyebrows. The poltergeist's pranks were often crude, but extremely effective. Following Professor Umbridge, then blowing raspberries whenever she spoke, is a prime and very Peeve-ish example.

➣ DRAWING OF PEEVES BY J.K. ROWLING (1991)
J.K. Rowling

NEARLY HEADLESS NICK

J.K. Rowling's drawing of Nearly Headless Nick shows the Gryffindor ghost demonstrating exactly how you can be *nearly* headless. As a ghost, Nick could not enjoy simple pleasures such as eating food, a fact that he lamented at Harry's first Hogwarts feast. He also nursed resentment at his botched beheading, which prevented him from joining the Headless Hunt. J.K. Rowling has elsewhere defined a ghost in Harry Potter's world as, 'the transparent, three-dimensional imprint of a deceased witch or wizard, which continues to exist in the mortal world'.

⮜ DRAWING OF NEARLY HEADLESS NICK BY J.K. ROWLING (1991)
J.K. Rowling

it was free: Harry's foot found ~~the~~ the crook of its ~~back~~ hind leg and he ~~scrambled~~ clambered up onto its back: its scales felt hard and rough as steel: ~~he~~ it did not seem even to feel him. ~~The~~ ~~H~~ He stretched out an arm, as high as he could, Hermione grabbed it and he pulled her up onto the back, too; Ron ~~was~~ climbed up behind them but Griphook was nowhere to be seen: he seemed ~~lost~~ to have vanished into ~~be somewhere~~ ~~amongst~~ the crowd of goblins but ~~but before Harry could~~ ~~but there was no chance~~ before Harry could ~~to~~ locate him: the dragon ~~that~~ realised it was free.

With a roar it reared: Harry dug in ~~his~~ ~~entire hands~~ knees, clutched with all his strength at the adamantine scales, and then the wings opened, ~~tossing~~ knocking goblins ~~aside, and the beast~~ aside as though they were ninepins, and it rose into the air, soaring ~~Harry glanced back~~ towards the passage opening, ~~a~~ and the goblins below could do nothing but throw daggers, which glanced off its flanks.

'We'll never get out, it's too big, much too big!' Hermione screamed, but the dragon opened its mouth again and a burst of flame such as Harry had never seen ~~exploded~~ blasted the tunnels, whose floors and ceiling ~~[illegible]~~ cracked and ~~the dragon~~ crumbled: and by sheer force the dragon clawed and fought its way forwards: ~~[illegible]~~ Harry's eyes were tight shut against the heat and ~~falling rock~~ dust: deafened by the crashing of rock and the dragon's ~~[illegible]~~ roars he ~~had~~ could only cling to its back and pray: and then

Still the dragon was belching flame; where the goblins ~~scattered~~ ~~to~~ began clashing again; maddened, its realising it carved into the wall

↑ [this way]

sword, seized Griphook's hand and pulled. The blistered, howling goblin emerged by degrees.

'X' yelled Harry and he landed on the bumpy surface of the swelling treasure with the goblin on his shoulder again, but now a hundred swords of Gryffindor were multiplying all around him.

'The real one —' he groaned: he had to destroy the Horcrux, 'where — it's got the cup on it —'

The jewelled hilt was shoved into his hand: Griphook had spotted and seized it. In one fluid action, the hot air full of screams, Harry swung the sword into the air, the cup flew up, turned over and fell, and he impaled it on the blade, the point of the sword penetrating the bottom of the cup.

He heard no sound, but a bloodlike liquid gushed from the punctured cup, splashing over Hermione who choked and gasped, and then they were sliding uncontrollably out of the vault on a great mass of gold and silver: the waiting goblins had removed the door.

only one thought in his head: goblins did not carry wands.

THE ESCAPE FROM GRINGOTTS

This is the very first handwritten draft of the scene in *Harry Potter and the Deathly Hallows* in which Harry, Ron and Hermione escape from Gringotts bank on the back of a dragon. The first page describes the dramatic escape, and a little arrow in the corner indicates that the scene continues on the previous page. There are many crossings-out and added sentences in both margins. The page on the right-hand side describes Harry destroying a cup, the Hufflepuff Horcrux, while his friends are still in the Lestranges' vault. This is an event that does not take place in the published text – instead Hermione is the one who destroys the cup.

> *"This manuscript demonstrates that J.K. Rowling did not necessarily write the scenes in her books in order, and that some of them were later rewritten. Note how Harry's dialogue is represented by a cross on the second page, to be filled in with something appropriate at a later stage."*
>
> JOANNA NORLEDGE
> *Curator*

◁ AN EARLY DRAFT OF *HARRY POTTER AND THE DEATHLY HALLOWS* BY J.K. ROWLING
J.K. Rowling

> *"When I'm planning I often have multiple ideas popping up at the same time, so I'm attempting to catch the best ones as they fly by and preserve them on paper. My notebooks are full of arrows and triple asterisks instructing me to move forward four pages, past the ideas I jotted down hurriedly twenty minutes ago, to continue the thread of the story."*

J.K. Rowling

ETHIOPIAN DRAGONS

On 13th May, 1572, the same day that Pope Gregory XIII was invested, a 'monstrous dragon' was found in the countryside near Bologna. Recognised as a bad omen, the dragon's body was consigned for analysis to the Pope's cousin, the celebrated naturalist and collector Ulisse Aldrovandi. Although Aldrovandi quickly wrote up his findings, his work was not published for nearly 60 years, appearing posthumously in 1640 as *A History of Snakes and Dragons.* Perhaps this is the sort of text that Hagrid might have needed when 'looking up stuff about dragons' for hatching Norbert, or when Harry was in the library pulling down 'every book he could find on dragons' for the Triwizard Tournament.

"Aldrovandi's study provides detailed descriptions of snakes, dragons and other monsters, explaining their temperament and habitat. Depicted here are two types of Ethiopian dragon, distinguishable by the ridges on their back."

ALEXANDER LOCK
Curator

ULISSE ALDROVANDI, *SERPENTUM ET DRACONUM HISTORIAE* (BOLOGNA, 1640)
British Library

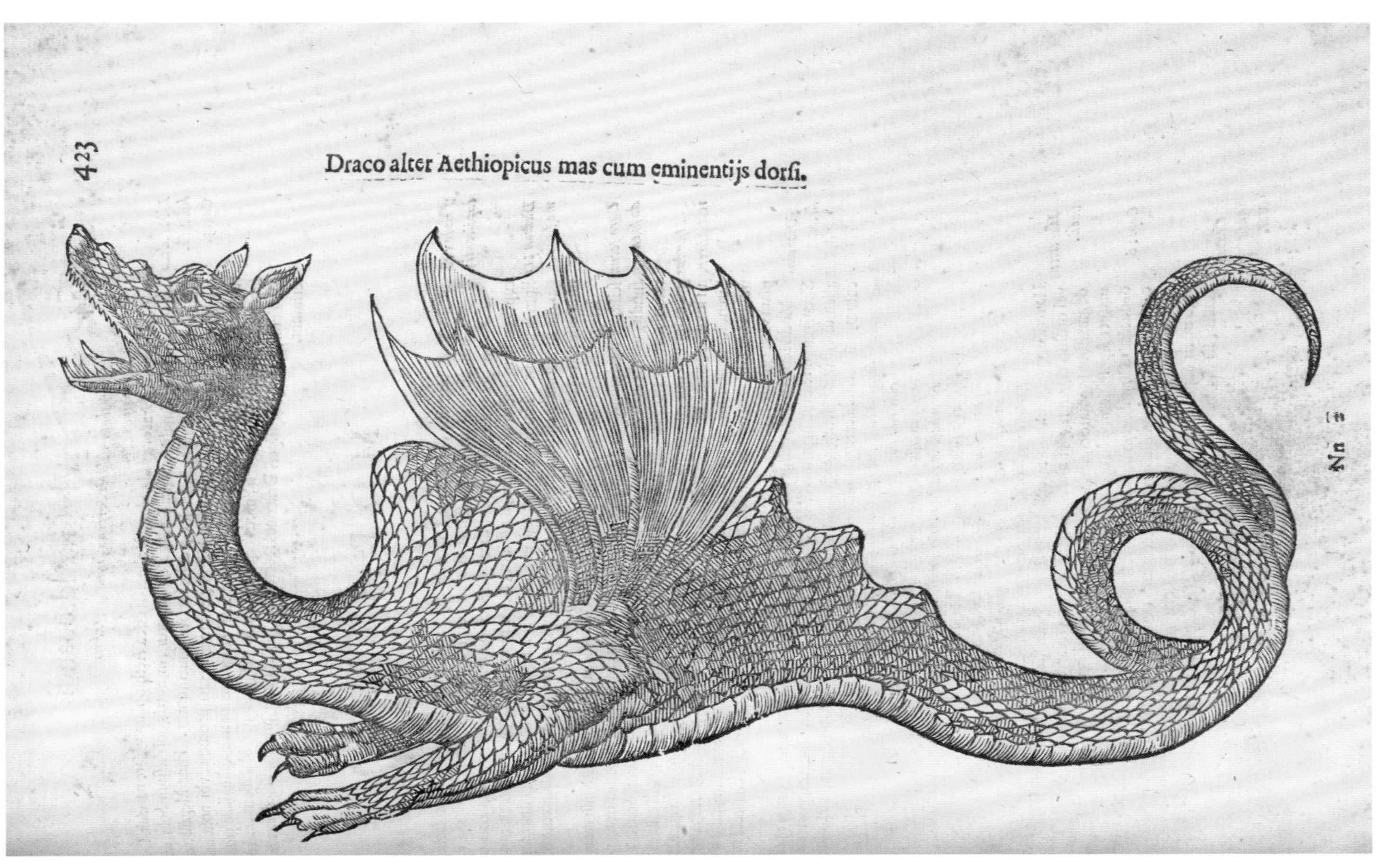

Probably the most famous of all magical beasts, dragons are among the most difficult to hide. The female is generally larger and more aggressive than the male, though neither should be approached by any but highly skilled and trained wizards.

Fantastic Beasts and Where to Find Them

All at once there was a scraping noise and the egg split open. The baby dragon flopped on to the table. It wasn't exactly pretty; Harry thought it looked like a crumpled, black umbrella.

Harry Potter and the Philosopher's Stone

DRAGON EGGS

Jim Kay's study of dragon eggs reflects the sheer variety of dragon species in Harry Potter's world. The artist painted the shape and base colours of the eggs first, then added and overlaid extra details and flecks of colour to the final versions. A scale to indicate the size of these eggs shows the smallest to be around six inches high (around the same size as an ostrich egg) and the largest up to fifteen inches. Some of the eggs are simple and almost ordinary looking, while others unmistakably belong in the magical world. All of the egg species would have been familiar, of course, to Newt Scamander.

DRAGON EGGS
BY JIM KAY
Bloomsbury

AN OUTSTANDING OWL

First Year students at Hogwarts were allowed to bring an owl, a cat or a toad to school – all animals with historic magical significance. In *The Philosopher's Stone*, Hagrid bought Harry a beautiful female snowy owl, which the boy named Hedwig. This hand-coloured and life-sized illustration of a pair of snowy owls appears in the enormous *Birds of America*, the first book to depict every bird native to North America. John James Audubon painted every bird at its actual size, fitting each illustration onto a giant sheet known as 'double elephant' paper. The finished book stands at just over a metre (three and a quarter feet) tall, requiring several people to lift it.

THE SNOWY OWL, IN JOHN JAMES AUDUBON, *THE BIRDS OF AMERICA* (LONDON, 1827–38)
British Library

> *"Snowy owls are native to Arctic regions of North America and Eurasia, their white feathers blending into a white landscape. The female snowy owl, perched in the foreground, has the more variegated feathers."*
>
> TANYA KIRK
> *Curator*

A CUNNING CAT

Conrad Gessner was a Swiss naturalist, whose *Historiae Animalium* is one of the earliest printed zoological texts. Gessner used realistic woodcuts to illustrate the animals being described, including enough detail to aid identification, unlike the earlier fable and bestiary collections. Cats already had a bad reputation – here they are said to possess '*ingenium calliditas*' (a cunning character). Edward Topsell, the first English translator of Gessner's work, noted, 'The familiars of witches do most ordinarily appear in the shape of cats, which is an argument that the beast is dangerous to soul and body.' Elsewhere, Gessner asserted that, 'men have been known to lose their strength, perspire violently, and even faint at the sight of a cat.'

➣ CONRAD GESSNER, *HISTORIAE ANIMALIUM* (ZÜRICH, 1551–87)
British Library

Something brushed his ankles. He looked down and saw the caretaker's skeletal grey cat, Mrs Norris, slinking past him. She turned lamplike yellow eyes on him for a moment before disappearing behind a statue of Wilfred the Wistful.

Harry Potter and the Order of the Phoenix

De Cato. A. Lib. I. 341

uulgò hodie apud Græ- ta, gatto. Hispanicè gá- t. Germanicè katz. An. czka. Furioz apud Al-) cato legitur, quod no- sumptum puto, & Ara- n esse: Albertus signifi- rauit, & alicubi pro ca- ice, ut supra dixi, ine- d catū esse constat, quo- bi Aristoteles de æluro; iusdem forsan originis n furo, quod uiuerram generem feli. Aegyptij cant, Stephanus: Hinc to ciuitati in Aegypto: bastin appellat: sacras habebant, ut infra di- lumellam (lib. 8. cap. 3.) .cap. 12.) feles accipi ui : enim uulgus appellat time infestam noxiāq; ta contrucidantē, Phi- eles Varronis & Colu marturellus uidetur, ibi, felis est, inquit, quę a: ictis, marturus uel a uero, donula. Sed de stela dicam. Meles a- um, puto esse id quod marturellum appellat, n litera M. in Enarra- uocum: citat aūt Var- st. lib. 3. cap. 12. ubi sic ignorat septa è mace-

in leporario, ut tectorio tecta sint, & sint alta. Alterum ne feles, aut meles, aliáu ossit: alterum, ne lepus transilire. Ego Ge. Alexandrinum felem interpretari uo memoria melem (quem suo loco taxum uulgò dictum esse docebo) posuisse pu o siue domestico siue syluestri apud ueteres authores semper acceperim. Erran it martem dici, Perottus. ¶ Γαλῆ Græcis mustelam significat, diuersum à fel- robat Perottus in Cornucop. Recentiores tamen quidam Græci, ut Galeomyo b ijs decepti quidam Latini, γαλῆν pro cato accipiunt. Sunt sanè quędam horun & cati, naturis communia, ut corporis ferè figura, & ingenium: calliditas, ui enatus: utrunq; fœtus suos ore de loco in locum transfert, ut & canes interdum non solum γαλῆν simpliciter, sed sæpe γαλῆν κατοικίδιον, id est domesticam, & ir uersantem uocitant: sunt autem ubiq; cati domestici, mustelæ nimirum nō item occasio fuisse illis uidentur, qui galen pro cato interpretantur. Miror autē no atus est apud ueteres Græcos, quo nomine mustelam ijdem appellarint. Michae iræcis scholijs in lib. 3. de gener. animal. cap. 29. γαλῆν exponit catam, ut refer iza γαλῆν non semper mustelam transfert, sed aliquando catum: ut galen agrian larcellum Vergilium quoq; mustelam domesticam, felem existimasse, appare is in Dioscoridis caput de mustela domestica, & in caput de lychnide. Feles ge abet: mustela, ictis, lupus & uulpes habent, Sipontinus. Mustelæ hyeme cubant ur, Aristot. Hoc mustelis accidere (inquit Sipontinus) compertum est: quod ips unc usum utriusq; generis (paruis & magnis, siue domesticis & rusticis) muste ti sumus: hoc cati non faciunt, sed neq; in cauernis uersantur, nec ingredi eas fa rent aues: quorum utrunq; mustelis tribuitur. Plinius certe pro æluro ex Aristo ddit, pro gale mustelam. Hæc si cui non satisfaciunt, collatis cati quam hic tradi M. litera, historijs, ipse iudicet. Carolus Figulus uir eruditus utraq; lingua, dialo idit, in quo similiter ęluron pro fele, galen pro mustela semper exponi debere con t. in prouerbijs γαλῆ ταρτησία, & γαλῆ κροκωτόν, pro gale felē posuit, dubitando ta his uerbis: Porrò uox hæc gale, felémne significet an mustelam, an quem uulgo

At long last, the train stopped at Hogsmeade station, and there was a great scramble to get out; owls hooted, cats miaowed, and Neville's pet toad croaked loudly from under his hat.

Harry Potter and the Prisoner of Azkaban

▲ J.B. VON SPIX, *ANIMALIA NOVA, SIVE SPECIES NOVÆ TESTUDINUM ET RANARUM, QUAS IN ITINERE PER BRASILIAM ANNIS 1817–1820 ... COLLEGIT, ET DESCRIPSIT* (MUNICH, 1824)
British Library

A TOXIC TOAD

Toads have long featured in magical folklore, their properties ranging from predicting the weather to bringing good luck. When Johann Baptist von Spix, the German biologist, visited Brazil he described this species of toad, *Bufo auga*, also known as the cane toad or giant marine toad. The cane is the world's largest toad, recognisable for its unwebbed hands and feet, its brown-coloured iris and the venom glands dotted across the surface of its skin, which produce a toxic milky secretion. Unfortunately, it is dangerous to many animals, such as dogs. At Hogwarts, Neville Longbottom's pet toad Trevor seemed much more benign.

"Toads often feature in old folk remedies for common ailments and complaints. Rubbing a toad on a wart was said to cure it, but only if you impaled the toad and left it to die."

JOANNA NORLEDGE
Curator

RON AND HARRY MEET ARAGOG

Imagine, if your greatest fear was spiders, how you might feel meeting an Acromantula. Jim Kay's image of the horrific spider captures every creepy detail of the carnivorous creature that Harry and Ron encountered in the Forbidden Forest. In the background, hundreds of spiders' legs become indistinguishable from the spiky trees around them. Strands of cobwebs gleam white in Harry's wandlight. Aragog is the originator of this spider colony – a combination of too many eyes and too many horribly hairy legs. This painting was layered with a watercolour tone and edited to create the final image.

ARAGOG BY JIM KAY
Bloomsbury

[...] a spider the size of a small elephant emerged, very slowly. There was grey in the black of his body and legs, and each of the eyes on his ugly, pincered head was milky white.

Harry Potter and the Chamber of Secrets

BIRD-EATING SPIDERS

Maria Sibylla Merian was a pioneering naturalist and zoological illustrator, celebrated for her ground-breaking work on South American insects. Between 1699 and 1701, Merian worked in the Dutch colony of Surinam, where she made the drawings of these arachnids for this book. This was a highly unusual place to visit, and Merian's scientific expedition was reputedly the first to be led by a European woman. Like Hagrid, who cared for Aragog when he 'was only a boy', Merian's fascination with insects developed in childhood. Many of the species first encountered by Merian in Surinam were unknown to Western science.

➢ MARIA SIBYLLA MERIAN, *METAMORPHOSIS INSECTORUM SURINAMENSIUM* (AMSTERDAM, 1705)
British Library

"When Merian published this image of giant, bird-eating spiders, she was denounced as a fantasist by her male peers. Her hand-painted books nevertheless sold well, but it was not until 1863 that the genuine existence of this bird-eating spider was finally accepted."

ALEXANDER LOCK
Curator

BUCKBEAK THE HIPPOGRIFF

In this Jim Kay illustration, Buckbeak has taken over his beloved owner's bed, a snack of dead ferrets resting under his claws. Hagrid received orders from the Ministry of Magic to tether the hippogriff, but he could not bear to leave 'Beaky' tied up outside, alone in the snow. The interior of Hagrid's cabin was drawn from the real life gardener's hut at Calke Abbey. The vibrant blue highlights echo the famous bluebells that grow there. The word *hippogriff* is derived from the ancient Greek for 'horse' and the Italian for 'griffin'. The griffin, with its eagle's head and lion's hindquarters, is said to be the hippogriff's ancestor.

▲ BUCKBEAK THE HIPPOGRIFF BY JIM KAY
Bloomsbury

CANTO . VI .

ORLANDO FURIOSO

Ludovico Ariosto was the first to describe the hippogriff in 1516 in his epic poem *Orlando Furioso*. The verse was inspired by the Roman author Virgil, who used the union of a horse with a griffin as a metaphor for the irrationality of ill-fated love – a central theme in *Orlando Furioso*. In this 18th-century illustration, the knight, Ruggiero, has tethered his hippogriff mount to a tree. Unbeknown to him, the tree was actually another knight who had been transformed by an evil sorceress. Her monstrous minions can be seen approaching in the background.

◄ LUDOVICO ARIOSTO, *ORLANDO FURIOSO* (VENICE, 1772–3)
British Library

> *"This luxury edition of* Orlando Furioso *was printed on vellum (calf skin). It once belonged to King George III."*
>
> ALEXANDER LOCK
> *Curator*

HUNTING THE UNICORN

Ever since the Greek physician Ctesias first described the medicinal properties of unicorns around 400 BC, these elusive animals have attracted human hunters. This image of the killing and skinning of the 'pirassoipi', a twin-horned unicorn, is found in a study by Ambroise Paré, surgeon to the French crown. Unsurprisingly, the hunters in the scene have a cruel appearance. As Firenze told Harry in *The Philosopher's Stone*, 'it is a monstrous thing, to slay a unicorn'.

➢ AMBROISE PARÉ, *DISCOURS D'AMBROISE PARÉ, CONSEILLER, ET PREMIER CHIRURGIEN DU ROY. ASÇAVOIR, DE LA MUMIE, DE LA LICORNE, DES VENINS, ET DE LA PESTE* (PARIS, 1582)

British Library

The unicorn is a beautiful beast found throughout the forests of northern Europe. It is a pure white, horned horse when fully grown, though the foals are initially golden and turn silver before achieving maturity.

Fantastic Beasts and Where to Find Them

A LION-LIKE UNICORN

This unusual unicorn appears in a 16th-century Greek manuscript. The accompanying text is a poem about the natural world composed by the Byzantine poet Manuel Philes. According to the poem, the unicorn was a wild beast with a dangerous bite – it had the tail of a boar and the mouth of a lion. If such a unicorn was encountered, the beast could only be snared by a woman. This is in line with medieval folklore stipulating that unicorns must be captured by female virgins. The unicorn would place its head in the virgin's lap and then fall asleep, allowing the hunter to sneak up on it unawares.

➢ MANUEL PHILES, *ON THE PROPERTIES OF ANIMALS* (PARIS, 16TH CENTURY)
British Library

des Drogues, Livre Premier. 9

CHAPITRE II.

De la Licorne.

LA LICORNE, eſt un animal que les Naturaliſtes nous dépeignent ſous la figure d'un Cheval, ayant au milieu du front une Corne en ſpirale, de deux à trois pied de long: mais comme l'on n'a pû, juſques aujourd'huy, ſçavoir la verité de la choſe; je diray que celle que nous vendons, ſous le nom de Corne de Licorne, eſt la Corne d'un Poiſſon que les Iſlandois appellent Narvual comme on le verra, cy-aprés, au chapitre des poiſſons.

Cette Corne eſtoit autrefois beaucoup en uſage, à cauſe des grandes proprietez que les anciens luy attribuoient, principalement contre les poiſons, c'eſt ce qui faiſoit que les grands Seigneurs en eſtoient fort amateurs, & pour ce ſujet elle eſtoit venduë au poids de l'or. Cette erreur a eſté tellement établie, & il y a encore quelques perſonnes qui en ſont ſi fort entêtées, qu'il leur en faut à quelque prix que ce ſoit.

» Ambroiſe Paré, dans un petit Traité qu'il a compoſé da la Licorne, dit que
» dans l'Arabie deſerte, il s'y trouve des Aſnes ſauvages, qu'ils appellent Camphurs, Camphurs.
» portant une corne au front, avec laquelle ils combattent contre les Taureaux,
» & dont les Indiens ſe ſervent pour ſe garantir de pluſieurs maladies, particulie-
» rement des veneneuſes; & qu'en Arabie, prés de la Mer rouge, il ſe trouve un

II. Partie. B

FIVE SPECIES OF UNICORN

The *Histoire générale des Drogues* was a practical manual that described an array of popular 17th-century medicinal ingredients. It was written by Pierre Pomet, a Parisian pharmacist and chief apothecary to King Louis XIV of France. In the chapter on the unicorn, Pomet would not confirm the animal's existence, conceding that 'we know not the real truth of the matter', but he did acknowledge that what was commonly sold as unicorn's horn 'is the horn of a certain fish called narwhal'. According to Pomet, whatever its origin, the horn was 'well used, on account of the great properties attributed to it, principally against poisons'.

◁ PIERRE POMET, *HISTOIRE GÉNÉRALE DES DROGUES, TRAITANT DES PLANTES, DES ANIMAUX ET DES MINERAUX* (PARIS, 1694)
British Library

"Accompanying Pomet's text are the images of five different species of unicorn. These are the camphur (a horned ass from Arabia), the pirassoipi (a unicorn with twin horns) and three unidentified breeds noted by the naturalist John Johnstone in 1632."

ALEXANDER LOCK
Curator

'Harry Potter, do you know what unicorn blood is used for?'
'No,' said Harry, startled by the odd question. 'We've only used the horn and tail-hair in Potions.'

Harry Potter and the Philosopher's Stone

FAWKES THE PHOENIX

Harry Potter first met Fawkes the phoenix in Dumbledore's office in his second year. It happened to be a 'Burning Day', meaning that the bird burst into flames and was reborn from the ashes before Harry's very eyes. Later, the fully grown Fawkes came to Harry's rescue in the Chamber of Secrets. Jim Kay's glorious painting of the bird captures the brilliant reds and golds of the phoenix's feathers. The image seems to soar across the surface of the page, almost taking off at the edges. Kay has also painted details of the feathers, the egg and the eye, which were used in the final composite image.

➢ STUDY OF THE PHOENIX BY JIM KAY
Bloomsbury

> *"Jim Kay's delicate study of the single phoenix feather shows how the different colours blend, in a similar way to that of less exotic birds such as the mallard."*
>
> JOANNA NORLEDGE
> *Curator*

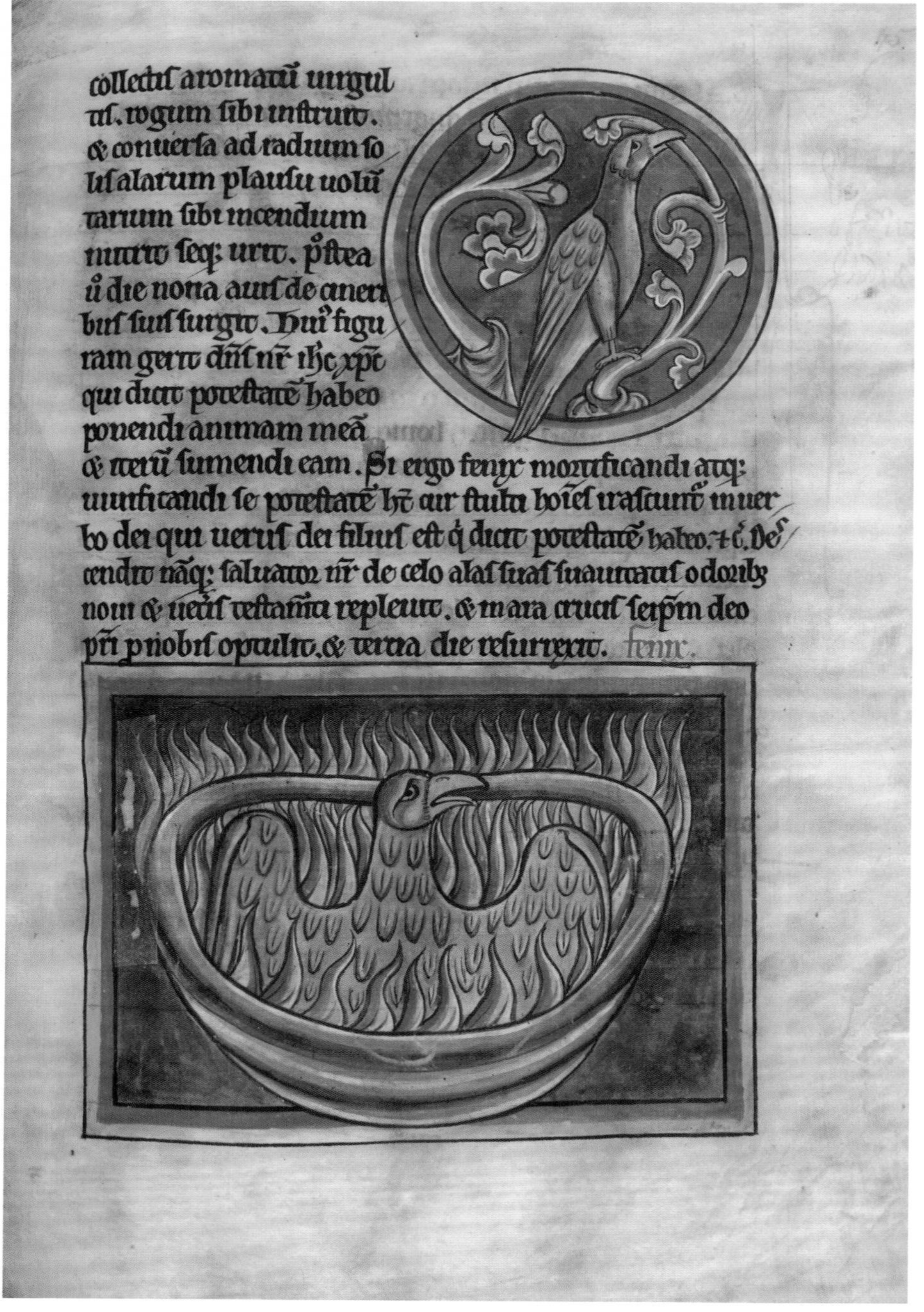
collectis aromatū uirgul
tis, rogum sibi instruit.
& conuersa ad radium so
lis alarum plausu uolū
tarium sibi incendium
nutrit seq; urit. p̄stea
ū die nona auis de cineri
bus suis surgit. Huius figu
ram gerit dn̄s nr̄ ih̄c xp̄c
qui dicit potestatē habeo
ponendi animam meā
& iterū sumendi eam. Si ergo fenix mortificandi atq;
uiuificandi se potestatē hn̄ cur stulti hoīes irascunt̄ in uer
bo dei qui uerus dei filius est q̄ dicit potestatē habeo. + c. Des
cendit naq; saluator nr̄ de celo alas suas suauitatis odorib;
noui & ueť testamenti repleuit. & in ara crucis se ipm̄ deo
pr̄i p nobis optulit. & tertia die resurrexit. fenix.

RISING FROM THE FLAMES

This 13th-century bestiary describes and illustrates the phoenix in wonderful detail. The bird's most remarkable attribute is its ability to resurrect itself in old age. It creates its own funeral pyre from branches and plants, before fanning the flames with its own wings, in order to be consumed by the fire. After the ninth day, it rises again from the ashes. This legendary ability has often been compared to the self-sacrifice and Resurrection of Christ – in some traditions, the phoenix signifies the eternal life of the faithful Christian.

THE PHOENIX IN A MEDIEVAL BESTIARY (ENGLAND, 13TH CENTURY)
British Library

"The phoenix is a semi-mythical bird, seldom spotted and, according to Newt Scamander, rarely domesticated by wizards. This bestiary claims that the phoenix dwells in Arabia, but Newt Scamander extended its distribution to Egypt, India and China."

JULIAN HARRISON
Lead Curator

The bird, meanwhile, had become a fireball; it gave one loud shriek and next second there was nothing but a smouldering pile of ash on the floor.

Harry Potter and the Chamber of Secrets

DESCRIPTION DV PHOE-
nix, & du lieu heureux de ſa reſidence, de
ſa longue vie, pure conuerſation, beaul-
té excellente, diuerſité de ſes cou-
leurs, & de ſa fin & reſur-
rection admirable.

LE ſouuerain Architecte du monde,
Voulut dreſſer ceſte machine ronde,
Comme vn parfaict & grand amphi-
teatre, C j. On

THE HISTORY AND DESCRIPTION OF THE PHOENIX

In 1550, when global exploration was in its infancy and new animals were being constantly discovered, the French author Guy de la Garde devoted an entire study to the phoenix. This fine volume features a hand-coloured picture of the creature emerging from a burning tree. The translated caption reads: 'A description of the phoenix and its fortunate place of residence, of its long life, pure conversation, excellent beauty, diverse colours, and of its end and remarkable resurrection.' De la Garde dedicated the book to Princess Marguerite, a patron of the arts and sister of King Henri II of France, probably in an attempt to gain her favour through association with this miraculous bird.

A PHOENIX, IN GUY DE LA GARDE, *L'HISTOIRE ET DESCRIPTION DU PHOENIX* (PARIS, 1550)
British Library

"Phoenixes are historically associated with the Sun. The crest of seven feathers on the bird's head corresponds to the seven rays which traditionally emit from the head of Helios, the Greek god of the Sun."

TANYA KIRK
Curator

THE SIMURGH, AN IRANIAN THUNDERBIRD

Like the phoenix or the thunderbird, its North American relative, the Iranian simurgh's exact form and qualities are much disputed. It was traditionally portrayed in pre-Islamic Iran as a composite creature with a snarling canine head, forward-pointing ears, wings and a 'peacock' tail. In Persian literature, however, the simurgh was usually depicted in flight with fantastic swirling tail feathers. It is best known in this culture as the bird who reared the hero Zal on a mountain top and healed the wounded warrior Rustam. Subsequently, as king of the birds, the simurgh became a metaphor for God in Sufi mysticism.

MAJMA' AL-GHARA'IB 'COLLECTION OF RARITIES', BY SULTAN MUHAMMAD BALKHI (INDIA, 1698)
British Library

> *"This bestiary was especially popular in Central Asia. In it the author describes the simurgh as strong enough to easily carry off an elephant. It is said to lay an egg once every three hundred years."*
>
> URSULA SIMS-WILLIAMS
> *Curator*

A REAL MERMAID

Here is proof, if proof were ever needed, that mermaids really do exist. This specimen was presented to the British Museum in 1942 by Princess Alexandra, second Duchess of Fife and granddaughter of King Edward VII. It had allegedly been caught in Japan some 200 years previously. According to an accompanying note, the mermaid had been given to Princess Alexandra's late husband, Prince Arthur of Connaught. Somewhat disappointingly, this particular mermaid is actually a fake. It has the upper body of a monkey and the tail of a fish. The creature is testament to an 18th-century East Asian fad for fabricating merpeople, often for display in European drawing rooms.

A MERMAID (JAPAN, 18TH CENTURY)
British Museum

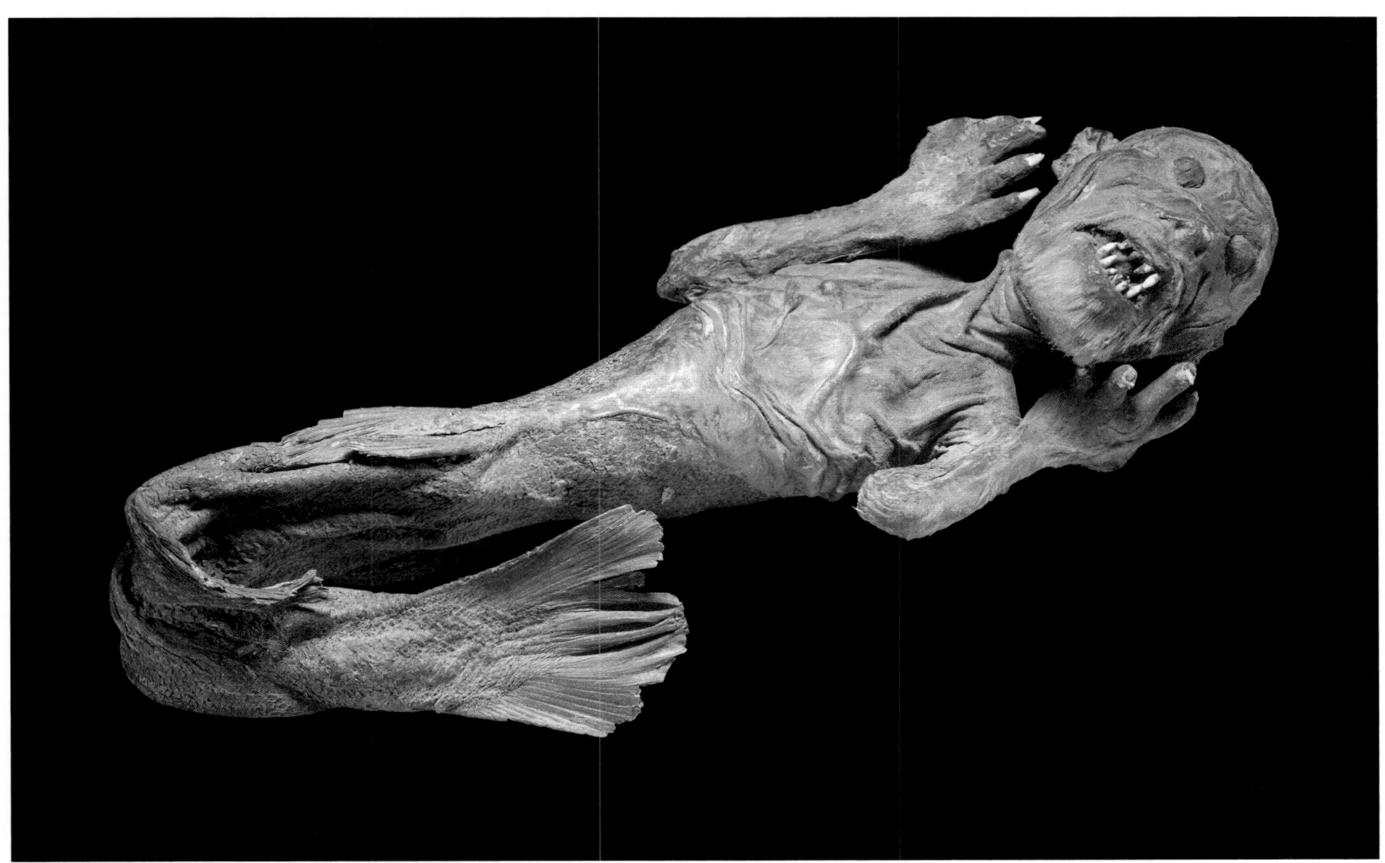

The merpeople had greyish skins and long, wild, dark green hair. Their eyes were yellow, as were their broken teeth, and they wore thick ropes of pebbles around their necks.

Harry Potter and the Goblet of Fire

I wondered whether the mer-people scene actually works? After all, we don't see them again... what if, as an alternative, the car suddenly develops underwater boosters or something – and suddenly shoots out of the water? Might help pace too?

64

"Oh, well - a fish -" said Harry, "A fish isn't going to do anything to us... I thought it might be the giant squid."

There was a pause in which Harry wished he hadn't thought about the giant squid.

"There's loads of them," said Ron, swivelling round and gazing out of the rear window.

Harry felt as though tiny spiders were crawling up his spine. Large dark shadows were circling the car.

"If it's just fish..." he repeated.

And then, into the light, swam something Harry had never expected to see as long as he lived.

It was a woman. A cloud of blackest hair, thick and tangled like seaweed, floated all around her. Her lower body was a great, scaly fishtail the colour of gun-metal; ropes of shells and pebbles hung about her neck; her skin was a pale, silvery grey and her eyes, flashing in the headlights, looked dark and threatening. She gave a powerful flick of her tail and sped into the darkness.

"Was that a *mermaid?"* said Harry.

"Well, it wasn't the giant squid," said Ron.

There was a crunching noise and the car suddenly shifted.

Harry scrambled about to press his face against the back window. About ten merpeople, bearded men as well as long haired women, were straining against the car, their tails swishing behind them.

"Where are they going to take us?" said Ron, pannicking.

The mermaid they had seen first rapped on the window next to Harry and made a circular motion with her silvery hand.

"I think they're going to flip us over," said Harry quickly, "Hold on -"

'WAS THAT A MERMAID?'

This deleted scene from *Harry Potter and the Chamber of Secrets* shows Harry and Ron crashing their enchanted Ford Anglia into the lake at Hogwarts instead of the Whomping Willow. In this version of the story, the boys are saved by the merpeople, who flip the car over and drag it to the safety of the bank. The first mermaid that Harry saw had a lower body that was 'a great, scaly fishtail the colour of gun-metal'. We are told that the creature's eyes, 'flashing in the headlights, looked dark and threatening'. At the top of page 64, the editor has written a note questioning this scene, perhaps prompting the rewriting of the chapter.

◂ THE DELETED MERPEOPLE SCENE BY J.K. ROWLING, FROM *HARRY POTTER AND THE CHAMBER OF SECRETS* ▸
Bloomsbury

"In this draft chapter, one of the mermaids speaks to Harry and Ron in English, above the surface of the water. This contrasts with the later published texts in which merpeople can only speak Mermish above water."

JOANNA NORLEDGE
Curator

They grabbed the door hands and slowly, as the mer-people pushed and strained, the car turned right over onto its wheels, clouds of silt fogging the water. Hedwig was beating her wings furiously against the bars of her cage again.

The mer-people were now binding thick, slimy ropes of lakeweed around the car and tying the ends around their own waists. Then, with Harry and Ron sitting in the front seats hardly daring to breathe, they pulled... the car was lifted off the bottom and rose, towed by the mer-people, to the surface.

"Yes!" said Ron, as they saw the starry sky again through their drenched windows.

The mer-people in front looked like seals, their sleek heads just visible as they towed the car towards the bank. A few feet from the grassy bank, they felt the wheels touch the pebbly ground of the lake again. The mer-people sank out of sight. Then the first mermaid bobbed up at Harry's window and rapped on it. He unwound it quickly.

"We can take you no further," she said. She had a strange voice, it was both screechy and hoarse. "The rocks are sharp in the shallows, but legs are not so easily torn as fins..."

"No," said Harry, nervously, "Look, we can't thank you enough..."

The mermaid gave a little flick of her tail and was gone.

"Come on, I need food..." said Ron, who was shivering.

They opened the doors of the car with difficulty, picked up Hedwig and Scabbers, braced themselves and jumped down into the freezing water, which came up above Harry's thighs. They waded to the bank and climbed out.

"Not as pretty as they look in books, are they, mermaids?" said Ron, trying to wring out his jeans. "Of course, they were lake people... maybe in a warm sea..."

Harry didn't answer; he was having trouble with Hedwig, who had clearly had enough of wizard transport. He let her out of her cage and she soared off at once towards a high tower which housed all the school owls.

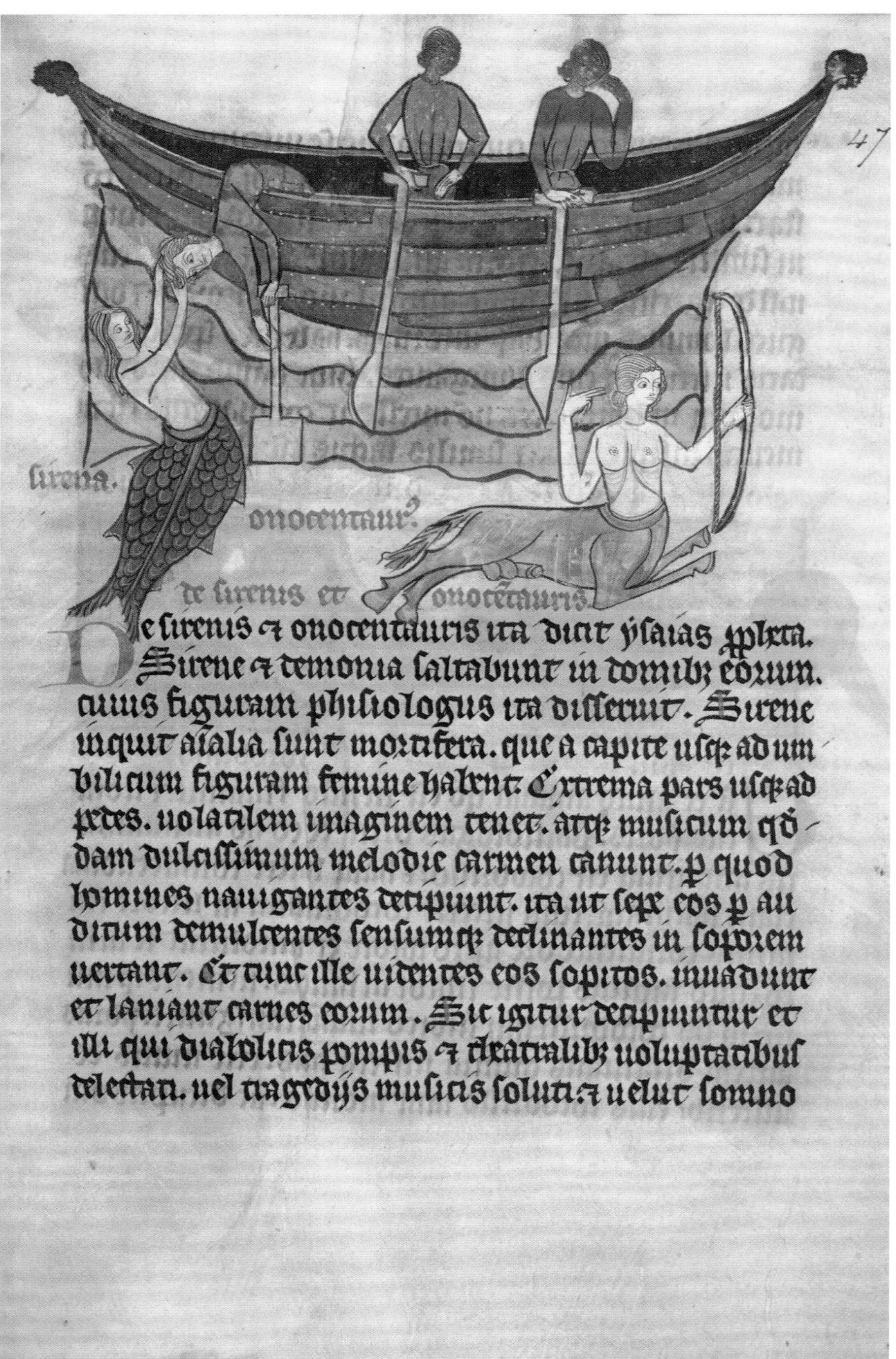

De sirenis et onocentauris ita dicit ysaias propheta.
Sirene et demonia saltabunt in domibus eorum.
cuius figuram phisiologus ita disseruit. Sirene
inquit animalia sunt mortifera. que a capite usque ad um
bilicum figuram femine habent. Extrema pars usque ad
pedes. uolatilem imaginem tenet. atque musicum quo
dam dulcissimum melodie carmen canunt. per quod
homines nauigantes decipiunt. ita ut sepe eos per au
ditum demulcentes sensumque declinantes in soporem
uertant. Et tunc ille uidentes eos sopitos. inuadunt
et laniant carnes eorum. Sic igitur decipiuntur et
illi qui diabolicis pompis et theatralibus uoluptatibus
delectati. uel tragedijs musicis soluti et uelut somno

AN ENCHANTING SIREN

Merpeople play a key role in the second task of the Triwizard Tournament, in *Harry Potter and the Goblet of Fire.* When Harry dives into the lake in search of Ron Weasley, he encounters 'A choir of merpeople [...] singing in the middle, calling the champions towards them [...] would they pull him back down to the depths when the time was up? Did they perhaps eat humans?' Such sinister qualities are shared by the sirens in this book. A medieval siren is usually a creature with a woman's head and a bird's body, but here it is depicted with a fish-like tail. The text reports that the siren has a violent nature – she enchants sailors with her birdsong and voluptuous body, before dragging them from their ships to eat their flesh.

A SIREN IN A MEDIEVAL BESTIARY (FRANCE?, 13TH CENTURY)
British Library

> *"Another fantastical creature appears in this illustration. An onocentaur is shown looking on from the shore. The onocentaur has the body of a man as far as the navel, and the body of an ass below."*
>
> JULIAN HARRISON
> *Lead Curator*

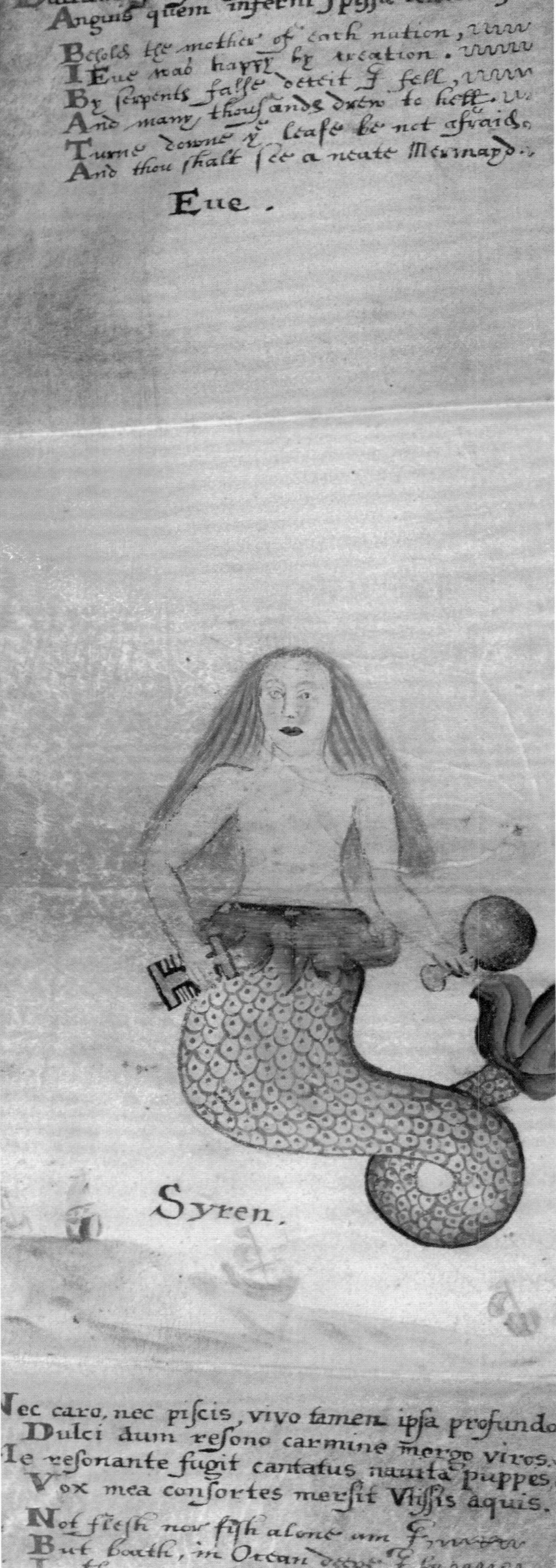

A GAME BOOK

This 'game book', dating from the early 17th century, was possibly made as a love token. The parchment has been folded into a concertina, with each section depicting an animal. A series of flaps overlays each portion of the manuscript, and can be opened or closed to create different types of creature. The game book includes mythical beasts such as dragons, manticores and griffins, which can be transformed using the features of real animals such as monkeys, snakes and lions. This mermaid can be given legs to become a woman or a man's head to become a fish-man. Although she appears different from the merpeople at Hogwarts, she is not to be trusted. The accompanying poem describes how the mermaid lured sailors, 'Who leaving off their ship were found, On shore, by my enchantments drown'd.'

A GAME BOOK
(ENGLAND, 17TH CENTURY)
British Library

The oldest recorded merpeople were known as sirens (Greece) and it is in warmer waters that we find the beautiful mermaids so frequently depicted in Muggle literature and painting.

Fantastic Beasts and Where to Find Them

THE GRAPHORN

This portrait of the aggressive Graphorn shows a large humped-back creature, with two horns and a heavy tail. According to Newt Scamander's *Fantastic Beasts and Where to Find Them*, the creature could be found in the mountainous regions of Europe. Olivia Lomenech Gill's evocative illustration shows how potentially dangerous J.K. Rowling's creation could be. The beast is shown scraping the ground with its 'large, four-thumbed feet' ready to take on anyone foolish enough to stray too close. The artist has skilfully used highlights of colour to add texture to the Graphorn's gnarled, greyish purple skin.

➢ DRAWING OF THE GRAPHORN BY OLIVIA LOMENECH GILL
Bloomsbury

Mountain trolls can occasionally be seen mounted on Graphorns, though the latter do not seem to take kindly to attempts to tame them and it is more common to see a troll covered in Graphorn scars.

Fantastic Beasts and Where to Find Them

Like the Snallygaster, the Hodag is a North American creature whose antics have excited considerable Muggle interest and curiosity.

Fantastic Beasts and Where to Find Them

A DRAWING OF THE SNALLYGASTER BY OLIVIA LOMENECH GILL

Bloomsbury

THE SNALLYGASTER

The Snallygaster is a creature of North American origin, said to have been named by Dutch settlers in the 1730s. The creature was added to the 2017 edition of *Fantastic Beasts and Where to Find Them.* Half bird, half serpent, the Snallygaster's name is derived from *schnell geiste*, a Pennsylvania Dutch term meaning 'quick spirit'. Despite its status as a mythological creature, numerous sightings of the flying beast have been reported in Frederick County, Maryland. *Valley Register*, a newspaper in Middletown, featured several stories from February to March 1909, describing the Snallygaster's enormous wings, long sharp beak and fierce claws. The next recorded sighting occurred 23 years later. The last unsuccessful search for the Snallygaster took place in 1976.

THE HODAG

The Hodag is another North American beast. Although rooted in legend, sightings have been reported in the Wisconsin area over the years, with many local stories springing up around it. The residents of Wisconsin describe a creature allegedly made of a frog's head with an elephant's face, a spiky, reptilian back and a long tail topped off with a hook-of-death. Painfully aware of its gruesome appearance, the Hodag was, according to legend, prone to fits of weeping over its ugliness. This atmospheric illustration by Olivia Lomenech Gill shows the beast as known to Magizoologists in *Fantastic Beasts and Where to Find Them.*

"The Hodag can reputedly be destroyed by dynamite, chloroform and lemons. The first person to catch and kill one, Eugene Shephard, also admitted to being behind many a Hodag hoax."

JOANNA NORLEDGE
Curator

DRAWING OF THE HODAG BY OLIVIA LOMENECH GILL
Bloomsbury

Past, Present, Future

Past, Present, Future

Steve Kloves

Steve Kloves is a writer and director. In addition to his seven Harry Potter film adaptations, his work includes Racing with the Moon, Wonder Boys, Flesh and Bone and The Fabulous Baker Boys, the latter two which he also directed.

About twenty years ago – remarkable to think it's been that long and then again, in some ways, it feels like a lifetime – I received an envelope from my literary agency. Contained within were half a dozen synopses of novels that – theoretically – could provide fodder for films. For someone like me, a screenwriter, these envelopes were a familiar sight. They arrived with relative consistency every few weeks and with absolute consistency I ignored them.

But for some reason – to this day I know not why – I decided to open this particular envelope.

I made quick work of the contents, moving from one synopsis to another, utterly unpersuaded, when I came to the last. It concerned a book with a fanciful title written by an author of whom I'd never heard: *Harry Potter and the Philosopher's Stone*, by J.K. Rowling.

The title was, as I say, undeniably fanciful, as was the author's name, but I still wasn't persuaded. Then my eye fell on the 'log line'. For those who don't know – and why would one? – a log line is a snappy summation of a book – a synopsis of a synopsis – ideally expressed in one sentence. More akin to ad copy than literature and about as reliable, it's meant to provide busy (i.e. lazy) screenwriters a quick way to sift the wheat from the chaff. For example, if the log line reads, 'Two teens start a detective agency on the Moon,' you know you can stop there. (Unless of course you actually think a movie about two teens who start a detective agency on the Moon is a good idea.) Anyway, in this instance, here was the log line:

A young boy goes to wizards' school.

On most days back then such a thing wouldn't have remotely intrigued me. I was hardly a fantasy aficionado. My tastes ran to Raymond Carver, not Tolkien. But I found myself reading it again.

A young boy goes to wizards' school.

Five minutes later I was standing in the bookshop down the street from my office asking the clerk if by any chance she'd heard of a book entitled *Harry Potter and*

Quirrell, however, must have be[...]
the weeks that followed he did
ner, but it didn't look as though
Every time they passed the th
Hermione would press their ears
was still growling inside. Snape
bad temper, which surely mean
Whenever Harry passed Quirrel
encouraging sort of smile, and Ro
for laughing at Quirrell's stutter.
Hermione, however, had mo
Philosopher's Stone. She had start
tables and colour-coding all her n
have minded, but she kept nagging
'Hermione, the exams are ages aw
'Ten weeks,' Hermione snapped.
second to Nicolas Flamel.'
'But we're not six hundred year
'Anyway, what are you revising for, yo
'What am I revising for? Are you n
pass these exams to get into the secon
tant, I should have started studying a
what's got into me ...'

— CHAPTER SEVENTEEN—

The Man with Two Faces

It was Quirrell.

'*You!*' gasped Harry.

Quirrell smiled. His face wasn't twitching at all.

'Me,' he said calmly. 'I wondered whether I'd be meeting you here, Potter.'

'But I thought – Snape –'

'Severus?' Quirrell laughed and it wasn't his usual quivering treble, either, but cold and sharp. 'Yes, Severus does seem the type, doesn't he? So useful to have him swooping around like an overgrown bat. Next to him, who would suspect p-p-poor st-stuttering P-Professor Quirrell?'

Harry couldn't take it in. This couldn't be true, it couldn't.

[...] kill me!' [...] friend Miss Granger acci-

the Philosopher's Stone. She wrinkled her brow and said, 'If we have it, it'll be in the International section.' Leading me there – the 'International section' wholly comprised of two short rows – she plucked a slim volume from the shelf and handed it to me.

While I would later come to have affection for it, the cover illustration of a distracted (and seemingly university-aged) Harry about to be run down by the Hogwarts Express was not promising on first encounter. At best, it looked like another run-of-the-mill children's book. Then I opened to the first page:

Mr and Mrs Dursley, of number four, Privet Drive, were proud to say that they were perfectly normal, thank you very much.

I stopped. Blinked. Read it again. Snapped the book shut, paid the clerk and five minutes later, back in my office, read that first sentence for a third time. And kept reading, through lunch, into the afternoon, stopping only once, about 30 pages in, to call my agent.

'I think I've found what I want to do next. It's called *Harry Potter and the Philosopher's Stone.*'

Silence. Then … 'Say that again?'

'It's about a boy who goes to wizards' school.'

Silence. Then … nothing.

'I'm serious. It's really good. It's better than good. It's special. If it stays special I want to do it.'

Suffice it to say, on that day, as I rushed headlong through the pages of this wonderfully strange book with the fanciful title, the light growing ever more faint outside the windows of an office I no longer possess, I could never have imagined I was about to embark on a remarkable journey, that I was but one of a legion of fellow travellers around the world embarking on the same journey, all of us falling under the spell of this unknown author, J.K. Rowling, a spell that, twenty years on, only grows more powerful.

Yes, it stayed special. Then, now, forever.

They gambolled and preened

> Undignified and foolish, dependent on the whims of a woman.

> Locked up his heart.

> His friends and his family laughed to see him so

not knowing what he had done

aloof. 'All will change,' they prophesied, 'when he ~~falls in love~~ meets the right ~~[illegible]~~ maiden.'

But the young man did not fall in love. All around him young ~~his friends~~ men and women ~~played~~ were raised to ecstasy or ~~else~~ plunged to despair by the vagaries of ~~love~~ desire and affection, ~~and~~ but the warlock walked unscathed through their midst, a cold smile upon his handsome mouth. He cared naught for anyone ~~or~~ or anything, ~~except~~ and he was proud ~~of it and for the fact to have~~ for ~~his own~~ ~~[illegible]~~ ~~untainted and uninjured heart, locked up safe in its enchanted box.~~ that it was so.

Now his friends began, first, to ~~marry~~ wed, and then to have children. More than ever he was pleased to ~~visit his untainted and uninjured heart,~~ think of his untainted and uninjured heart, safe in its enchanted box. '~~They are at~~ Their hearts must be ~~torn~~ ~~shrivel~~,' he ~~said~~ told himself, ~~'they give and give,~~ and ~~'endlessly they give to their~~ ~~by the needs of~~ these brats, ~~these brats'~~ ~~parasites~~ ~~sucked~~ shrivelled and dry ~~by~~ with the demands of their brats!'

His own ~~mother~~ father fell ill and died. He watched his mother weep for days, ~~and sp~~ heard her speak of a broken heart. In vain did she ~~implore him to~~ ask him why he did not cry. But the ~~heartless~~ warlock ~~merely~~ ~~smiled, and congratulated~~ ~~pleased to flatt~~ congratulated himself again on his heartless state, for he had escaped ~~the~~ her suffering.

~~There came a day when a beautiful~~ ~~maiden, a pri~~

One day, soon after his father's death, a beautiful

THE WARLOCK'S HAIRY HEART

This is an original handwritten draft of one of the stories for *The Tales of Beedle the Bard*. It is one of four wizarding fairy stories written by J.K. Rowling to accompany 'The Tale of the Three Brothers', which Hermione reads out aloud to Harry and Ron in Chapter 21 of *Harry Potter and the Deathly Hallows*. This draft outlines the plot and captures the essence of the story, but it was extended for the published version. The tale is another example of a wizard attempting to use Dark Magic to protect himself from human vulnerability. In the Harry Potter novels, love has its own powerful magic. By rejecting his heart and starving it of love, the warlock's heart becomes 'savage' and leads him to tragedy. Professor Dumbledore notes that this kind of Dark Magic would not be possible outside of fiction.

◁ DRAFT OF 'THE WARLOCK'S HAIRY HEART' BY J.K. ROWLING ▷

J.K. Rowling

"It was about five years to finish the first book and to plot the remaining six books, because they were already plotted before the first book was published."

J.K. Rowling in conversation with Christopher Lydon, The Connection, WBUR Radio, 12th October, 1999

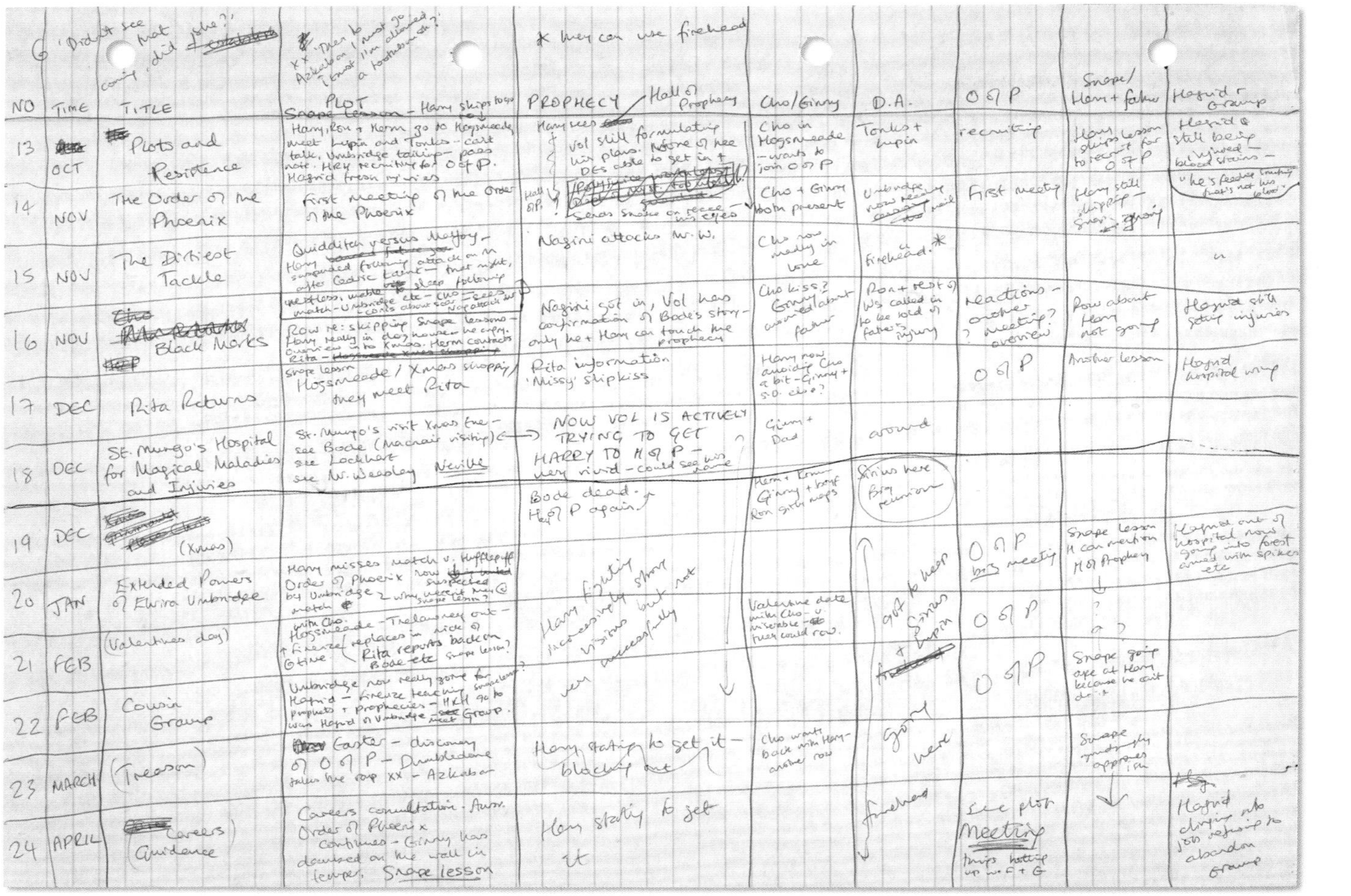

PLANNING THE ORDER OF THE PHOENIX

These plans for the fifth book, *The Order of the Phoenix*, show the complexity of the later storylines, and how they were carefully intertwined. Employing the 'series' method, the charts acted as early plotting aids for the author, with the titles and ordering of the chapters varying from the published versions. The plans also noted the whereabouts of individual characters – for example, Hagrid is 'still with giants' for the first nine chapters – and the discovery of new information – Harry is at the Department of Mysteries when he realises that prophecies are held there. In these plans, the secret Defence Against the Dark Arts organisation is called the 'Order of the Phoenix', while the official resistance is called 'Dumbledore's Army'.

PLANS FOR *HARRY POTTER AND THE ORDER OF THE PHOENIX* BY J.K. ROWLING

J.K. Rowling

NO.	TIME	TITLE	PLOT	PROPHECY	CHO/GINNY	D.A.	O.P.	Harry/Dad/Snape	Hagrid + Grawp
1	Aug	Dudley Demented	Harry desperate for information – contact – letters circumspect – desperate to rejoin Weasleys – listening to news – Dudley showdown – meets Dementor – Mrs. Figg	→ but Dudley informed – Arabella anyone can take – L.M. + Nott [illegible] joint. Vol plotting Bode under Imperius to put B. under Imperius					Still with giants
2	Aug	A Peck of Owls	Confused letters from Ministry – Harry to bed very worried – newspapers (D.P.s) 'Missy' Stiplkiss	"				Mention of Snape obliquely by Aunt P.	Still with giants
3	Aug	The Auror's Guard	Moody, Tonks and Lupin turn up to take Harry to Grimmauld. Finish on entry to kitchen – announce rental of small room in D.A.	"					Still with giants
4	Aug	12, Grimmauld Place	(Percy) F+G planning Dinner + [illegible] of information 'Missy Stiplkiss' → Sirius explains Fudge's standpoint. Ginny cheeky + funny. Mrs. W. worried House-elf George + F. + Hermione	LM to put Bode / anyone from Dept Myst under Imperius if get chance	See plot	Meet for 1st time – [illegible]		Snape not present – hint Shy	Still with giants
5	Aug	The Ministry of Magic	Interrogation – Mrs. Figg witness – Dumbledore there. See entrance (Percy) Dept. of Mysteries	LM hanging around Min. on excellent terms with Fudge (puts Bode under)		Still around			Still w. giants
6	Aug	Mrs. Weasley's Worst Fears	The clock – Mrs. W's premonitions of doom – (Percy) etc – 'Missy' S? [illegible] More info + House-elf + Hermione discussion – Harry Ron prefects?	↓ Bode is under / and under orders to proceed v. cautiously	Ginny here. Ginny / Hermione / Tonks	around. Sirius farewell until Xmas			Still with giants

+ Sorting hat sings lament? about sad future + wisdom being made again?

NO	TIME	TITLE	PLOT	PROPHECY	Cho/Ginny	DA	OP	Harry/Snape/Father	Hagrid + Grawp
7	SEPT	Night Mares	Journey to Hogs – Cho to speak to Harry [illegible] Cho on train – arrival + see Thestral Horses – Grubbly-Plank speaks – up to castle for Sorting – [illegible] Hagrid + Harry [illegible]	Bode lessons on some level no can't do it. Vol impatiently awaits Bode's news but it is difficult (Harry wins? Confused visions?)	Cho speaks some clues are [illegible]				Hag still w. giants
8	SEPT	Danger + Denial	Feast – Prof Umbridge introduced – her speech – D's contrasting speech –						"
9	SEPT	Joyce Umbridge	Exam emphasis – McGonagall 1st – prefect conversation – promise of Careers guidance to whole class – Herm + Ron given prefect badges keys + privileges – 1st Umbridge lesson – GP substituting Hagrid			Can write in guarded way – HRH write + ask [illegible] Hagrid			"
10	SEPT / OCT	Blackout	Weekend – careers pamphlets – starting to get annoyed with Umbridge – Quid. practice – Umbridge stalking – Scar – Dumbledore – Snape lessons set up.	Bode hurt – 'elementary mistake' Harry sees Vol's subsequent fury	Cho very attracted by scar – [illegible] Ginny practical	Bill says Madame Maxime was back for [illegible]			
11	OCT	[closed ward]	Trelawney – Umbridge meddles – Snape lesson. Lights in H's hut – Harry + co go to see – giants + general background – Hagrid badly injured – Umbridge [illegible]	Vol plotting – can't make fresh attempt too soon, suspicion. Harry reads of Bode's 'elementary mistake' – all connects with V's fury – [illegible] DA [illegible]		writing in guarded fashion		Snape + Harry 1st lesson	Hagrid returns badly injured with Grawp
12	OCT	Offense Against The Dark Arts	Grapple now with Umbridge re: teaching methods and Hagrid, Dumbledore! Umbridge comes? O of P idea – Umbridge [illegible] to Dumbledore [illegible] Care of M.C. lesson – 1st [illegible]	Vol concocting new plan – still doesn't realise Harry + he have 2 way connection – or in 13	Cho still more attracted but in morbid way. Contrast Ginny.		Idea for OP	Snape lessons continue	Mysterious injuries continue

NO	TIME	TITLE	PLOT	PROPHECY	Cho/Ginny	DA	OP	Snape/Harry/Father	Hagrid + Grawp
13	OCT	Plots + Resistance	Harry skips Snape lesson to go to Hogsmeade – Umbridge tailing – [illegible] HRH recruiting for OP – [illegible] refuses – Herm wants to incorporate SPEW in OP. Daily Prophet [illegible] Dumbledore's	Harry sees Hall of P 1st time. Not sinister – beautiful. Vol still plotting –	Cho wants to join OP	Tonks + Lupin	Recruiting	Harry skips – Snape furious	New injuries [illegible]
14	NOV	The Order of the Phoenix – Dobby finds	First meeting – named. Umbridge now reading mail – Hedwig attacked – bad Snape lesson (skipped last)	can't follow that went wrong with Bode – decides to send Nagini on	Cho + Ginny both present	Umbridge intercepting mail	1st meeting	Snape lesson?	
15	NOV	The Dirtiest Tackle	Quidditch v. Malfoy – Cedric taunt – Harry [illegible] following foul – restless – can't sleep – Malfoy – Cho – Umbridge [illegible] finally falls asleep – sees Nag. attack on Mr. Weasley	Nagini attacks Mr. Weasley. Vol sees Harry [illegible]	Cho [illegible]? Harry's tackle – [illegible] Ginny [illegible]	forehead?			Hagrid's lessons falling apart
16	end NOV	Black Lake	'Missy' Stiplkiss reaction to Mr. Weasley's injury – Gryffindors angry at Harry same form. Fred + George [illegible] action? Harry contacts Rita. OP meeting	Vol has explanation of Bode – Nagini saw [illegible] more concerned in the prophecy [illegible]	Cho, [illegible] Harry [illegible] Kiss? [illegible]	forehead re: Arthur?	meeting	Snape lesson v.v. bad – Harry saw snake [illegible] enough	Hagrid in bad way – Umbridge [illegible]
17	DEC	Rita Returns	Hogsmeade – Xmas shopping – meet Rita →	Rita into 'Missy' Stiplkiss Bargain struck	Harry now avoiding Cho a bit. Ginny + S.O. else? Seamus? [illegible] OP?		OP		Hagrid hosp wing. Grubbly-Plank back
18	DEC	St. Mungo's Hospital for Magical Maladies + Injuries	See Lockhart – Neville – Bode – Arthur – Macnair	Vol now playing Harry v. subtly. Sees H of P again. Scar hurting only v. slightly. See own name?	Ginny + Dad	around Moody + [illegible] eye?			"

NO	TIME	TITLE	PLOT	PROPHECY	Cho/Ginny	DA	OP	Snape/Harry/Father	Hagrid/Grawp
19	DEC	(Xmas)		Bode dead. Hall of Prophecy again	Herm/Ron Ginny + ? Seamus	Big reunion			
20	JAN	Extended Powers of Joyce Umbridge	Harry misses match v. Hufflepuff. OP now suspected by Umbridge – why weren't they all @ match. Snape lesson [illegible]	Harry learning – more fighting increasingly strong visions but natural curiosity [illegible] echo of [illegible] Patronus	Cho + Harry back on (ish)		Big meeting	Snape lesson overview ?	Hagrid out of [illegible] purposefully into forest armed with spikes etc
21	FEB	(Valentine's Day)	Date with Cho in Hogsmeade – thoroughly depressing – row – Cho in tears – Harry joins HR, depressed, at Rita meeting – Rita [illegible] for details of Harry's [illegible]		miserable Valentine date – row	forehead – got to keep		Snape lesson overview keep in view	Hagrid cooking things up still
22	FEB	Cousin Grawp	Umbridge persecuting Hagrid. Firenze teaching prophecies + prophets – HRH go to [illegible] Hag – meet Grawp – nightmare waiting to happen		Ginny great. Cho wants back – Harry can't take	lump in	OP overview	keep in view	They meet Grawp
23	MARCH	Treason	Easter – discovery of OP – Dumbledore takes the rap. Then to Azkaban I must surely go. [illegible] DA			+ Sirius grip [illegible]			Hagrid [illegible] job by skin of teeth
24	APRIL	Careers Guidance	Careers consultation – Auror – OP meeting – Ginny, Fred + George extremely defiant to U. doubts wall – Snape lesson?	getting better Harry starts to get it now. → Rita comes out for Dumbledore in 'The Quibbler'	Harry back with Cho at meeting – Dumbledore has [illegible]	well		overview mention of progress	Hagrid sacked – Grubbly-Plank back again

No	Time	TITLE	PLOT	PROPHECY	Cho/Ginny	DA	O of P	Snape/Harry/Father	Hagrid + Grawp
25	APRIL	James Potter's Worst Hour	Snape [illegible] Harry sees Snape's worst day in Pensieve – Snape won't teach any more.	Harry now at V's mercy	Ginny recipient of confidences	[illegible]	keep in view – meeting	See PLOT	Hagrid + Grawp continue (unseen) H won't [illegible] Grawp
26	APRIL	Umbridge Ascendant	Hagrid sacked – misses lesson. Harry sees Lupin / Sirius in fire – long discussion re: his father. [illegible] Fred + George expelled	Still fighting	Cho not happy		[illegible] considers etc	Sirius furious with Snape	
27	MAY	Azkaban Breakout	Quid – F & G gone. Gryff flattened – Azkaban breakout – Rita	Now like speeded up film sees H of P where it is, close up on name, how to get in	Cho breaks it off				
28	JUNE	Thestral Horses	Vol breaks through. Horses + Neville + Ginny	Vol has decided to go for it – breakout from Azkaban – unfortunately for him, D goes too, [illegible] in hot pursuit – distract Auror, draw them away from [illegible]					
29	JUNE	Dept of Mysteries	Entrance – death – love – Hall of P – no dying (?) but his name on Prophecy – arrival of DEs	new vision of ? dying in H of P	DOESN'T REALISE UNTIL THERE THAT THE HALL CONTAINS PROPHECIES				
30	JUNE	Battle DEs	arrival S + Co (alerted by Snape) Harry [illegible] Prophecy S dies						

	TIME	CHAP TITLE	
23	APRIL		Harry sees Snape's worst memory in Pensieve – Snape won't teach any more
24	MAY		Fred + George expelled and Azkaban breakout
25	JUNE		Vol breaks through – Harry sets off – Thestral horses
26	JUNE		Arrival at Ministry – Invisibility cloak on Dept of Mysteries (must fight way in)
27	JUNE		• Death room • Love room seen • Into prophecy room – Harry gets prophecy – arrival of DEs
28	JUNE		Battle DEs – arrival of Sirius + co
29	JUNE		Harry runs for it with prophecy but S is in trouble – goes back – Sirius chooses death rather than the Dementor – Snape there – Vol comes
30	JUNE		Harry and Ron pull Harry from death – now Vol, enraged, furious, goes for Harry – Ministry wizards coming – Dumbledore – Vol throws Crabbe in front of himself – gone
31	JUNE		Back Hogs – from Dumbledore – fall out – full explanations – letter – prophecy – Neville etc
32			Journey home
33			
34			
35			

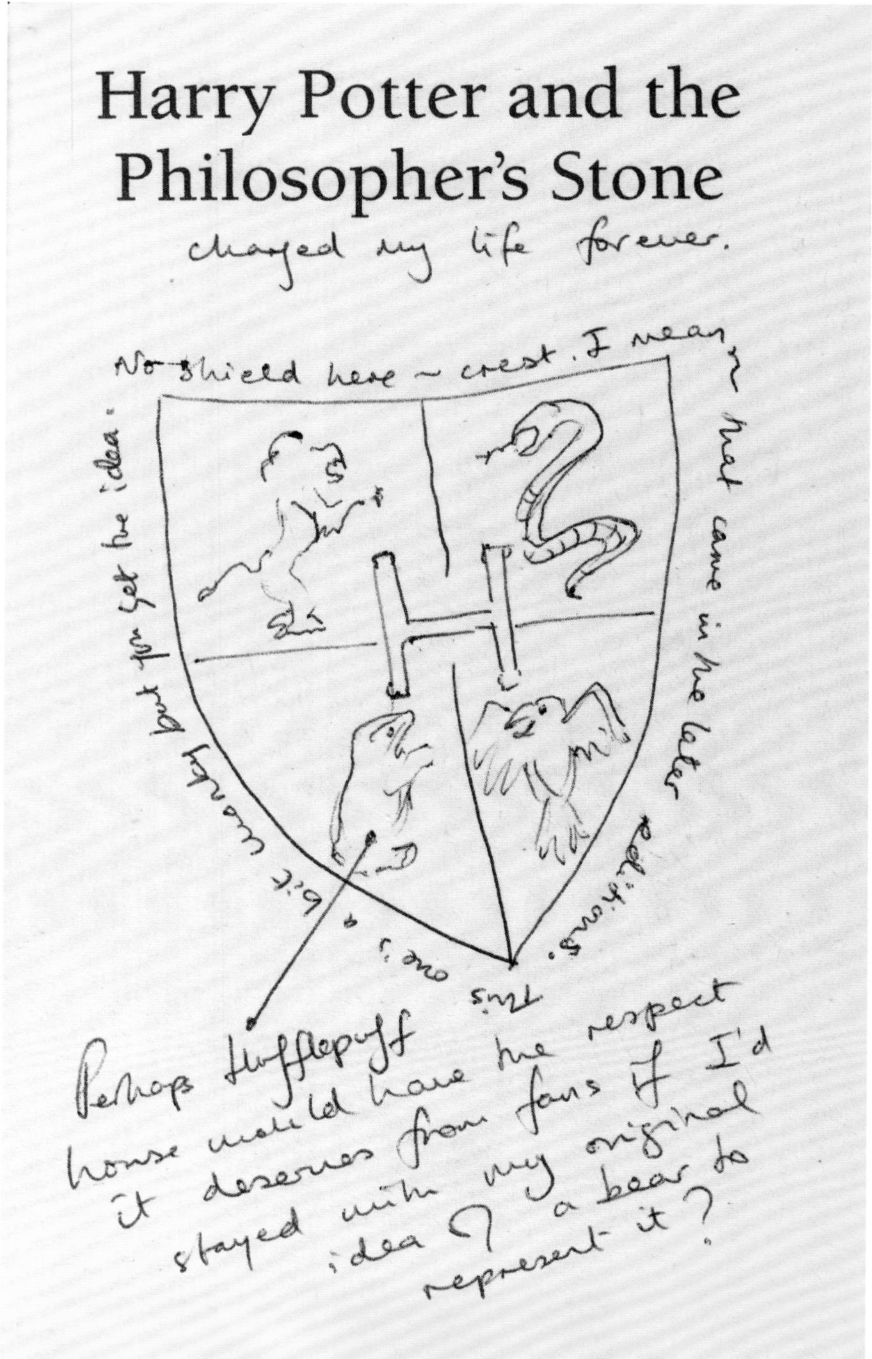

J.K. ROWLING'S ANNOTATED PHILOSOPHER'S STONE

This unique first edition of *Harry Potter and the Philosopher's Stone*, with drawings and annotations by J.K. Rowling, was sold at a charity auction in aid of English PEN and Lumos in 2013. Forty-three of the pages have annotations or illustrations, among them reflections on and references to the Harry Potter series and films. In this copy, J.K. Rowling points out sections of text she refused to cut, and comments on an anomaly in Chapter Four relating to snapped wands. She also describes the circumstances of the invention of Quidditch. On the first page, under the typeset title *Harry Potter and the Philosopher's Stone*, the author has written the simple words, 'changed my life forever'.

"This wonderful treasure contains twenty original illustrations by the author. They include drawings of a swaddled Harry Potter on the Dursleys' doorstep, a menacing Professor Snape, an annotated sketch of the Hogwarts coat of arms, an Albus Dumbledore Chocolate Frog Card, Norbert the Norwegian Ridgeback, and the man with two faces."

JOANNA NORLEDGE
Curator

Harry Potter and the Philosopher's Stone, illustrated and annotated by J.K. Rowling (c. 2013)

Private Owner

Professor McGonagall turned to Harry and Ron.

'Well, I still say you were lucky, but not many first years could have taken on a full-grown mountain troll. You each win Gryffindor five points. Professor Dumbledore will be informed of this. You may go.'

They hurried out of the chamber and didn't speak at all until they had climbed two floors up. It was a relief to be away from the smell of the troll, quite apart from anything else.

'We should have got more than ten points,' Ron grumbled.

'Five, you mean, once she's taken off Hermione's.'

'Good of her to get us out of trouble like that,' Ron admitted. 'Mind you, we *did* save her.'

'She might not have needed saving if we hadn't locked the thing in with her,' Harry reminded him.

They had reached the portrait of the Fat Lady.

'Pig snout,' they said and entered.

The common-room was packed and noisy. Everyone was eating the food that had been sent up. Hermione, however, stood alone by the door, waiting for them. There was a very embarrassed pause. Then, none of them looking at each other, they all said 'Thanks', and hurried off to get plates.

But from that moment on, Hermione Granger became their friend. There are some things you can't share without ending up liking each other, and knocking out a twelve-foot mountain troll is one of them.

This was the cut I refused to make – my editor wanted to lose the whole troll-fighting scene. I'm glad I resisted ♡

out that grubby little package. Had that been what the thieves were looking for?

As Harry and Ron walked back to the castle for dinner, their pockets weighed down with rock cakes they'd been too polite to refuse, Harry thought that none of the lessons he'd had so far had given him as much to think about as tea with Hagrid. Had Hagrid collected that package just in time? Where was it now? And did Hagrid know something about Snape that he didn't want to tell Harry?

Snape, brooding on the unfairness of life

HARRY POTTER AND THE PHILOSOPHER'S STONE, ILLUSTRATED AND ANNOTATED BY J.K. ROWLING (C. 2013)

Private Owner

corner he stopped and took out the silver Put-Outer. He clicked it once and twelve balls of light sped back to their street lamps so that Privet Drive glowed suddenly orange and he could make out a tabby cat slinking around the corner at the other end of the street. He could just see the bundle of blankets on the step of number four.

'Good luck, Harry,' he murmured. He turned on his heel and with a swish of his cloak he was gone.

A breeze ruffled the neat hedges of Privet Drive, which lay silent and tidy under the inky sky, the very last place you would expect astonishing things to happen. Harry Potter rolled over inside his blankets without waking up. One small hand closed on the letter beside him and he slept on, not knowing he was special, not knowing he was famous, not knowing he would be woken in a few hours' time by Mrs Dursley's scream as she opened the front door to put out the milk bottles, nor that he would spend the next few weeks being prodded and pinched by his cousin Dudley ... he couldn't know that at this very moment, people meeting in secret all over the country were holding up their glasses and saying in hushed voices: 'To Harry Potter – the boy who lived!'

ur-posters hung with deep-red velvet curtains. Their
ready been brought up. Too tired to talk much, they
r pyjamas and fell into bed.
, isn't it?' Ron muttered to Harry through the hang-
Scabbers! He's chewing my sheets.'
going to ask Ron if he'd had any of the treacle tart,
eep almost at once.
rry had eaten a bit too much, because he had a very
. He was wearing Professor Quirrell's turban, which
o him, telling him he must transfer to Slytherin at
it was his destiny. Harry told the turban he didn't
Slytherin; it got heavier and heavier; he tried to pull
htened painfully – and there was Malfoy, laughing at
uggled with it – then Malfoy turned into the hook-
, Snape, whose laugh became high and cold – there
green light and Harry woke, sweating and shaking.
over and fell asleep again, and when he woke next
remember the dream at all.

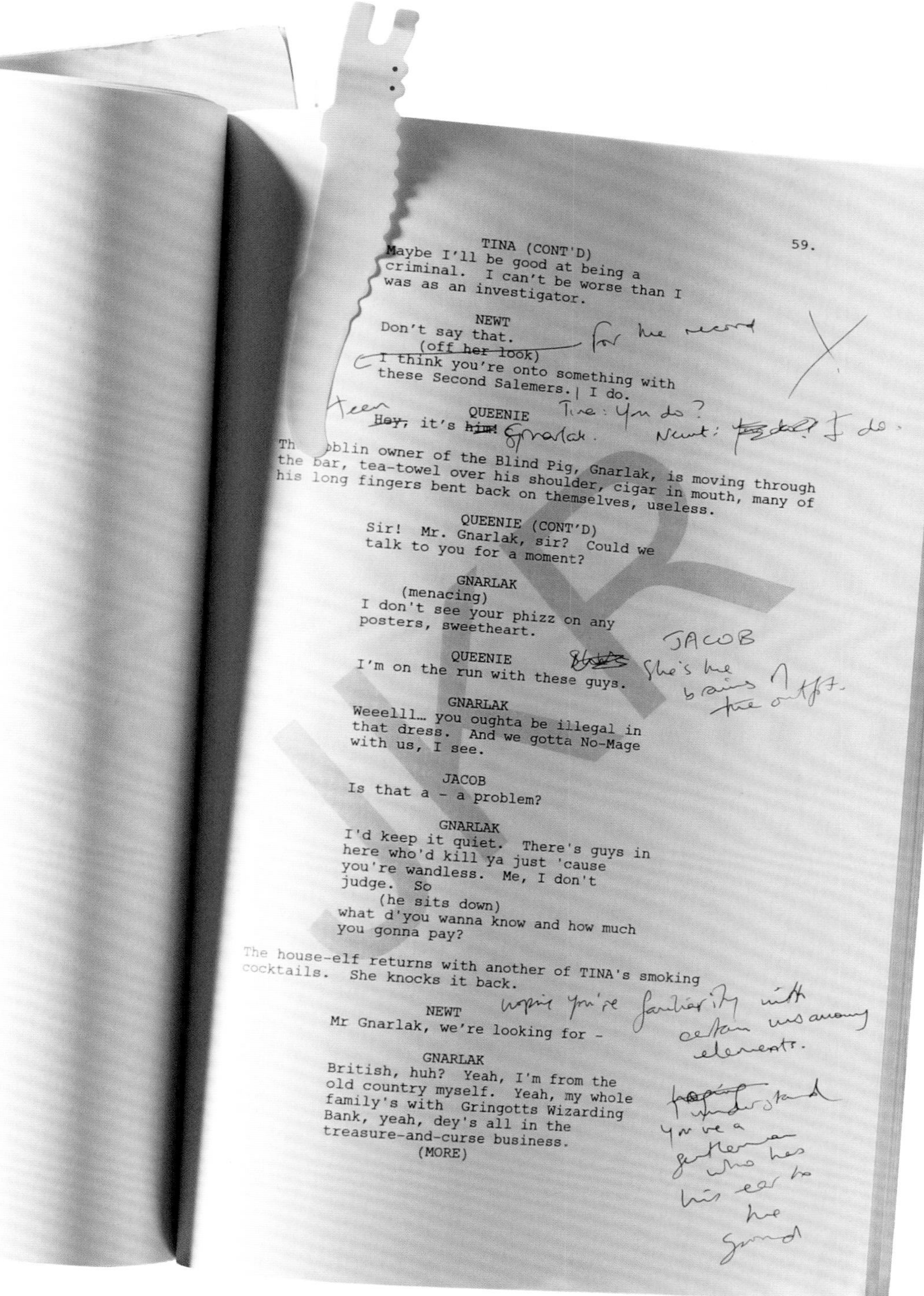

TINA (CONT'D) 59.

Maybe I'll be good at being a criminal. I can't be worse than I was as an investigator.

NEWT

Don't say that.

~~(off her look)~~

I think you're onto something with these Second Salemers. I do.

QUEENIE

~~Hey~~, it's ~~him!~~

The goblin owner of the Blind Pig, Gnarlak, is moving through the bar, tea-towel over his shoulder, cigar in mouth, many of his long fingers bent back on themselves, useless.

QUEENIE (CONT'D)

Sir! Mr. Gnarlak, sir? Could we talk to you for a moment?

GNARLAK

(menacing)

I don't see your phizz on any posters, sweetheart.

QUEENIE

I'm on the run with these guys.

GNARLAK

Weeelll… you oughta be illegal in that dress. And we gotta No-Mage with us, I see.

JACOB

Is that a - a problem?

GNARLAK

I'd keep it quiet. There's guys in here who'd kill ya just 'cause you're wandless. Me, I don't judge. So

(he sits down)

what d'you wanna know and how much you gonna pay?

The house-elf returns with another of TINA's smoking cocktails. She knocks it back.

NEWT

Mr Gnarlak, we're looking for -

GNARLAK

British, huh? Yeah, I'm from the old country myself. Yeah, my whole family's with Gringotts Wizarding Bank, yeah, dey's all in the treasure-and-curse business.

(MORE)

FANTASTIC BEASTS AND WHERE TO FIND THEM

This annotated screenplay of *Fantastic Beasts and Where to Find Them* contains J.K. Rowling's additions in her own handwriting. The screenwriting process is very different from writing a novel – it can be much more collaborative and require edits at almost any stage in the process of filming. The script must be technically filmable, and so the limits of imagination are potentially more restricted. Although *Fantastic Beasts* was J.K. Rowling's first screenplay, she did not appear to be confined by this new format. Filmmaker David Yates has talked about working on this script with her, describing how the author would rewrite, reinvent and add astonishing detail to her characters and world, with seemingly no limit to her imagination. This draft represents the skeleton on which the film and the world of Newt Scamander were based.

TYPEWRITTEN SCREENPLAY OF *FANTASTIC BEASTS AND WHERE TO FIND THEM* BY J.K. ROWLING, WITH AUTOGRAPH ANNOTATIONS

J.K. Rowling

> *"She has so much flowing through her head."*

David Yates on working with J.K. Rowling

HARRY POTTER AND THE CURSED CHILD MODEL BOX

Based on an original new story by J.K. Rowling, Jack Thorne and John Tiffany, *Harry Potter and the Cursed Child* is a play by Jack Thorne, produced by Sonia Friedman Productions, Colin Callender and Harry Potter Theatrical Productions. It had its official premiere at the Palace Theatre, London, on 30th July 2016 and among the many awards it has received since then is the Olivier for Best Set Design. This model box shows an evocative and flexible set design, which is integral to the theatrical magic that takes place on stage. Model boxes such as this one, designed by Christine Jones, help the creative team to work out the crucial detail of staging a play – ultimately making Harry Potter's world come alive before the audience's eyes.

CHRISTINE JONES PRESENTING THE *HARRY POTTER AND THE CURSED CHILD* MODEL BOX TO THE ORIGINAL WEST END COMPANY DURING REHEARSALS

"This model box by Christine Jones includes steel arches reminiscent of familiar London train stations. The versatile set walls have rich wooden panelling and a beautiful round clock in the centre. Her design is rich in symbolism and Harry Potter heritage."

JOANNA NORLEDGE
Curator

MODEL BOX DESIGNED BY CHRISTINE JONES WITH BRETT J. BANAKIS, AND BUILT BY MARY HAMRICK, AMELIA COOK, A RAM KIM, AMY RUBIN AND KYLE HILL

ORIGINAL WEST END COMPANY OF *HARRY POTTER AND THE CURSED CHILD* AT THE PALACE THEATRE, LONDON

Index of Exhibits

ABOUT J.K. ROWLING

J.K. Rowling is the author of the record-breaking, multi-award-winning Harry Potter novels. Loved by fans around the world, the series has sold over 450 million copies, been translated into 79 languages, and made into 8 blockbuster films. She has written three companion volumes in aid of charity: *Quidditch Through the Ages* and *Fantastic Beasts and Where to Find Them* (in aid of Comic Relief and Lumos), and *The Tales of Beedle the Bard* (in aid of Lumos), as well as a screenplay inspired by *Fantastic Beasts and Where to Find Them.* J.K. Rowling has also collaborated on a stage play, *Harry Potter and the Cursed Child Parts One and Two,* which opened in London's West End in the summer of 2016. In 2012, J.K. Rowling's digital company Pottermore was launched, where fans can enjoy news, features and articles, as well as original content from J.K. Rowling. J.K. Rowling has written a novel for adult readers, *The Casual Vacancy,* and also writes crime novels under the pseudonym Robert Galbraith. She has received many awards and honours, including an OBE for services to children's literature, France's Légion d'honneur and the Hans Christian Andersen Award.

THE CURATORS

JULIAN HARRISON

Julian Harrison is the Lead Curator of the British Library exhibition *Harry Potter: A History of Magic*. He is a specialist on medieval and early modern manuscripts, and previously curated major exhibitions on Magna Carta (The British Library, 2015) and William Shakespeare (The Library of Birmingham, 2016). He writes for and edits the British Library's Medieval Manuscripts Blog, which was named UK Arts and Culture Blog of the Year in 2014.

ALEXANDER LOCK

Alexander Lock is Curator of Modern Archives and Manuscripts at the British Library and co-curator of the exhibition *Harry Potter: A History of Magic*. He is a specialist of modern historical manuscripts and was lead researcher for the exhibition *Magna Carta: Law, Liberty, Legacy* (The British Library, 2015). His most recent book, *Catholicism, Identity and Politics in the Age of Enlightenment*, was published by Boydell and Brewer in 2016.

TANYA KIRK

Tanya Kirk is the British Library's Lead Curator of Printed Heritage Collections, 1601–1900, and a co-curator of *Harry Potter: A History of Magic*. She is a specialist in rare books and English Literature and has curated six literary exhibitions, including most recently *Shakespeare in Ten Acts* (2016) and *Terror and Wonder: The Gothic Imagination* (2014/15). She is the editor of a collection of ghost stories, *The Haunted Library*, published by the British Library in 2016.

JOANNA NORLEDGE

Joanna Norledge is Lead Curator of Contemporary Literary and Creative Archives and co-curator of the British Library exhibition *Harry Potter: A History of Magic*. She is a trained archivist and specialist in literary and theatrical archives at the British Library.

THE BRITISH LIBRARY

The British Library is the national library of the United Kingdom and one of the world's greatest research libraries. The Library's collection has developed over 250 years – it exceeds 150 million separate items representing every age of written civilisation. Its vast archive includes books, journals, manuscripts, maps, stamps, music, patents, photographs, newspapers and sound recordings in all written and spoken languages. Among the greatest treasures in the Library's collection are two copies of Magna Carta from 1215, the Lindisfarne Gospels, Leonardo da Vinci's notebook, the first edition of *The Times* from 18th March, 1788, manuscripts of the Beatles' song lyrics, and the recording of Nelson Mandela's speech given at his trial. The oldest items in the collection are Chinese oracle bones that date back over 3,000 years – the most recent are today's newspapers and websites.

Picture Credits

Items on pages 17, 24–5, 27, 31, 48–9, 62, 66–7, 75, 99, 104, 106, 107, 108 (top), 124, 125, 171, 176–7, 196, 197–9, 201 (both), 202–3, 224–5, 238–9, 240–1 © J.K. Rowling
26 © Alice Newton-Rex
34 Private Collection. Photo courtesy Sotheby's
35 The Museum of Witchcraft and Magic, Boscastle, Cornwall
45 © The Trustees of the British Museum
51 Science Museum/Wellcome Images
53 © Science Museum/Science & Society Picture Library
54 (top) Science Museum/Wellcome Images
60 Photo © RMN-Grand Palais (musée de Cluny – musée national du Moyen Âge)/Gérard Blot
63 Birmingham Museum and Art Gallery
64–5 Derby Museum/Bridgeman Art Library
70 © George Wright
78 The Museum of Witchcraft and Magic, Boscastle, Cornwall
91 (bottom) © Science Museum/Science & Society Picture Library
95 The Garden Museum, London
110 (top) The Museum of Witchcraft and Magic, Boscastle, Cornwall
117 The Museum of Witchcraft and Magic, Boscastle, Cornwall
120 ESA – M. Koell, 2009
131 © The Trustees of the British Museum
133 © Science Museum/Science & Society Picture Library
143 The Museum of Witchcraft and Magic, Boscastle, Cornwall. Photo © Sara Hannant
149 The Museum of Witchcraft and Magic, Boscastle, Cornwall
150–1 © The Trustees of the British Museum
154 (top) The Museum of Witchcraft and Magic, Boscastle, Cornwall. Photo © Sara Hannant
154 (bottom) The Museum of Witchcraft and Magic, Boscastle, Cornwall
158 The Museum of Witchcraft and Magic, Boscastle, Cornwall. Photo © Sara Hannant
160 The Museum of Witchcraft and Magic, Boscastle, Cornwall
165 © Tate, London 2017
166 © NMP Live Ltd
173 (both) The Museum of Witchcraft and Magic, Boscastle, Cornwall
181 (bottom) © The Trustees of the British Museum
186 © Tate, London 2017
187 The Museum of Witchcraft and Magic, Boscastle, Cornwall. Photo © Sara Hannant
223 © The Trustees of the British Museum
233 Photography by Manuel Harlan
234 Photography by Hopper Nash
235 Private Collection
242–4 Private Collection
245 Photography by www.studio68b.com
246 Photography by Manuel Harlan
247 (top) Photography by Brett J. Banakis
247 (bottom) Photography by Manuel Harlan
250 Photography by Debra Hurford Brown © J.K. Rowling 2014
252 Joanna Norledge image by Tony Antoniou

British Library Shelfmarks

Title page G.10992
9 Or.11390, f. 57v
10–11 Cotton MS Tiberius B V/1, f. 37r
12 452.f. 2
15 Sloane MS 278, f. 47r
36 Sloane MS 2523B
37 IB.344
39 8905.a.15
43 IB.344
44 IA.5209
46–7 Royal MS 12 D XVII, ff. 41v–42r
50 Sloane MS 1977, f. 49v
52 7511.c.30
55 Additional MS 25724, f. 50v
56–7 Sloane MS 2523B
58 Harley MS 3469, f. 4r
59 Additional MS 17910, ff. 13v–14r
61 8905.a.15
68 Additional MS 22332, f. 3r
69 Harley MS 5294, f. 22r
71 10.Tab.29
76–7 1601/42
79 Additional MS 22332, f. 3r
80–1 Harley MS 5294, ff. 21v–22r
82–3 Sloane MS 4016, ff. 37v–38r
84–5 35.g.13
86 Additional MS 78334, f. 3r
87 10.Tab.29
88 452.f. 2
89 10.Tab.40
91 (top) Or.3366, f. 144v
92–3 Harley MS 3736, ff. 58v–59r
96–7 Or.13347B, ff. 6v–7r
98 Additional MS 36674, f. 10r
101 Additional MS 32496, f. 49r
108 (bottom) Additional MS 36674, f. 10r
110 (bottom) Additional MS 32496, f. 49r
111 1078.i.25.(5.)
114 Papyrus 46 (5)
115 Royal MS 12 E XXIII, f. 20r
116 Or.11390, f. 97r*
118 Maps C.6.d.5
119 Maps C.44.a.42.(2.)
121 Maps G.55
126–7 Or.8210/S.3326
128–9 Cotton MS Tiberius B V/1, ff. 36v–37r
130 Cotton MS Tiberius C I, f. 28r
131 (bottom) Additional MS 24189, f. 15r
132 Maps G.55
134–5 Arundel MS 263, f. 104r + f. 107v
136 48.f. 7
137 Maps C.6.d.5
138–9 Maps C.44.a.42.(2.)
140 C.194.a.825(2)
141 Or.4830, ff. 20–21
147 Or.7694/1595
148 117.d.44.(2.)
152–3 Or.4830 , ff. 20–21
155 YA.1988.a.9195
156–7 Royal MS 12 C XII, ff. 106v–107r
159 C.194.a.825.(2.)
161 8633.c.9
162–3 8633.eee.31
164 43.k.3–10
166 16084.d.15
172 Royal MS 12 C XIX, f. 67r
174 43.k.3–10
175 3835.c.26
179 Additional MS 82955, f. 129r
180 1256.d.9
181 (top) 16084.d.15
182 435.h.6
183 (left and top) Or.12859
183 (bottom) Or.9178
184–5 Or.11390, ff. 57v–58r
188 37.h.7
189 G.10992
191 N.L. Tab.2
195 32.k.1
204–5 38.g.10
207 N.L. Tab.2
208 460.c.1
209 505.ff. 16
211 649.c.26
213 C.7.d.7
214–15 461.b.11.(1.)
216 Burney MS 97, f. 18r
217 37.h.7
220 Harley MS 4751, f. 45r
221 G.10992
222 Additional MS 15241, f. 64r
226 Sloane MS 278, f. 47r
227 Additional MS 57312

With thanks to

J.K. Rowling for the use of items from her personal collection
Jim Kay and Olivia Lomenech Gill for allowing us to use their artwork

Contributors: Mandy Archer from 38a The Shop;
Stephanie Amster, Mary Berry, Elaine Connolly, Isabel Ford, Claire Grace,
Saskia Gwinn and Bronwyn O'Reilly from Bloomsbury;
Robert Davies, Abbie Day and Sally Nicholls from British Library Publishing;
Ross Fraser from The Blair Partnership

Design: Sally Griffin
Cover design: James Fraser